Corpus Linguistics and Translation Tools for Digital Humanities

Also Available from Bloomsbury

Extending the Scope of Corpus-Based Translation Studies,
Sylviane Granger and Marie-Aude Lefer
Corpus-Based Translation Studies, Alet Kruger
Thomas Pynchon and the Digital Humanities, Erik Ketzan
Electronic Literature as Digital Humanities, Dene Grigar and
James O'Sullivan

Corpus Linguistics and Translation Tools for Digital Humanities

Research Methods and Applications

Edited by
Stefania M. Maci
Michele Sala

BLOOMSBURY ACADEMIC
LONDON • NEW YORK • OXFORD • NEW DELHI • SYDNEY

BLOOMSBURY ACADEMIC
Bloomsbury Publishing Plc
50 Bedford Square, London, WC1B 3DP, UK
1385 Broadway, New York, NY 10018, USA
29 Earlsfort Terrace, Dublin 2, Ireland

BLOOMSBURY, BLOOMSBURY ACADEMIC and the Diana logo are trademarks
of Bloomsbury Publishing Plc

First published in Great Britain 2022
This paperback edition published 2024

Copyright © Stefania M. Maci and Michele Sala, 2022

Stefania M. Maci and Michele Sala have asserted their right under the Copyright,
Designs and Patents Act, 1988, to be identified as Authors of this work.

Cover image © Dirk Hoffmann / EyeEm

All rights reserved. No part of this publication may be reproduced or transmitted
in any form or by any means, electronic or mechanical, including photocopying,
recording, or any information storage or retrieval system, without
prior permission in writing from the publishers.

Bloomsbury Publishing Plc does not have any control over, or responsibility for,
any third-party websites referred to or in this book. All internet addresses
given in this book were correct at the time of going to press. The author and publisher
regret any inconvenience caused if addresses have changed or sites have
ceased to exist, but can accept no responsibility for any such changes.

A catalogue record for this book is available from the British Library.

A catalog record for this book is available from the Library of Congress.

ISBN:	HB:	978-1-3502-7522-5
	PB:	978-1-3502-7526-3
	ePDF:	978-1-3502-7523-2
	eBook:	978-1-3502-7524-9

Typeset by Integra Software Services Pvt. Ltd.

To find out more about our authors and books visit www.bloomsbury.com
and sign up for our newsletters.

Contents

List of Figures — vii
List of Tables — viii
List of Contributors — ix
Foreword *Mike Scott* — xiii

1 Corpus linguistics and translation tools for digital humanities: An introduction *Michele Sala and Stefania M. Maci* — 1

Part 1 Corpus linguistics for digital humanities: Research methods and applications

2 Digital humanities: An adaptive theory approach *Paola Catenaccio* — 19
3 Comparable corpora in cross-cultural genre studies: Tools for the analysis of CSR reports *Marina Bondi* — 37
4 Applying a corpus-driven approach in linguistic analyses: The case of lexical bundles and phrase frames *Miguel Fuster-Márquez* — 65
5 Data triangulation using Sketch Engine and WMatrix: Ketogenic diet on *Twitter* *Stefania M. Maci* — 81

Part 2 Translation for digital humanities: Research methods and applications

6 The legal translator as a digital humanist: On the use of digital corpora in professional legal translation *Patrizia Anesa* — 107
7 A comparative study of emotive language in English and Italian migrant narratives in digital museums *Cinzia Spinzi and Anouska Zummo* — 127
8 Learning analytics at the service of interpreter training in academic curricula *Francesca Bianchi, Davide Taibi, Philipp Kemkes and Ivana Marenzi* — 153

9 Exploring the construction and translation of film characters through a parallel corpus: The case of *Little Women* adaptations *Gianmarco Vignozzi*   177

10 Subtitling in the digital era: TV crime drama series in domestic languages *Alessandra Rizzo*   201

Index   225

Figures

5.1	Tweet by sentiment	87
5.2	Corpus breakdown	87
7.1	Quantitative distribution of overt Affect in English subcorpus	137
7.2	Quantitative distribution of covert Affect in English subcorpus	137
7.3	Quantitative distribution of overt Affect in Italian subcorpus	139
7.4	Quantitative distribution of covert Affect in Italian subcorpus	140
8.1a	Glossary interface with sample entries: 'creation mode'	161
8.1b	Glossary interface with sample entries: 'consultation mode'	161
8.2	General information on students' activity (class view)	166
8.3	Number of concepts and terms entered into the glossary, and number and types of sources the students declared to use most frequently (class view)	166
8.4	Whether and to what extent each student completed the compulsory and optional fields (class view)	166
8.5	A list of the definitions entered and their lengths (class view). In the picture, the student's names have been replaced with placeholders for privacy reasons	167
8.6	Preferred sources and reference pages (referring to a single student)	167
8.7	List of Web addresses visited, tracked by the WAPS tool (referring to a single student)	167
8.8	Group view of the data entered by the students in the source field	170
9.1	Pairs of tagged texts taken from *Little Women* (Armstrong 1994)	182
9.2	*Sketch Engine* document metadata editor	182
9.3	Sample of the parallel concordance of *Marmee* in LWT	191

Tables

3.1	Top fifty keywords in Italian	48
3.2	Positive keywords in the English corpus	50
3.3	Statements of understanding/belief ('Vision statements')	54
4.1	Features of Lexical Bundles	71
5.1	Breakdown of the top 50 *keto*_3-4n-grams* by frequency	88
5.2	Key semantic domains generated against the spoken sampler of the BNC	97
7.1	Overt instantiations of Affect	134
7.2	Covert instantiations of Affect	135
9.1	Total numbers in *LittleWomenTalk* corpus after the compilation	183
9.2	Number of tokens in the four subcorpora	185
9.3	List of top twenty-five keywords in the subcorpora	186
9.4	Distribution of *Marmee* in LWT and its dubbing solutions	191
9.6	Apologies in LWT	194
10.1	Linguistic features analysed in the corpus	212
10.2	Dialogic interaction between Luther and Rose and Italian subtitling	213
10.3	Dialogic interaction between Luther and Ripley and Italian subtitling	216
10.4	Dialogic interaction between Luther and Reed and Italian subtitling	216
10.5	Dialogue between Luther and Alice Morgan and Italian subtitling	217
10.6	Dialogue between Luther and Zoe and Italian subtitling	217
10.7	Translation strategies adapted from different taxonomies	220

Contributors

Patrizia Anesa is a Associate Professor in English Language and Translation at the University of Bergamo, Italy. She holds a Ph.D. in English Studies, with a specialization in professional communication. She is a member of the Research Centre on Specialized Languages (CERLIS) and is also an Associate Editor of the IDEA project (International Dialects of English Archive). Her research interests lie mostly in the area of specialized discourse. In particular, she is currently interested in the applications of Conversation Analysis in LSP and the investigation of knowledge asymmetries in expert-lay communication.

Francesca Bianchi (PhD) is Associate Professor of English Language and Linguistics at the University of Salento (Lecce, Italy), where she teaches interpreting and audiovisual-translation. She has long been involved in the creation of pedagogical units using multimedia authoring systems and in the development of computerized interactive teaching environments. She has over fifty publications focusing on the use of technologies in either language learning or linguistic research, and has organized several international conferences on linguistics and/or translation.

Marina Bondi is Professor of English Language and Translation at the University of Modena and Reggio Emilia, where she is coordinator of the PhD programme in Human Sciences. Founding Director of the *CLAVIER* centre (*Corpus and LAnguage Variation in English Research*), she has published extensively in the field of genre analysis, EAP and corpus linguistics, with a focus on argumentative dialogue and language variation across genres, disciplines and cultures. Her recent interest centres on knowledge dissemination and the impact of digital media on specialized discourse. She has recently coordinated a national project on the issue.

Paola Catenaccio is Full Professor of English Linguistics and Translation at Università degli Studi di Milano. Her research interests lie primarily in the field of discourse analysis, which she applies to a variety of domains (legal discourse, business communication, professional discourse, ELF communication, the discourse of science and of scientific popularization) in combination with other methodological perspectives (most notably corpus linguistics), adopting a multi-methods approach to linguistic research, especially in an intercultural perspective. She has authored numerous articles which have appeared in international journals and edited collections. She has also coedited several volumes on various aspects of domain-specific discourse.

Miguel Fuster-Márquez is Associate Professor in English Language and Linguistics at the *Universitat de València* (UV), where he teaches in the Department of English and German. In his master courses he deals with methodological and corpus issues. He is a member of the research group CORPLING (Corpus Linguistics: developments and applications) and GENTEXT (Gender and social/sexual (in)equality) at UV. Currently, he is vice-president of the Spanish Association for Corpus Linguistics. In his research, Fuster Márquez has applied corpus methods to the study of lexis and phraseology, critical discourse analysis, stylistics and tourism discourses.

Philipp Kemkes (M.Sc.) is a Researcher at the L3S Research Center of the Leibniz University of Hannover, Germany. His main research interests are Information Retrieval, Data Mining, Machine Learning and e-Learning. He leads the development of the collaborative learning platform LearnWeb (https://learnweb.l3s.uni-hannover.de/).

Stefania Maci (PhD, Lancaster University, UK) is Full Professor of English Language and Translation at the Dept. of Foreign Languages, Literatures and Cultures (University of Bergamo, Italy), Department of Excellence (*Translation and Digital Humanities project*) and Director of CERLIS (Research Centre on Specialised Languages). Her research is focused on English in academic and professional contexts, in particular on tourism and medical discourse.

Ivana Marenzi (PhD) is Senior Researcher at the L3S Research Center of the Leibniz University of Hannover, Germany. Throughout her career she has specialized in the relationship between technology and communication. As educational technologist her main interest is dealing with issues related to the adoption of new technologies in education (***Multiliteracies and e-learning2.0, 2014***). She works as a referee for international conferences and journals and collaborates in international European projects such as LA4S (Learning Analytics and Learning Process Management for Small Size Organizations in

Higher Education): and Cleopatra (Cross-lingual Event-centric Open Analytics Research Academy. MSCA Innovative Training Network).

Alessandra Rizzo is Associate Professor in the Department of Humanities at the University of Palermo, where she teaches ESP and audiovisual translation. She holds a PhD and a Master of Arts in Translation from the University of Essex. She is a member of the Centre for Research in Translation and Transcultural Studies and of the AIA, ESIST and EST associations. Her research interests focus on audiovisual translation, creative domestication, accessibility, ELF in the context of migration and the visual arts and subtitling as counter discourse. She has extensively published in national and international journals, and in dedicated volumes.

Michele Sala (PhD) is Associate Professor of English Language at the University of Bergamo, Faculty of Foreign Languages, Literatures and Cultures. He is a member of AIA (Associazione Italiana di Anglistica), of CERLIS (Centro di Ricerca sui Linguaggi Specialistici) and of the CLAVIER group (Corpus and Language Variation in English Research Group). He has been an assistant editor of the *European English Messenger* (2009–12) and a member of the scientific and editorial board of the *CERLIS Series*. His research field and publications are mainly concerned with the application of genre analysis to academic and legal discourse, and with the analysis of the linguistic

Cinzia Spinzi is Associate Professor at the University of Bergamo. She holds a PhD in English for Specific Purposes, a Master's Degree in Translation Studies from the University of Birmingham and a Research Fellowship from the City University of London. Her research interests include Language Mediation and Translation, Corpus Linguistics and Functional Grammar applied to the study of ideology and metaphors in specialized communication. She is member of the Research Centre on Languages for Specific Purposes and of the EU funded Project on Teaching and Training in the field of Language for Specific Purposes. She is co-editor of an international journal *Cultus: The Journal of Intercultural Mediation and Communication*.

Davide Taibi is a Tenured Researcher at the Institute of Educational Technology of the National Research Council of Italy and part-time lecturer at the Department of Computer Science, University of Palermo. His research activities focus mainly on the application of innovative technologies that assist both Secondary and

Higher Education in such domains as Mobile Learning, Semantic Web and Linked Data for e-learning, Open Education, Learning Analytics, Augmented Reality and Virtual Reality for education. He has participated, as partners, to several European funded projects and he is currently coordinating two two-year European Union funded projects in the field of Data Literacy.

Gianmarco Vignozzi (PhD in English linguistics) is a Research Fellow in English language and translation at the University of Pisa where he teaches ESP in the Department of Law. His main research interests are in the field of corpus-assisted discourse analysis, audiovisual translation and English for specific purposes (legal and political domains). His most recent publications include: '**The Representation of Spoken discourse in Little Women: A journey through its original and dubbed adaptations**' (2021), '**Disney animated films vis-à-vis their live-action remakes: A study on the representation and the Italian dubbing of vocative forms**' (2021), '**"What are Miranda rights?": The case of video FAQs on a criminal law firm website**' (2021)'.

Anouska Zummo holds a PhD in Translation Studies from Durham University, UK. Her doctoral study concerned the translation of Sicilian dialect poetry in English. She is a freelance editor, English language teacher and translator whose interests include the representation of minority languages and cultures in translation, migration studies and translation and creative writing.

Foreword

This volume invites us to bring together three research and applied fields of human endeavour, Corpus Linguistics, Translation, Digital Humanities.

Translation is the first of these in terms of the development of humanity, having been a subject of controversy involving both speech and (hand-)writing for millennia. For much of that time issues centred on appropriacy and fidelity to rhetorical or literary purpose. Corpus linguistics arose first in the middle of last century with the birth of computers the size of a small room and continued now they can fit into a chip. CL was largely concerned in the 1960s and 1970s with describing languages in terms of their grammar and lexis, and in those days mostly regardless of the notion of structured text or text purpose, taking as its units chiefly the word, the lemma, the sentence. Digital humanities as a term is much more recent, but people (including many corpus linguists especially since the 1990s) have studied DH since there have been humanities texts available in digital format, and such DH researchers have mostly required a strong sense of text, text purpose and text structure.

The chapters in this volume bring together these three strands, exemplifying how one may seek specific answers to much more general questions: How can existing texts, literary, journalistic, historical, legal, philosophical etc. be best processed so as to identify patternings? Will such methods illuminate texts originally produced in or between different languages, and how will the act of translation affect findings? Where will research or practical implications fit in with other issues of interest to the DH reader and researcher? Welcome to the volume. Enjoy.

Mike Scott
Lexical Analysis Software & Aston University

1

Corpus linguistics and translation tools for digital humanities: An introduction

Michele Sala and Stefania M. Maci

Introduction

Although much research has been carried out on Corpus Linguistics (CL) – methodologies and applications – and on Digital Humanities (DH), on the one hand, and, on the other, extensive scientific literature is available on translation and Translation Studies (TS), there is still a critical gap as to how the three research domains relate and interact with one another, and how the combination of their specific methods and approaches may be used, firstly, for better understanding texts – on the basis of the quantitative and structural distribution of micro- and macro-linguistic elements – and, then, for such understandings to be effectively managed and exploited for translation purposes.

Another possible gap resides in the fact that, although CL and DH are indeed contiguous domains – both dealing with the investigation of digitalized texts – there is still little consensus as to their relation, interconnections and even possible overlaps (cf. Hockey 2004, Svensson 2010, DHM 2011, Burdick *et al.* 2012, among others).

This, arguably, has to do with the fact that they pertain to two different macro-domains: CL is a branch of Linguistics, based on 'data and methodology, analysis, and interpretation [...] referring to the use of corpora and computers as tools for analysis and to the use of the results as a basis for interpretation in the study of any aspect of language' (Kirk 1996: 251), whereas DH is a much broader domain, nested in the Humanities, studying or, more generally, handling digitalized versions of knowledge products 'in the arts, human and social sciences' (DHM2 2011: 2) not just for quantifications and frequency counting (which is typical of

CL), but also, for instance, for text editing, text mapping, transposition and other applications made possible by the digital format.

Secondly, the difficulty in defining how CL and DH at the same time differ and relate owes to the fact that the term DH has often been taken to mean different things in the course of the last decades. Unlike CL, which is a much older language-based discipline and domain of practice in data retrieval and investigation through digital tools – established in the 1960s and steadily growing with the development of computer technologies (Kirk 1996, Owens 2011, McEnery/Hardie 2012) – what is meant by DH is not discrete and clear-cut: as a matter of fact, as the introductory chapter of this collection will detail, the label DH has been used to refer at the same time to a field of investigation (i.e. what DH is), a domain of practice (i.e. what DH does) and a set of methodologies (i.e. how DH processes texts). Indeed, most of the literature on the subject was – and still largely is – focused on the definition of DH as a research domain, and on outlining its most central concerns and debates (Gold 2012, Terras *et al.* 2013) – often with the purpose of neutralizing scepticism within the Humanities on the part of the academic establishment and more traditionally oriented scholars (who considered 'toying' with machines not proper and solid academic work,[1] cf. Leech 1991, Fillmore 1992, Cohen 2010). Other scholars discussing DH, instead, focus on the practical usefulness of computational methods applied to text analysis for a variety of purposes, ranging from pedagogy, to text analysis or to editing (Cohen/Scheinfeldt 2013, Santos 2019). Finally, for another group of DH scholars the main aim of their research is to describe the range of applications and computational resources that can be applied to digitalizated texts (Carter 2013). Although these different approaches are coherent in themselves and internally consistent, the drastically different critical angle through which they assess the domain (i.e. analytic, operative and technical) impedes a cohesive framing of DH as a whole.

Another element of possible confusion as to how DH and CL relate comes from the quite restricted view that sees them as simply two parallel methodologies for carrying out research on different types of digitalized material. According to this view, for instance, CL appears to be a much more quantity-oriented set of methods, focussed on identifying or attesting patterns of language use in extended but structured collections of texts (typically, non-literary ones), whereas DH would appear to be an essentially quality-oriented method meant to locate and identify specific linguistic, discursive or stylistic elements within the same text (typically, a literary one[2]). This necessarily brings about a set of methodological considerations. In DH, for instance, text digitalization is perceived as a tool for text- and data-mining performed on unstructured data and 'raw' material (i.e. text simply usable in its electronic format, rather than material collected on the basis of some discursive or pragmatic similarity or family membership, cf. Ebensgaard Jensen 2014), thus being best suited for texts in the humanities (notably, literature, the arts, etc.). In contrast, CL works on structured collections of texts, where corpora are designed on the basis of specific criteria (ranging from text-type, to genre, domain, content, contexts, time and place of their production, channel, users, length or other extra-linguistic and contextual parameters etc.) for them to be representative of some specific language use and, at the same time, for corpora to be usable. As a matter of fact, in CL approaches, such structuring is organized on the basis of – or would allow for – annotation (i.e. part-of-speech annotation, syntactic, semantic, pragmatic, etc., cf. McEnery/Wilson 2001, Ide 2004, Baker et al. 2006), in order to make language material easily workable, that is, not only for occurrences to be systematically located and quantified, but for frequencies to be easily connected to specific patterns and for such patterns to be associated to recognizable pragmatic functions.

In sum, as will be amply discussed in the introductory chapter, DH is neither just the digital processing of literary texts, nor can it be only reduced to the exploitation of computer resources in human science investigations, or in the arts; similarly, CL is not purely concerned with quantity-based research at the expenses of quality-related analysis, and is not entirely carried out by machines, but does require human intervention for fine-tuning searches and for a fine-grained result interpretation.

For the purpose of this volume, DH and CL are neither parallel, quasi-synonymical or overlapping terms, but have distinctively different referents and are related according to a meronymic type of relationship (part-whole).

DH in fact is the extended domain, intended as the 'digital archiving of a body of human-made artefacts (i.e. the text and the usage-event therein) that are processed and interpreted via a plethora of digital methods' (Ebensgaard Jenses 2014: 124). In other words, DH is the overarching term for the macro-area of research which analyses texts produced in the humanities and social sciences – either taken singularly or collected in databases – by processing their electronic versions through an array of digital tools and for a variety of purposes, ranging from establishing frequencies, locating specific occurrences, finding internal or cross-references, quantifying distribution, evidencing similarities and differences otherwise difficult to find by manual text processing.

CL instead refers precisely to the 'plethora of methods' mentioned above, namely the set of principled approaches and tools based on or including criteria concerning corpus design (i.e. selection and organization of texts), corpus collection (i.e. on the basis of text affinity, representativeness, (proto)typicality, family membership, etc., or simply in terms of corpus size and exhaustiveness, especially for extended archives and databases) and corpus annotation (on the basis of linguistic, textual or pragmatic functions identified in connection to specific occurrences, etc.). Such collections then – structured and purpose-built ones or extended and unstructured archives – would allow for data searchers via both corpus-based approaches (i.e. from hypothesis to testing, meant 'to expound, test or exemplify theories and descriptions', Tognini-Bonelli 2001: 65) and corpus-driven ones (i.e. from quantification to hypotheses, cf. Tognini-Bonelli 2001), both to be carried out through annotation-oriented searches or via data-mining procedures – and thanks to a variety of dedicated software, concordancing programs, etc. (such as Wordsmith Tools, Sketch Engine, WMatrix, Antconc, etc.). In other words, where DH is the territory, CL is the map to chart it and make it manageable; where DH is the field, CL is the trajectory along which to navigate it.

Digital humanities and corpora

The importance of corpora for linguistic analysis in all its related domains and subdomains (i.e. from pragmatics to applied linguistics, from typology- and genre-based studies to cognitive analysis, etc.) can hardly be overstated.

After a long research tradition where the scholar's intuition was the sole, or the most relevant, parameter for linguistic investigation and language description – especially before the development of computer science and technologies, but also in the decades between the 1960s and the late 1980s, where Generative Linguistics was the dominant approach to language analysis (with its focus placed on the notion of native speaker's intuition as the basis for understanding how natural language occurs) – corpora started to be considered as invaluable resources owing to the quality, type and range of evidence they could provide, which could prove to be more solid, reliable and even quasi-empirical with respect to hypotheses and abstractions (cf. Sinclair 1991). As a matter of fact, since 'language is a human construct and its interpretation involves a degree of subjectivity, whatever the methodology employed' (Gotti/Giannoni 2014: 10), resorting to corpora and searching large amount of naturally occurring texts in order to test theories may not only keep any confirmation bias at bay, but may indeed produce unexpected results which falsify expectations, thus evidencing how 'our intuition about the patterns of use is often inaccurate' (Biber 2009: 190).

The awareness of the usefulness of textual evidence for substantiating possible abstractions is not restricted to modern research. In fact, as has been noted:

> The study of language use through documentary evidence gleaned from variously large collections of authentic texts pre-dates by centuries the modern science of corpus linguistics. Since Samuel Johnson's landmark Dictionary of the English Language (1755), lexicographers and the reading public have become aware that in language matters intuition is not enough, for the actual meaning/usage of words varies over time, from place to place and contextually. Driven by a similar interest, medieval scholars pioneered the first bible Concordances and similar concordances were compiled after the advent of print from the works of literary classics such as Chaucer, Shakespeare and Milton, to name but a few.
> (Gotti/Giannoni 2014: 9)

This concern acquired relevance and started to become central in linguistic investigations from the 1950s onwards, when computational techniques started developing and became more and more reliable and (relatively) easy to use (Sinclair *et al.* 1970), and especially when their applicability began being implemented for text analysis, in the late 1980s, making it possible to, firstly, gather and manage extended amount of text and, secondly, to use a variety of computing software for text processing purposes.

The availability of material that could be accessed both offline and online has made it possible to compile corpora of variable size – from relatively small ones (yet too large to be handled manually) to extended ones, to even larger Big Data archives – depending on the rationale behind their compiling. As we have briefly anticipated above, the factors that contribute to conferring structure to corpora and their designing may include the language of the sample texts included (i.e. national dialects, language used by native vs non-natives, etc.), the medium (i.e. written vs spoken), the format and type of the items collected (i.e. genre, register, text type, etc.), the domain (i.e. specialized vs non specialized, hard knowledge sciences vs humanities, etc.) and the type of users (i.e. their gender, profession, role within the community, level of expertise, status and recognizability for the audience, etc.).

Moreover, corpus collection is always necessitated by very a specific purpose (Pearson 1998, Teubert/Cermakova 2004, that is, 'in view of some kind of benefit' cf. Gotti/Giannoni 2014: 10), and this not only influences corpora's inherent organization, but will also determine the way they are going to be used.

On the basis of this, different types of corpus and approach to their use can be distinguished. The first is between *reference* and *disposable* corpora. The former are extensive – even gigantic – collections of texts meant to provide a testimony to and a representative sample of language use in either a given time/context or across times/contexts (*British National Corpus* (BNC), *Corpus of Contemporary American English* (COCA), *Cobuild Bank of English* (CBE), etc.). Disposable ones instead contain material collected by analysts in view of the type of research they are carrying out, therefore on the basis of specific requisites texts need to respect for them to be included (Pearson 1998).

Strictly connected to this is the type of investigation to be carried out with such materials, which, as we have seen above, can be intended to test hypotheses, substantiate theories, and validate assumptions (corpus-based approaches, cf. Tognini-Bonelli 2001) or instead to observe and quantify patterns of naturally occurring language in order to possibly find trends, commonalities or divergence in language use (corpus-driven approaches) – the former approach being typically the case with disposable purpose-built corpora, even though also reference corpora (or specially selected section of them) can be mined for purpose-oriented searches.

Finally, corpora can be investigated for either speculative or operative reasons, that is to say to either see how language is used with the aim to further its understanding or else to find regularities that can be singled out and taught in practical and applied contexts (i.e. for the pedagogy of general language or of specialized discourses, for highlighting terminological preferences, stylistic trends, rhetorical choices, etc., Hyland *et al*. 2012).

Chapters in the first part of this volume will be devoted to showing how compiling and scanning purpose-based disposable corpora, or resorting to existing ones as reference, may help trace discoursal traits and prosodic or semantic preferences which indicate how meanings are usually codified within specific contexts, how expectations are anticipated and managed and, eventually, how given interpretation may be favoured over others.

Corpora and translation

The potential offered by corpora in terms of locating items, collocations, recurring patterns, typical uses of the language in naturally occurring texts (i.e. not crafted ad hoc by analysts) was eventually appreciated also by translation scholars, and even welcomed as a 'new paradigm in translation studies' (Laviosa 1998: 1).

One of the earliest applications of corpus-based methods to TS was first hypothesized, in the mid-1990s (Baker 1993, 1995), primarily as a way of pointing to 'the nature of translated text as a mediated communicative event' (Baker 1993: 243), that is, as a way of detecting – with the purpose of becoming aware of their frequencies and, then, of possibly neutralizing them – the 'typicalities' of translated texts (TT), that is those forms of homogenization, normalization, conventionalization, reduction of idiosyncrasies (or 'universals of translation', cf. Toury [1978] 2012, 1995) that make the language of translation clearly distinguishable from that of non-translated text – as if a dialect of its own right – and whose features appear to be common to all translations irrespective of the type of the source texts (ST), their authors, the domains and the time of their production (such was, for instance, the purpose of the *Translational English Corpus* – TEC – compiled at the University of Manchester, cf. Olohan/Baker 2002, Olohan 2004). This emphasis on quantifiable evidence was also meant to address specific criticisms by some translation scholars (notably Toury 1980 and Holmes 1988, among others) who expressed concerns regarding idealizations and speculations made about translation, translation practices and processes, without them being based on observable data.

A part of said studies on corpus-based approach to TS, especially the early ones (Baker 1995, Olohan 2000, Laviosa 2002), indeed assessed core and philosophical issues concerning how 'to match theory, data, and methodology in a coherent whole' (Laviosa 1998: 2), or about corpus composition and possible bias, the representativeness of texts in translation corpora, etc. (cf. Halverson 1998, Malmkjaer 1998).

Another branching off of CL applied to TS is instead represented by the focus on corpora as a tool for translators or for translator training (Bernardini *et al.* 2003, Baker/Saldanha 2019), in order to facilitate translation as an activity rather than understand it as a communicative event. In operative contexts, translators have distinctive needs which are different from those of the linguists and language scholars, the main one residing in the fact that translation-oriented corpora should not only provide large amounts of searchable material, but should allow for comparison and contrast between texts written in different languages, hence the need for collections containing material from more than one language.

In these contexts, different types of corpus can be used and for different purposes – especially when computer-assisted translation (CAT) methods, allowing access to previous translations, are involved.

Monolingual corpora – intended as archives collecting authentic texts in a specific language – may serve as reference corpora by which to measure the naturalness and frequency of use of expressions and collocations the translator may be trying to transfer in the TL, hence representing 'the yardstick of the language against which to measure deviation' (Munday 2008: 181).

Comparable bilingual/multilingual corpora are collections of texts with similar pragmatic purposes and features (in terms of genre, content, domain, etc.) written in different source languages (SL) without being the translation of each other. They can be effectively resorted to for contrastive language analysis in that they allow for comparison, thus making it possible to find correspondences or terminological and referential forms of equivalence (Bowker/Pearson 2002, Granger *et al.* 2003, Williams 2007) – even though caution should always be used in that discursive practices in different languages may not match (Baker 1995, Aijmer/Altenberg 1996).

Finally, parallel (bilingual/multilingual) corpora are specific types of corpora which contain the STs and their respective translation – either from a SL *a* to a TL *b* (unidirectional corpora) or both from SL *a* to a TL *b* and vice versa (bidirectional corpora, cf. Olohan 2004) – thus favouring a closer investigation into the language of translation (Kenny 2001, Johansson 2007) in quantitative terms (i.e. by allowing comparison of concordancing software produced statistics in terms of words frequency, distribution, keywords, etc.) and in qualitative terms (i.e. by comparing concordance lines and collocations for various entries).

The second part of the present volume is expressly intended to explore the potential of these types of corpora from a translational perspective, namely as resources by which to measure, for instance linguistic unmarkedness (vs markedness), naturalness (vs idiosyncrasy) and typicality (vs atypicality) in SL uses in given contexts, or to detect possible differences between ST and TT, thus producing linguistic evidence upon which to try and understand translational variation.

Contents of the volume

Part One. Corpus linguistics for digital humanities: Research methods and applications

The first part of the volume expands upon the domain that is the object of investigation of this collection by assessing the assets offered by corpora, on the one hand, and CL tools and methodologies, on the other, when they are used to investigate texts, bring to light linguistic/prosodic features, understand language use and, ultimately, see how it may guide interpretation. The present collection opens with an introductory chapter – Digital Humanities: An adaptive theory approach, by Paola Catenaccio – which discusses the broad and multifarious concept of DH with the purpose of making it a coherent notion and an essential framing resource for a clear understanding of the contents in this volume. The chapter provides an overview of the main strands within DH, organizing them according to three broad categories – namely, DH as the study of digital artefacts, as the development and deployment of digital practices, and, finally, as the use of digital methods of analysis in the humanities – evidencing also how, despite being conceptually distinct, the boundaries between these three areas may often merge and overlap. Discussing the evolving cultural and methodological landscape of such areas, the chapter also evidences the challenges (or possibilities) represented by such a rapid evolution, which requires approaches to DH to be flexible and adaptable and, at the same time, capable of crossing and stretching boundaries and methods. In the light of this an adaptive theory approach is presented as being necessary in order to effectively address the many questions raised by DH.

The next chapter – Comparable corpora in cross-cultural genre studies: Tools for the Analysis of CSR Reports, by Marina Bondi – details how corpora – even comparable ones, which are usually relegated to translation-related types of analysis – can indeed be effectively used as investigation tools within the framework of established research domain, as is, for instance, genre analysis. Corpora, in fact, extend the range of resources available for contrastive investigation and CL tools allow for frequency calculations and for the retrieval of combination of elements (in terms of keyness or concordances) which provide essential insights into salient features of conventional and established genres – Corporate Social Responsibility reports in this case. The chapter shows that cross-cultural comparison of genres, made possible by comparable corpora, both facilitates and benefits from integrating analyses at different levels – namely, the lexical, semantic and functional-pragmatic – and different procedures – namely, bottom-up (from lexis to semantics and function) and top-down (from function to lexis) – and this contributes to a solid understanding of genres.

After having seen how CL affordances may complement research parameters in specific research domains and traditions (where the focus is distinctively on text and macro-language as much as on micro-language), the next chapter – Applying a corpus-driven approach in linguistic analyses: The case of Lexical Bundles and Phrase Frames, by Miguel Fuster-Márquez – discusses specifically micro-linguistic and phraseological units which are typically exploited for corpus-related researches, namely lexical bundles and phrase frames, that is, those multiword sequences which, mainly due to their frequency within given texts, can be taken to be distinctive of specific registers or text types. The chapter outlines the state of the art on such resources, and also offers an updated account on the criteria applied to their identification and quantification – distinguishing between the classical phraseological approach (focused on idioms and pre-selected phraseological expressions) and the distributional approach (focused on frequency and distribution) – their feature analysis – based on the tendency for given bundles to co-occur, their syntactic, semantic, pragmatic and discursive function – and extraction and operationalization – distinguishing between frequency-defined bundles and association-defined ones.

The last chapter in Part One – Data triangulation using Sketch Engine and WMatrix: Ketogenic diet on Twitter, by Stefania M. Maci – details how different CL computational methodologies can be used jointly to evidence trends in language use and identify semantic preferences in specific types of discourse – e-health communication, in this case. The author collects a corpus of posts on the ketogenic diet from Twitter – this platform being one of the loci where health literacy is developed and popularized, where specialized contents are transmitted and commented upon, on the one hand, and, on the other, corroborated or (possibly) transformed in the (interactional) process. Through a triangulation of quantitative and qualitative investigation, namely by using concordancing software such as Sketch Engine, in order to observe concordance lines and semantic preferences, and WMatrix4, to find key semantic domains – which are in turn determined by comparison with the British National corpus (spoken Sampler) – the chapter shows how given clusters (lexical choices and collocations) are associated to very specific semantics, hence establishing preferred interpretation on health-related issues on the part of and/or for Twitter users.

Part Two. Translation for digital humanities: Research methods and applications

Chapters in Part Two of the present volume discuss DH applications to translation and, more precisely, investigate how corpora and computational techniques are essential resources in translation-related context in order, for instance, to understand TTs with reference to STs, to find correspondences and forms of equivalence between STs and TTs, to help and train translators, and to help produce TTs which are as comprehensible and effective as STs.

In the first chapter of this section – The legal translator as a digital humanist: On using digital corpora in professional legal translation – Patrizia Anesa discusses the relevance of corpora in legal translation, how their use in professional practice has increased over the years for the optimization of translation processes and how the use of CL and DH resources in legal translation may contribute to knowledge construction (also due to the expansion of traditional semiotic, and representational and hermeneutic practices). The chapter offers a critique of existing legal corpora (that can be resorted to as reference corpora), and illustrates their main features, potential applications and also limitations. As the author claims, corpora can in fact be exploited not just for their application in the TT production, but they can also be useful for the translator in terms of vocabulary extraction and comparison, analysis of terminological collocability, awareness gaining of stylistic issues and for the evaluation of legal concepts across languages, cultures and legal systems. As such, legal corpora may help evidence and highlight the connection existing between the micro level of individual texts and the macro level of legal discourse.

The following chapter – A comparative study of emotive language in English and Italian migrant narratives – explores the relevance of comparable corpora in order to understand cross-cultural variation (and forms of continuity) in specific types of discourse. In their study, Cinzia Spinzi and Anouska Zummo focus specifically on emotive language (expressing anger, anxiety, nostalgia, etc.) used by migrants in their digital narratives in order to establish empathy within the community for inclusion purposes and, for this reason, the authors compile an *ad hoc* corpus containing 'stories' in English (collected from digital museums in London, New York and Melbourne) and in Italian (form museums in Genoa, Belluno and the virtual museum *Migrador Museum*). By offering the possibility of tracing and comparing lexical units and expressions conveying emotion-laden meanings, CL techniques applied to such materials allow migrants' discourse to be approached and understood as the first-hand and authentic expression of uprooted, 're-located' and adapted identities, thus eschewing stereotyped and other-mediated (both xenophobic patronizing) representations which are necessarily biased in terms of cultural acceptability and expectedness.

The next chapter – Learning analytics at the service of interpreter training in academic curricula, by Francesca Bianchi, Davide Taibi, Philipp Kemkes and Ivana Marenzi – assesses the potential that digital databases hold in pedagogical contexts, and in this specific case, for interpreter training (in modules offered by the University of Salento, Lecce, Italy). The authors provide a detailed overview of, first, the software tools now available for supporting terminology management, and then, of LearnWeb – an online competence developing environment, which has been recently complemented by a set of affordances specifically meant to help students create and manage glossaries and acquire terminology (and for teachers to monitor students' progress). Among such affordances particularly notable – especially as far as DH techniques are concerned – is the integration of Web resources (content-based databases such as Wikipedia, encyclopaedia, institutional websites, scientific publications, non-institutional websites or blogs, etc., and language-based databases such as monolingual and bilingual dictionaries, glossaries, Linguee or Reverso) and data tracking and data analysis systems, which allows investigations into the way students use the Web as source for relevant material in the creation of glossaries, and provides insight into the learning, cognitive and/or material processes that students of interpreting apply during the preparation phase and in glossary compilation, and into their preferences.

The final chapters of this collection show how CL methodologies – data extraction, quantification, comparison – can be exploited in investigating DH multimedia products in order to locate and highlight forms of equivalence or variation between STs and the related translation. In the chapter – Exploring the construction and translation of film characters through a parallel corpus: The case of *Little Women* adaptations – Gianmarco Vignozzi explores how computational techniques can be implemented in analysing character construction strategies in SL and dubbed film dialogues by considering the English original and Italian dubbed cinematic adaptations of *Little Women*. By organizing the film dialogues into a digital annotated parallel corpus, the material is made readily usable for systematic textual analysis across characters, film adaptations and translations. The chapter then provides a corpus-driven analysis on the texts focusing, on the one hand, on the characterization cues used in the ST to shape the identities of the four protagonists of the story (i.e. some conversational routines that typify each one of the March sisters) and, on the other, through a parallel concordance analysis, on the translation solutions used in the TT. In the chapter that closes this collection – Subtitling in the digital era: TV crime drama series in domestic languages – Alessandra Rizzo focuses on the use of crime and legal jargon as found in TV crime drama series (namely, the British *Luther,* the Scandinavian *Deadwind* and the Icelandic *TVM*). By collecting an *ad hoc* corpus of original dialogues and their translated versions, the chapter analyses subtitles and subtitling strategies as localization resources in order to evidence differences in the rendering of expressions or culture-based meanings from a source to a target language (Italian, in this case) and see how the 'prefabricated' or fictive orality which is typical of audiovisual drama series may vary and range between (pseudo) authenticity and (pretended) realism, on the one hand, and the stereotyped language of crimes drama series, on the other.

As we can see in the chapters of this volume, the digitalization of texts, while a necessary condition in DH, is just a first step into a wide, multifaceted and complex domain of investigation. When texts are collected in corpora, when corpora are designed on the basis of specific parameters (i.e. extended/reference vs disposable and purpose-based) allowing for data-mining, tagging, frequency counting, etc., and especially when CL methods, tools and applications are used to investigate samples in digital collections or to evidence differences between sets of texts through comparison (i.e. by resorting to reference, comparable or parallel corpora), then frequencies, commonalities and even idiosyncrasies can reveal more about texts and their meaning than (or beyond) their actual semantics. And this is of uttermost importance for both scholars in DH investigating language use, practitioners working with the language (notably translators, teachers, interpreters and even those working in the editorial and publishing domain), but, ultimately, also for researchers and developers of CL tools, for them to be able to refine and fine-tune applications in order to make texts more easily 'searchable' and readable and make their interpretation and understanding more accurate.

Notes

1   In a similar way, from the 1960s to the late 1980s, when Generative Linguistics was the dominant approach within the domain of Linguistics, generative linguists overlooked CL, privileging the notion of native speakers' (abstract) competence rather than performance-based evidence collected in corpora.
2   An item of '"traditional" literature, written and "frozen" in a publish text, and usually by a single author' (Santos 2019: 91).

References

Aijmer, K. and B. Altenberg (1996), 'Introduction', in K. Aijmer, B. Altenberg and M. Johansson (eds), *Languages in Contrast. Papers from a Symposium on Text-based Cross-linguistic Studies, Lund 4–5 March 1994. LundStudies in English 88*, 11–16, Lund: Lund University Press.

Baker, M. (1995), 'Corpora in Translation Studies: An Overview and Some Suggestions for Future Research', *Target. International Journal of Translation Studies*, 7 (2): 223–43. DOI: https://doi.org/10.1075/target.7.2.03bak

Baker, M. (1993), 'Corpus Linguistics and Translation Studies: Implications and Applications', in M. Baker, G. Francis and E. Tognini-Bonelli (eds), *Text and Technology: In Honour of John Sinclair*, 233–50, Amsterdam: John Benjamins.

Baker, M. and G. Saldanha (2019), *Routledge Encyclopedia of Translation Studies*, London: Routledge.

Baker, P., A. Hardie and T. McEnery (2006), *A Glossary of Corpus Linguistics*, Edinburgh: Edinburgh University Press.

Bernardini, S., D. Stewart and F. Zanettin, (2003), 'Corpora in Translator Education: An Introduction', in S. Bernardini, D. Stewart and F. Zanettin (eds), *Corpora in Translator Education*, 1–13, Manchester: St. Jerome.

Biber D. (2009), 'Corpus-based and Corpus-driven Analyses of Language Variation', in B. Heine and H. Narrog (eds), *The Oxford Handbook of Linguistic Analysis*, 159–92, Oxford: Oxford University Press.

Bowker, L. and J. Pearson (2002), *Working with Specialised Language. A Practical Guide to Using Corpora*, London: Routledge.

Burdick, A., J. Drucker, P. Lunenfeld, T. Presner and J. Schnap (2012), *Digital_Humanities*, Cambridge, MA: MIT Press.

Carter, B. W. (2013), *Digital Humanities: Current Perspective, Practices, and Research*, Bingley, UK: Emerald.

Cohen, D. J. and T. Scheinfeldt, eds (2013), *Hacking the Academy: New Approaches to Scholarship and Teaching from Digital Humanities*, Ann Arbor: University of Michigan Press.

Cohen, P. (2010), 'Humanities Scholars Embrace Digital Technology', *The New York Times*, 16 November. Available online: http://dbhs_sensei.tripod.com/webonmediacontents/Humanities%20Scholars%20Embrace%20Digital%20Technology%20-%20NYTimes.com.pdf (accessed 6 June 2021).

DHM - Digital Humanities Manifesto 2.0 (2011), Available online: http://www.humanitiesblast.com/manifesto/Manifesto_V2.pdf (accessed 6 June 2021).

Ebensgaard Jensen, K. (2014), 'Linguistics and the Digital Humanities: (Computational) Corpus Linguistics', *MedieKultur*, 57: 115–34.

Gold, M. K., ed. (2012), *Debates in the Digital Humanities*, Minneapolis: University of Minnesota Press.

Gotti, M. and D. S. Giannoni (2014), 'Introduction', in M. Gotti and D. S. Giannoni (eds), *Corpus Analysis for Descriptive and Pedagogical Purposes*, 9–21, Bern: Peter Lang.

Granger, S. and S. Petch-Tyson, eds (2003), *Extending the Scope of Corpus-based Research: New Applications, New Challenges*, Amsterdam and New York: Rodopi.

Fillmore, C. (1992), '"Corpus Linguistics" or "Computer-Aided Armchair Inguistics"', in J. Svartvik (ed.), *Directions Proceedings of Nobel Symposium 82, Stockholm 4–8 August 1991*, 35–60, Berlin: Mouton de Gruyter.

Halverson, S. (1998), 'Translation Studies and Representative Corpora: Establishing Links between Translation Corpora, Theoretical/Descriptive Categories and the Conception of the Object of Study', *Meta (Special issue: The corpus-based approach*, ed. S. Laviosa), 43 (4): 494–514.

Hockey, S. (2004), 'History of Humanities Computing', in S. Schreibman, R. Siemens and J. Unsworth (eds), *A Companion to Digital Humanities*, 3–19, Oxford: Blackwell.
Holmes J. S. (1988), *Translated! Papers on Literary Translation and Translation Studies*, Amsterdam: Rodopi.
Hyland, K., M. H. Chau and M. Handford, eds (2012), *Corpus Applications in Applied Linguistics*, London: Continuum.
Ide, N. (2004), 'Preparation and Analysis of Linguistic Corpora', in S. Schreibman, R. Siemens and J. Unsworth (eds), *A Companion to Digital Humanities*, 289–305, Oxford: Blackwell.
Johansson, S. (2007), *Seeing through Multilingual Corpora: On the Use of Corpora in Contrastive Studies*, Amsterdam and Philadelphia: John Benjamins.
Kenny, D. (2001), *Lexis and Creativity in Translation: A Corpus-based Study*, Manchester: St. Jerome Publishing.
Kirk, J. M. (1996), 'Corpora and Discourse: Transcription, Annotation, and Presentation', in C. E. Percy, C. F. Meyer and I. Lancashire (eds), *Synchronic Corpus Linguistics: Papers from the Sixteenth International Conference on English Language Research on Computerized Corpora, Toronto 1995*, 263–78, Amsterdam: Rodopi.
Laviosa S. (1998), 'The Corpus-based Approach: A New Paradigm in Translation Studies', *Meta - Special Issue: The Corpus-based Approach*, 43 (4): 1–6.
Laviosa, S. (2002), *Corpus-based Translation Studies. Theory, Findings, Applications*, Amsterdam: Rodopi.
Leech, G. (1991), 'The State of the Art in Corpus Linguistics', in K. Aijmer and B. Altenberg (eds), *English Corpus Linguistics*, 8–29, London: Longman.
Malmkjaer, K. (1998), 'Love Thy Neighbour: Will Parallel Corpora Endear Linguists to Translators?', *Meta - Special Issue: The Corpus-based Approach*, 43 (4): 534–41.
McEnery, T. and A. Hardie (2012), *Corpus Linguistics*, Cambridge: Cambridge University Press.
McEnery, T. and A. Wilson (2001), *Corpus Linguistics*, Edinburgh: Edinburgh University Press.
Munday, J. (2008), *Introducing Translation Studies*, 2nd edn, London: Routledge.
Olohan, M., ed. (2000), *Intercultural Faultlines: Research Models in Translation Studies. Textual and Cognitive Aspects*, London: Routledge.
Olohan, M. (2004), *Introducing Corpora in Translation Studies*, London: Routledge.
Olohan, M. and M. Baker (2002), 'Reporting *That* in Translated English: Evidence for Subconscious Processes of Explicitation?', *Across Languages and Cultures*, 1 (2): 141–58.
Owens, T. (2011), 'Defining Data for Humanists: Text, Artifact, Information or Evidence?', *Journal of Digital Humanities*, 1 (1): 6–8.
Pearson, J. (1998), *Terms in Context*, Amsterdam/Philadelphia: John Benjamins.
Santos, D. (2019), 'Literature Studies in *Literateca*: Between Digital Humanities and Corpus linguistics', in M. Doerr, Ø. Eide, O. Grønvik and B. Kjelsvik (eds),

Humanists and the Digital Toolbox: In Honour of Christian-Emil Smith Ore, 89–109, Oslo: Novus Forlag.

Scott, M. (2012), *Wordsmith Tools, Stroud: Lexical Analysis Software*. Available at: https://lexically.net/wordsmith

Sinclair, J. (1991), *Corpus, Concordance, Collocation*, Oxford: Oxford University Press.

Sinclair, J., S. Jones and R. Daley (1970), *English Lexical Studies*, Birmingham: University of Birmingham.

Svensson, P. (2010), 'The Landscape of Digital Humanities', *DHQ: Digital Humanities Quarterly*, 4 (1). Available online: http://digitalhumanities.org/dhq/vol/4/1/000080/000080.html (accessed 6 June 2021).

Terras, M., J. Nyhan and E. Vanhoutte, eds (2013), *Defining Digital Humanities: A Reader*, Farnham: Ashgate Publishing Limited.

Teubert, W. and A. Cermakova (2004), 'Directions in Corpus Linguistics', in M. A. K. Halliday *et al.* (eds), *Lexicology and Corpus Linguistics, An Introduction*, 113–67, London: MPG Book Ltd.

Tognini-Bonelli, E. (2001), *Corpus Linguistics at Work*, Amsterdam: John Benjamins.

Toury, G. ([1978] 2012), 'The Nature and Role of Norms in Literary Translation', in L. Venuti (ed.), *The Translation Studies Reader*, 168–81, London: Routledge.

Toury, G. (1980), *In Search of a Theory of Translation*, Tel Aviv: The Porter Institute.

Toury, G. (1995), *Descriptive Translation Studies and beyond*, Amsterdam: John Benjamins.

Williams, I. (2007), 'A Corpus-based Study of the Verb *Observar* in English-Spanish translations of Biomedical Research Articles', *Target*, 19 (1): 85–103.

Part One

Corpus linguistics for digital humanities: Research methods and applications

2

Digital humanities: An adaptive theory approach

Paola Catenaccio

1. What is digital humanities?

Digital humanities is by all accounts one of the most rapidly growing fields of research, as testified by the plethora of projects, courses and publications (including this one) devoted to it. One key feature of this field – which has rapidly moved from niche to mainstream – is that it seems to escape definition. The webpage https://www.whatisdigital-humanities.com/, which would appear to hold the promise of such a definition, fails to deliver on its pledge – and programmatically so. Upon landing on the website, a definition does indeed appear, except that it is accompanied by a caption which reads as follows:

> **NB**: Refresh the page to get a new definition. Quotes were pulled from participants from the 'Day of DH' between 2009–2014. As of January 2015, the database contains 817 rows and randomly selects a quote each time the page is loaded.

The point of the webpage is, of course, to highlight the broadness and instability of any definitions of digital humanities. Five years on, the concept of digital humanities has been no doubt refined, and the discipline (or method(s)?) has placed itself firmly at the forefront of the humanities as a field of human endeavour and academic research.

There remains a broadness – a vagueness, even – in the very idea of digital humanities, however, which appears to be constitutive to it. The multifaceted nature of the domain was indeed apparent from its very inception. The *Digital*

Humanities Quarterly, established in 2007, was one the first journals to be devoted to DH research. In the 'About Us' section of its website, the journal features this passage:

> Digital humanities is a diverse and still emerging field that encompasses the practice of humanities research in and through information technology, and the exploration of how the humanities may evolve through their engagement with technology, media, and computational methods. DHQ seeks to provide a forum where practitioners, theorists, researchers, and teachers in this field can share their work with each other and with those from related disciplines. In identifying the scope of DHQ, we define both 'the humanities' and 'the digital' quite broadly, and we invite contributions that probe the boundaries of the domain or re-examine its foundational premises.
>
> (http://www.digital humanities.org/dhq/about/about.html)

This description contains in a nutshell all that is needed to get an overview of the plethora of approaches subsumed under the label of Digital Humanities. By defining DH as a field encompassing the '*practice* of humanities research *in* and *through* information technology', the founders of the journal highlight, first of all, the nature of DH as a *practice*, and, secondly, the different roles that IT can have in DH – most notably, that of target of the investigation, of – possibly – medium for conducting/presenting humanities research (*in* information technology), and of analytical tool (*through* information technology). By defining the relationship between the humanities and technology as one of *engagement*, the passage also suggests that the humanities as we (used to) know them at the beginning of the twenty-first century are expected to be affected by their encounter with technology. A relationship of engagement is not one of mere use – technology is not just a new tool, or a new medium, but something which can in fact bring about changes in the very notion of humanities.

A similar point is made in *The Digital Humanities 2.0 manifesto* (2009), drafted at around the same time as the passage above. Here the point of departure is the acknowledgement that the world has changed, and that the changes that have occurred not only call for new knowledge paradigms, but also offer novel tools and techniques that can dramatically alter the way traditional humanistic knowledge is produced and disseminated:

> Digital Humanities is not a unified field but an array of convergent practices that explore a universe in which: (a) print is no longer the exclusive or the normative medium in which knowledge is produced and/or disseminated; instead, print finds itself absorbed into new, multimedia configurations; and (b) digital

tools, techniques, and media have altered the production and dissemination of knowledge in the arts, human and social sciences.

(http://www.humanitiesblast.com/manifesto/Manifesto_V2.pdf)

Again, the word chosen to introduce the field is *practices* – a term which places DH firmly in the world of empirical research – devoted to the exploration of a universe where the digital is, on the one hand, an object of study and, on the other, part of the technological tools and affordances whereby knowledge is created and disseminated.

The latter point conflates in a single definition both digital techniques for the analysis of humanities artefacts (most notably in the form of text) and digital tools and environments for the dissemination of results – to put it crudely (extremely crudely), text processing tools on the one hand, and digital methods of knowledge (re)presentation on the other, most notably hypermedia.

Given these premises, it is no surprise that to this day DH continues to mean different things to different scholars. A cursory overview of the literature that has been produced on the topic, as well as of the university modules and degrees in Digital Humanities which have been developed worldwide, suggests that the field remains as various and multifaceted as ever. Back in 2008, Zorich's survey of digital humanities centres in the United States described them as 'centres where new media and technologies are used for humanities-based research, teaching, and intellectual engagement and experimentation', with their goals being 'to further humanities scholarship, create new forms of knowledge, and explore technology's impact on humanities-based disciplines' (Zorich 2008: 4). By and large, this description holds to this day, though the parallel rise of (new) media studies has added a further dimension to the field (cf. Sayers 2018), with frequent overlaps (as well as divergences) between the two.

The reasons for this are easy to surmise. The topics subsumed under the umbrella term 'Digital Humanities' cover digital artefacts and digital practices (including digital ways of creating and disseminating knowledge in the humanities), as well as digital methods of enquiry for text and discourse analysis. The latter derive from an established tradition of humanities computing which all but dominated early DH projects, but which has now been complemented by other conceptualizations of DH covering a broader area of enquiry. All in all, it can be argued that the digital humanities cover three main strands:

1. The study of computer-mediated communication in its various forms, which has developed into a tradition of new media studies;

2. The use of computer-based techniques for text analysis;
3. The development of computer-based methods of knowledge organization (from digital libraries to multi-media databases).

To these, we must add natural language processing, with its various applications in text analytics, sentiment analysis, opinion mining, etc., as well as automatic translation, all of which have made huge progress in the last few years. These applications are beyond the scope of this chapter, not least because they involve technical knowledge which is not within my competences. Their relevance to the evolution of the field of DH as a whole is, however, huge, also in view of the development of truly transdisciplinary approaches (cf. Lin 2012). As for the third strand of DH, it also carries an enormous importance in terms of knowledge producing potential. For the purposes of this study, however, I will focus on the first two strands – the new forms of textuality enabled by the rise of computer-mediated communication, and the use of computer-based techniques for text analysis. To the discourse analyst, these two areas of the digital humanities – one centring around the impact of the new affordances provided by new media on traditional textualities, and the other exploring the potentials of corpus linguistics methods and techniques for a better understanding of language and discourse – are of special relevance because they challenge existing theoretical and methodological approaches, and can indicate new avenues for the development of innovative theoretical approaches. It is on the latter aspect that this chapter will focus.

2. The digital in the humanities: the rise of computer-mediated communication and the evolution of humanities computing

Computer-mediated communication predates the birth of the Internet, but it was the advent of the latter which marked its exponential rise. In a recent editorial appearing in a special issue of the *Journal of Computer-Mediated Communication* devoted to the state-of-the-art in CMC research, the editors ask themselves what the focus of such research should be:

> At a time when nearly all social activities could be, and likely are, mediated in some ways by some forms of computing technology, what should be the focus of CMC research? How do we theorize and study computer-mediated (or should we say digitally-mediated) communication when the topics of our

research – the technology, the concepts and processes of mediation, our sense of what constitutes communication, as well as the theories and methods used to examine these – are all in flux?

(Yao and Ling 2020: 5)

Yao and Ling's questions aptly underscore the theoretical and methodological difficulties of dealing with materials whose actual or potential configuration is constantly evolving, and where new technological affordances and changing communication patterns give rise to ever new phenomena which we are ill-equipped to address in all their implications.

Within this complex scenario, where multimodality has become the norm, one may be justified in believing that the written text has lost its centrality. And to an extent, this is true. Yet, the tradition of humanities computing – which has typically focused on verbal text – has continued to thrive. Besides technical improvements, which have led to the development of ever more sophisticated software for automated text analysis, there has been a surge in interest for corpus linguistics. Research in this now well-established tradition has both broadened and deepened in scope, and has often been aided and supported – for its interpretive component – by discourse analysis, giving rise to a robust tradition of quali-quantitative research (cf. Gabrielatos and Duguid 2014). Humanities computing in its most traditional meaning is alive and well, having benefited from the technological advances of the last thirty years or so.

In the remainder of this section, I will address some theoretical and methodological issues at the heart of new media studies and of corpus linguistic. After outlining some of the crucibles with which both are grappling, I will discuss the challenges they pose, arguing that addressing them can lead to synergic theoretical and methodological developments.

2.1. Computer-Mediated Communication and (New) Media Studies: theoretical and methodological issues

Computer-Mediated Communication (CMC) rapidly gained pace in the mid-1990s, becoming ubiquitous in later years as use of the Internet became more widespread. Research carried out in this tradition focuses on the study of digital (and increasingly multimodal) forms of communication. Starting from Susan Herring's 1996 edited volume (*Computer-Mediated Communication: Linguistic, Social and Crosscultural Perspectives*), which pioneered the era of CMC studies, scholarly work on CMC has come in a steady flow, its methodological focus shifting and developing with the evolution of computer-mediated practices and the rise of new technological affordances. Other key collections are Brenda Danet and Susan Herring's *The Multilingual Internet: Language, Culture, and Communication Online* (2007) and then, in 2009, Charley Rowe and Eva Wyss's *Language and New Media: Linguistic, Cultural, and Technological Evolutions*. Herring *et al.*'s *Handbook of the Pragmatics of CMC*, published in 2011, provides an excellent overview of the research carried out in the field in the first decade of the twenty-first century. Other collections which came out around the same time are Thurlow and Mroczek's *Digital Discourse: Language in the New Media* (2011) and Tannen and Trester's *Discourse 2.0: Language and New Media* (2013). The emergence, mainstreaming and evolution of new media, with their enhanced affordances and evolving patterns of communication, brought about methodological challenges in linguistics and discourse analysis which the research included in the above-mentioned volumes both testifies to and seeks to address.

Developing new analytical frameworks for the study of digital communication has proven, however, often elusive. As Jones, Chik and Hafner (2015) have pointed out,

> although there have been numerous attempts in discourse analysis (see for example Herring 2007), and sociolinguistics more broadly (see for example Androutsopoulos 2011), to formulate new analytical frameworks especially designed for the study of digital communication, the range of social practices associated with digitally mediated discourse, and the rapid pace at which new technologies are being introduced, make it difficult for any single framework to meet the challenge of understanding all of the complex relationships between discourse and digital practices.
>
> (Jones, Chik and Hafner 2015: 1)

The three scholars further stress the need to take stock of existing analytical approaches as well as to develop new ones:

> in order to cope with the fast-changing landscape of digital media, discourse analysts need to both draw upon the rich store of theories and methods developed over the years for the analysis of 'analogue' discourse, and to formulate new concepts and new methodologies to address the unique combinations of affordances and constraints introduced by digital media.
>
> (Jones, Chik and Hafner 2015: 1)

Formulating new concepts and methodologies, however, has not always been easy nor straightforward. Much research into the new media has relied extensively on ethnographic methods (cf., for instance, Androutsopoulos 2006, 2008, Georgakopoulou 2006, Kozinets 2010), though there have been early calls for combining qualitative and quantitative methods (cf. Georgakopoulou 2003). This was only normal at a time in the development of a new communicative environment when, literally, finding out 'what goes on' was of crucial importance. Digital ethnography has indeed been a prolific field, and a crucial one for the development of an understanding of computer-mediated communication. The proper analysis (as opposed to the description) of computer-mediated communication has relied by and large on a toolkit developed by Susan Herring in the late 1990s–early 2000s. Herring coined the term 'computer-mediated discourse analysis' (or CMDA) in 1994. The analytical framework she developed later evolved into a model 'organized around four levels of CMDA: structure, meaning, interaction management, and social phenomena' (Herring 2013: 4). The 'basic idea' of the CMDA toolkit is

> to adapt existing methods, primarily from linguistics (but in principle from any relevant discipline that analyzes discourse), to the properties of digital communication media. The methods and the phenomena, along with broader issues they address, are then loosely mapped onto four levels of hierarchy, from the microlinguistic, more context-independent level of structure to the macrolevel of contextualized social phenomena.
>
> (Herring 2013: 4)

The four different levels identified by Herring are structure, meaning, interaction management and social phenomena. At the level of structure, the issues to address comprise aspects such as orality, formality, complexity, efficiency, expressivity etc.; the attendant phenomena cover – in an ascending scale of complexity – typography, orthography, morphology, syntax, discourse schemata etc.; and the methods suited to the study of such phenomena are structural/descriptive linguistics, text analysis and stylistics.

At the level of meaning, the issues involved revolve around what is intended/communicated/accomplished; accordingly, the phenomena to be investigated are related to the meaning of words, utterances (in particular speech acts), exchanges etc.; as for the methods, they comprise semantics and pragmatics.

The third level is interaction management, with issues such as interactivity, timing, coherence, repair, co-construction etc; the phenomena involved are turns, sequences, exchanges, threads etc., and the methods conversation analysis and ethnomethodology.

The last level is that of social phenomena; it covers social dynamics, power, influence, identity, community etc.; the phenomena to be analysed are linguistic expressions of status, negotiation, face management etc., for the investigation of which recourse is had to methods such as interactional sociolinguistics, critical discourse analysis and the ethnography of communication (CMDA toolkit – Herring 2013: 5; revised version of Herring 2004).

As Herring herself pointed out in later contributions, while suited to tackling digital communication during its emerging phase, the capabilities of this toolkit have proven to have limited explanatory power as computer-mediated communication has become more complex. In particular, the rise of multimodality has challenged existing paradigms and methodological approaches – an aspect that has long been recognized in the literature, and which has been the object of considerable research since the turn of millennium (see, amongst others, Garzone 2007; cf. also Garzone 2019). As Herring puts it,

> the current conceptualization of CMC, which has not been updated substantially since the term first started appearing in print nearly 40 years ago, retains connotations of textual, one-mode-at-a-time transmission. Thus, as a first step, I propose reconceptualizing CMC as fundamentally multimodal. Indeed, if the proverbial Martian scholars were to come to the Earth and encounter CMC for the first time in 2018, they would undoubtedly perceive its transmission via multiple semiotic modes to be inherent in its nature – as, I assume, do young people who have never known a world in which CMC involved only textual exchanges. A consequence of conceptualizing CMC as multimodal is that non-multimodal CMC ceases to exist, except historically. This reconceptualization does not exclude text-only CMC; rather, text is one of a number of possible modes of transmission that also include voice, audio, video, and – I suggest – graphics and certain kinds of robotic devices […].
>
> (Herring 2019: 41)

This, in a way, puts theory and method development back at square one. How do we go about analysing the complexity of computer-mediated communication in its latest (and still developing) forms? For the linguist in particular, the 'broader question' is whether to 'remain within the borders of known linguistics methods and approaches, including traditional CMDA, or to "follow the technology where it leads, including beyond linguistics, to study CMD in all its forms"' (Herring 2019: 48). Again, the starting point may have to be descriptive; but – again – description is not enough. While it may be useful 'to gain an overall initial sense of what is going on in a complex environment', in order to systematically analyse digital communication 'more rigorous empirical approaches' are needed – 'methods that direct the researcher's attention to phenomena in systematic and principled ways, and that are informed by theory and research about the interactions of multiple semiotic systems' (Herring 2011: 344). More specifically, in a recent article on the co-evolution of computer-mediated communication and computer-mediated discourse analysis (2019) Herring has stressed the need for linguists who study CMD 'to move beyond the confines of familiar methods and approaches, including traditional CMDA, and to follow CMD where it leads, including beyond linguistics, in order to analyze emergent and unprecedented discourse phenomena in all their manifestations' (Herring 2019: 26).

This is where developments in what started as 'humanities computing' come into play.

2.2. From humanities computing to multimodal corpus linguistics and beyond

In a 2009 article on 'Humanities Computing as Digital Humanities', Patrick Svensson points out that the 'foundational story' of humanities computing, relies on 'two important epistemic commitments': (1) 'information technology as a tool' and (2) 'written texts as a primary object of study (for linguistic analysis)', arguing that commitments such as 'computer as instrumental tool' and 'text as object' end up 'helping decide what are legitimate types of questions and study objects for the field' (Svensson 2009: 18). Corpus linguistics has evolved precisely from this definition, and has traditionally focused on exclusively verbal text, or – for documents featuring contents relying on a variety of semiotic systems – on the verbal components of such documents. Corpus analysis techniques and other statistics-based methods of text analysis have been successfully used to investigate discourse in its broadest meaning. Corpus linguistic approaches are many and multifarious, suited to different kinds of analysis and to pursuit different but complementary goals. A recently published volume of collected papers, for instance, was specifically designed to provide 'a systematic comparison of various methodological approaches in corpus linguistics through a series of parallel empirical studies that use a single corpus dataset to answer the same overarching research question' (Baker and Egbert 2016: 1), testifying to the broad range of methods which go under the umbrella term 'Corpus Linguistics'.

In the case of the above-mentioned volume, the text around which all the analyses revolve is the digitalized version of an originally analogue text. This indeed was the norm in the early days of humanities computing. Today, however, the use of automated methods of text analysis is not confined to the investigation of conventional written texts. A growing number of studies use corpus techniques to study other forms of textuality, including spoken interaction and computer-mediated communication. The works referenced below are only some of the growing number of examples of text analysis using automated computerized routines and sophisticated statistical tools. In an early example of the potential of this kind of research, for instance, Niederhoffer and Pennebaker (2002) used automated text-analysis techniques to assess the degree to which people coordinated their word use in natural conversations, finding that individuals in dyadic interactions exhibited linguistic style matching (LSM). Interactional aspects of communication were also explored by Dürscheid and Stark (2011), who carried out a large-scale, corpus-based study of text messaging (thus introducing the digital element in the object of analysis); and at the heart of a study by Danescu-Niculescu-Mizil *et al.* (2013) is the investigation of the development of interactionally negotiated norms, whose variation over time in an online community was measured by the authors using statistical methods.

Automated techniques have therefore been used to explore verbal text produced in new digital environments, sometimes with the aim to identify similarities and differences with analogue texts. Research conducted by Emigh and Herring in 2005, for instance, measured formality in traditional and online encyclopaedia entries, finding that Wikipedia entries do not differ from traditional encyclopaedias in this respect. Another digital genre – the blog – was the topic of a study by Huffaker and Calvert (2005), who started from a qualitative analysis of gender differences in teenage blogs and then proceeded to quantitatively measure such differences. Herring and Paolillo (2006) assessed gender-related features of computer-mediated communication using the online tool *Gender Genie* to measure them, but finding that instead of being purely gender-related, such features were in fact related to the genre of the text analysed. Other important studies were devoted to computer-based methods for the automated classification of web-genres based on their recurrent linguistic features (Mehler, Sharoff and Santini, 2010); and the list could go on, and is indeed getting longer by the day.

As this brief overview shows, digital methods of text analysis have increasingly been applied to digital texts – but for the most part their application has been limited to the verbal component of such texts. Digital texts, however, are increasingly multimodal, develop along spatial and temporal coordinates and involve multiple semiotic resources; moreover, they are structurally unstable because of their hypertextual and hypermodal nature (Lemke 2009). As mentioned above, this has meant that research on digital texts of a multimodal nature has been mostly qualitative. Attempts have been made to develop tools that can enable multimodal corpus linguistics with a view to 'gaining insights into the meaning-making processes found in multimodal texts, including insights into the role language has to play in these processes' (Baldry/Thibault 2008: 12, cf. also Baldry/Thibault 2007, Baldry 2000, 2004, 2005, 2006, 2007). This research has related mainly to the development of multimodal corpus linguistics as a *theoretical* rather than as an *applicative* discipline; bridging the gap between the two has proven particularly challenging. Rather than pursuing this path, recent research seeking to account for some of the key features of new media communication has focused on measures of spatio-temporal dispersion/evolution and for network analysis (cf. Segev 2020 for a recent article on *textual* network analysis). Sentiment analysis, opinion mining and other data-mining techniques have also grown exponentially. All these methods provide valuable insights into the way digital communication works, identify prevalent themes and trends, and spot crucial information which interfaces with textual data (such as, for instance, user metadata), but fall short of accounting for textual aspects *strictu sensu*. There is no doubt that digital communication demands new methods of analysis, and that such methods must be capable of dealing not only with large amounts of data, but also with data that come in many shapes and forms, and which evolves diachronically in ways which are still largely unexplored. As Herring pointed out as early in 2013, especially needed in the field of web-communication are integrated multimodal analysis and longitudinal analysis, the latter being 'increasingly feasible given the preservation of digital records and computer-assisted corpus analysis methods' (Herring 2013: 22).

3. An adaptive theory approach

The brief discussion of DH as digital methods, on the one hand, and digital materials, on the other, has shown the extent to which these two originally separate strands have progressively converged, mutually influencing each other. It has also shown the challenges posed by the rise of digital communication – both theoretical and analytical. Heeding Herring's suggestion that we should 'follow the technology where it leads' (Herring 2019: 48) has indeed become an unescapable need. The technology may well lead us beyond linguistics, as Herring observes in the continuation of the above-mentioned quote; but it may also lead linguistics into unchartered territories which may stimulate theoretical development.

The topic of theory is an important one in the digital humanities. As has been shown above, the very nature of digital artefacts represents a theoretical challenge for linguists and communication scholars, as it involves a huge variety of mutually interconnected variables, each influencing the others. Capturing all these variables – which are themselves unstable and subject to continuous changes due to technological developments – and factoring in their possible modes of interaction can be difficult, especially if one wants to move beyond descriptive studies and reach generalizable results.

Because of the above-mentioned factors, theory development in the digital humanities is inevitably, I believe, the result of an ongoing interplay between emerging evidence and largely pre-existing theoretical constructs which are adapted and updated to account for such evidence. A theory capable of dealing with this kind of data needs to be adaptive, not only in the sense that it must be able to deal with the fast evolutionary pace of the world of digital communication, but also in the sense that it must be amenable to being shaped by such world. The notion of 'adaptive theory' was coined by Layder (1998), who explained that

> [t]he word 'adaptive' is meant to convey that the theory either adapts to, or is shaped by, incoming evidence while the data itself is filtered through, and is thus adapted by, the prior theoretical materials (frameworks, concepts, ideas) that are relevant to their analysis.
>
> (Layder 1998: 19)

Adaptive theory shares many features with grounded theory (Glaser and Strauss 1967), from which it derives. Grounded theory arose as a reaction to theory-testing approaches in sociological research which dominated the 1960s and was characterized by a qualitative focus aimed at generating theory 'by the systematic collection and analysis of data [which] is a very powerful way to bring concepts of reality to a substantive area both to others and subjects in the area itself' (Glaser 1992:14). In grounded theory, theory is inductively derived from data analysis. While not purely descriptive (a theory should *explain* and not only describe data), and whereas amenable to generalization (Glaser 1992), grounded theory relies essentially on empirical data and on the research process whereby such data are collected (Glaser and Strauss 1967). Adaptive theory departs from grounded theory in that it does not exclude reliance on previously existing theories; rather, it argues that the dynamic of adaptive theory is the result of an interchange and dialogue between prior theory (models, frameworks, concepts, conceptual clusterings) and emergent theory (Layder 1998: 27).

The field of the digital humanities is a prime candidate for an adaptive theory approach. Studies of digital discourse have been, on the one hand, informed by previous theoretical constructs in the field of linguistics. As stressed by Herring (section 2.1 above), the methodologies used to analyse digital discourse were originally the same conventionally used to investigate analogue discourse. Studies of digital genres (Garzone 2007, Santini *et al.* 2010), for instance, set out to explicitly adapt genre-theory and text-grammar principles to digital genres. At the same time, the realization that digital discourse worked in ways which could not be fully accounted for by using theoretical constructs traditionally applied to analogue discourse prompted extensive ethnographic investigation, which has yielded results that, in turn, have contributed to updating existing linguistic theories so as to make them capable of accounting for new, emerging phenomena (cyberpragmatics being a case in point). The rise of multi- and hypermodality in digital environments has added further layers of complexity which have been investigated in their own right, but which still lack an integrated theoretical framework.

The complexity of the digital environment has also exposed the limitations of some traditional humanities computing methods, in particular those subsumed under the umbrella term of corpus linguistics. The combination of multiple semiotic resources in digital discourse has proved difficult to codify in ways which may make it amenable to investigation using corpus analysis techniques. While patterns and regularities in digital discourse have been explored using a plethora of statistical methods (big data analysis having progressed enormously over the last decade or so), the explanatory potential of the application of quali-quantitative methods to multimodal corpora is still underexplored. Developing adequate digital methods for the analysis of large corpora of multisemiotic and multimodal texts capable of accounting for their mutual relationships and applicable to large corpora is essential if we are to identify regularities and patterns, and develop theoretical models that can accommodate and explain them. It has often been pointed out that corpus analysis is not a theory – but the evidence it produces can – and does – lead to theoretical development. This is true of 'traditional' corpus analysis (cf. McEnery and Gabrielatos 2006), and there is no reason to believe it would not be true of integrated multimodal corpus analysis.

In a recent contribution, Susan Herring (2019) has discussed the co-evolution of computer-mediated communication and computer-mediated discourse analysis. This co-evolution testifies to the fact that the process of theory building is inextricably bound with the evolving characteristics of the phenomena under investigation as well as with the development of analytical techniques suited to identifying the characterizing features of such phenomena.

Theory development in the digital humanities must be adaptive to capture the evolution of our object of analysis; but must also be adaptive in the sense that it must rely on evidence emerging from corpus (or data) driven investigation. Experimenting with computer-based analytical techniques for the analysis of multimodal data is essential if we are to collect evidence that may lead to theory development. Doing so involves multiple expertises, and is therefore bound to be a multidisciplinary effort. Methodological triangulation is essential to develop an integrated theory of discourse and communication open to challenges of a rapidly evolving digital world. Digital humanities, therefore, can gain enormously from applying the 'digital' to both the object and the method of study. It is in the interplay of these two strands in the Digital Humanities that lies the future of DH theory and methodologies.

References

Androutsopoulos, J. (2006), 'Introduction: Sociolinguistics and Computer-mediated Communication', *Journal of Sociolinguistics*, 10 (4): 419–38.

Androutsopoulos, J. (2008), 'Potentials and Limitations of Discourse-centered Online Ethnography', *Language@Internet*, 5. Available online: https://www.languageatinternet.org/articles/2008/1610 (accessed 1 July 2021).

Androutsopoulos, J. (2011), 'From Variation to Heteroglossia in the Study of Computer-Mediated Discourse', in C. Thurlow and A. Trester (eds), *Discourse 2.0: Language and the New Media*, 277–298, New York and London: Oxford University Press.

Baker, P. and J. Egbert (2016), 'Introduction', in P. Baker and J. Egbert (eds), *Triangulating Methodological Approaches in Corpus-Linguistic Research*, 1–19, London and New York: Routledge.

Baldry, A. (2000), 'English in a Visual Society: Comparative and Historical Dimensions in Multimediality and Multimodality', in A. Baldry (ed.), *Multimodality and Multimediality in the Distance Learning Age*, 41–89. Campobasso: Palladino.

Baldry, A. (2004), 'Phase and Transition, Type and Instance: Patterns in Media Texts as Seen through a Multimodal Concordancer', in K. O'Halloran (ed.), *Multimodal Discourse Analysis*, 83–108, London and New York: Continuum.

Baldry, A. (2005), *A Multimodal Approach to Text Studies in English. The Role of MCA in Multimodal Concordancing and Multimodal Corpus Linguistics*, Campobasso: Palladino.

Baldry, A. (2006), 'Promoting Comparative Multimodal Concordancing: Its Role in Language Education, Teacher Training, Subtitling and Minority Language Learning', in N. Vasta (ed.), *Forms of Promotion: Texts, Contexts and Cultures*, 97–124. Bologna: Pàtron.

Baldry, A. (2007), 'The Role of Multimodal Concordancers in Multimodal Corpus Linguistics', in T. Royce and W. Bowcher (eds), *New Directions in the Analysis of Multimodal Discourse*, 173–93, New Jersey: Lawrence Erlbaum Associates.

Baldry, A. and P. J. Thibault (2007), *Multimodal Transcription and Text Analysis. A Multimodal Toolkit and Coursebook*, London: Equinox.

Baldry, A. and P. J. Thibault (2008), 'Applications of Multimodal Concordances', *Hermes*, 41 (2): 11–42.

Danescu-Niculescu-Mizil, C., R West, D. Jurafsky, J. Leskovec and C. Potts (2013), 'No Country for Old Members: User Lifecycle and Linguistic Change in Online Communities', *Proceedings of the 22nd International Conference on World Wide Web (WWW '13)*, 307–18. Available online: https://doi.org/10.1145/2488388.2488416.

Danet, B. and S. Herring (2007), *The Multilingual Internet: Language, Culture, and Communication Online*, Oxford: Oxford University Press.

Dürscheid, C. and E. Stark (2011), 'SMS4science: An International Corpus-based Texting Project and the Specific Challenges for Multilingual Switzerland', in C. Thurlow and K. Mroczek (eds), *Digital Discourse: Language in the New Media*, 299–320, New York: Oxford University Press.

Emigh, W. and S. C. Herring (2005), 'Collaborative Authoring on the Web: A Genre Analysis of Online Encyclopedias', *Proceedings of the Thirty-Eighth Hawai'i International Conference on System Sciences (HICSS-38)*, Los Alamitos: IEEE Press.

Gabrielatos, C. and A. Duguid (2014), 'Corpus Linguistics and CDA: A Critical Look at Synergy', *CDA20+ Symposium,* University of Amsterdam, 9 September 2014.

Garzone, G. (2007), 'Genres, Multimodality and the World-Wide-Web: Theoretical Issues', in G. Garzone, P. Catenaccio and G. Poncini (eds), *Multimodality in Corporate Communication: Web Genres and Discursive Identities*, 15–30, Milano: FrancoAngeli.

Garzone, G. (2019), *Sharing Professional Knowledge on Web 2.0 and beyond. Discourse and Genre*, Milano: LED.

Georgakopoulou, A. (2003), 'Computer-mediated Communication', in J. Verschueren, J-O. Ostman, J. Blommaert and C. Bulcaen (eds), *Handbook of Pragmatics*, 1–20, Amsterdam and Philadelphia: John Benjamins.

Georgakopoulou, A. (2006), 'Postscript: Computer-mediated Communication in Sociolinguistics', *Journal of Sociolinguistics*, 10 (4): 548–57.

Glaser, B. (1992), *Basics of Grounded Theory Analysis*, Mill Valley, CA: Sociology Press.

Glaser, B. G. and A. L. Strauss (1967), *The Discovery of Grounded Theory: Strategies for Qualitative Research*, Chicago: Aldine Publishing Company.

Herring, S. C. (1994), 'Politeness in computer culture: Why women thank and men flame', in M. Bucholtz, A. Liang, L. Sutton, & C. Hines (eds), *Cultural performances: Proceedings of the Third Berkeley Women and Language Conference*, 278–94, Berkeley, CA: Berkeley Women and Language Group.

Herring, S. C., ed. (1996), *Computer-mediated Communication: Linguistic, Social and Crosscultural Perspectives*. Amsterdam: John Benjamins.

Herring, S. C. (2004). Computer-Mediated Discourse Analysis: An Approach to Researching Online Behavior. In S. A. Barab, R. Kling and J. H. Gray (eds), *Designing for virtual communities in the service of learning*, 338–376, Cambridge: Cambridge University Press.

Herring, S. C. (2011), 'Commentary', in C. Thurlow and K. Mroczek (eds), *Digital Discourse: Language in the New Media*, 340–8, New York and London: Oxford University Press.

Herring, S. C. (2007). A Faceted Classification Scheme for Computer-Mediated Discourse. *Language@Internet*, 4, article 1. https://www.languageatinternet.org/articles/2007/761

Herring, S. C. (2013), 'Discourse in Web 2.0: Familiar, Reconfigured, and Emergent', in D. Tannen and A. Trester (eds), *Discourse 2.0: Language and New Media*, 1–26, Washington, DC: Georgetown University Press.

Herring, S. C. (2019), 'The Co-evolution of Computer-mediated Communication and Computer-mediated Discourse Analysis', in P. Bou-Franch and P. Garcé-Conejos Blitvich (eds), *Analyzing Digital Discourse. New Insights and Future Directions*, 25–67, London: Palgrave.

Herring, S. C. and J. C. Paolillo (2006), 'Gender and Genre Variation in Weblogs', *Journal of Sociolinguistics*, 10 (4): 439–59.

Herring, S. C., D. Stein and T. Virtanen, eds. (2011), *Handbook of the Pragmatics of CMC*, Berlin and New York: Mouton de Gruyter.

Huffaker, D. and S. Calvert (2005), 'Gender, Identity, and Language Use in Teenage Blogs', *Journal of Computer-mediated Communication*, 10 (2). Available online: https://doi.org/10.1111/j.1083-6101.2005.tb00238.x.

Jones, R. H., A. Chik and C. A. Hafner (2015), 'Introduction. Discourse Analysis and Digital Practices', in R. H. Jones, A. Chik and C. A. Hafner (eds), *Discourse and Digital Practices. Doing Discourse Analysis in the Digital Age*, 1–17, Abingdon, Oxon and New York, NY: Routledge.

Knight, D. (2011), 'The Future of Multimodal Corpora', *Revista Brasileira de Linguística Aplicada*, 11 (2): 391–415. Available online: https://doi.org/10.1590/S1984-63982011000200006

Kozinets, R. V. (2010), *Netnography: Doing Ethnographic Research Online*, London: Sage Publications.

Lemke, J. (2009), 'Multimodal Genres and Transmedia Traversals: Social Semiotics and the Political Economy of the Sign', *Semiotica*: 283–97.

Layder, D. (1998), *Sociological Practice: Linking Theory and Social Research*, London: Sage.

Lin Y. (2012), 'Transdisciplinarity and Digital Humanities: Lessons Learned from Developing Text-Mining Tools for Textual Analysis', in D. M. Berry (ed.) *Understanding Digital Humanities*, 314–35, London: Palgrave Macmillan.

McEnery, T. and C. Gabrielatos (2006), 'English Corpus Linguistics', in B. Aarts and A. McMahon (eds), *The Handbook of English Linguistics*, 33–71, Oxford: Blackwell.

Mehler, A., S. Sharoff and M. Santini (eds) (2010), *Genres on the Web. Text, Speech and Language Technology*, vol. 22, Dordrecht: Springer.

Niederhoffer, K.G. and J. W. Pennebaker (2002), 'Linguistic Style Matching in Social Interaction', *Journal of Language and Social Psychology*, 21 (4): 337–360.

Rowe, C. and Wyss E. (eds) (2009), *Language and New Media: Linguistic, Cultural, and Technological Evolutions*. New York: Hampton Press.

Santini M., A. Mehler and S. Sharoff (2010), 'Riding the Rough Waves of Genre on the Web', in A. Mehler, S. Sharoff and M. Santini M. (eds), *Genres on the Web. Text, Speech and Language Technology*, 3–30. Dordrecht: Springer.

Sayers, J., ed. (2018), *The Routledge Companion to Media Studies and Digital Humanities*, New York: Routledge.

Segev, E. (2020), 'Textual Network Analysis: Detecting Prevailing Themes and Biases in International News and Social Media', *Sociology Compass*, 14 (4): 1–14.

Svensson, P. (2009), 'Humanities Computing as Digital Humanities', *Digital Humanities Quarterly*, 3 (3). Available online: http://digitalhumanities.org/dhq/vol/3/3/000065/000065.html (accessed 2 July 2021).

Tannen, D. and A. Trester, eds (2013), *Discourse 2.0: Language and New Media*, Washington, DC: Georgetown University Press.

Thurlow, C. and K. Mroczek, eds (2011), *Digital Discourse: Language in the New Media*, New York and London: Oxford University Press.

Yao, M. and R. Ling (2020), 'What Is Computer-mediated Communication? An Introduction to the Special Issue', *Journal of Computer-Mediated Communication*, 25: 4–8.

Zorich, D. M. (2008), *A Survey of Digital Humanities Centers in the United States*. Washington, DC: Council on Library and Information Resources. Available online: http://www.clir.org/pubs/reports/pub143/pub143.pdf (accessed 21 January 2021).

Comparable corpora in cross-cultural genre studies: Tools for the analysis of CSR reports

Marina Bondi

1. Introduction

The chapter explores the potential of corpus tools in cross-cultural studies of genres. The discussion is based on important assumptions about corpus linguistics and cross-cultural genre analysis.

The first assumption is that a cross-cultural comparison of genres requires integration of lexical categories with semantic and functional pragmatic perspectives. Studies on specialized discourse have witnessed a constant interest in genre analysis over the past thirty years. Different approaches to genre in the 1990s (Swales 1990, Berkenkotter/Huckin 1994, Christie/Martin 1997) were clearly marked by an interest in the definition of the organizational structure of genres. Identifying the rhetorical functions of a genre became a primary preoccupation, especially in the pedagogically oriented fields of ESP and EAP, largely influenced by Swales's two-layered move/step models. The early focus of genre analysis promptly extended to the linguistic features of the communicative functions and to cross-cultural comparison. Cross-cultural perspectives have rapidly caught the interest of scholars interested in different aspects of intercultural communication, often in relation to the expansion of English as the international language of knowledge and business. The need to communicate cross-culturally requires an awareness of convergences and divergences that may characterize both linguistic and rhetorical features of the discourses that identify the communicative event in various cultural contexts.

A second assumption regards corpus linguistics. Corpus-based and corpus-driven approaches have had enormous influence on all linguistic disciplines over the past thirty years or so. The most important contributions of corpus linguistics appear to me to lie in providing tools for the calculation of frequencies and for the study of the combination of elements, that is, phraseology in a wider sense. Corpus tools like frequency lists and keywords provide us with immediate and accurate access to quantitative data that may either substantiate our analysis or drive it. Corpus tools like concordancing have offered new perspectives to the study of words in combination and therefore to the study of meaning in text and of the interface between lexis and grammar. Sinclair's extended-units-of-meaning model (Sinclair 1991, 1996, 1998, Stubbs 2001, 2007, 2013), for instance, explores the phraseological tendency in language through four levels of analysis: collocation (words that occur regularly with the node word), colligation (grammatical categories that define the immediate context of the node word), semantic preference (the tendency to co-occur with words sharing the same semantic features) and semantic prosody (the tendency of the word to occur in specific pragmatic contexts, its connection to a specific speech act and/or evaluation).

The first corpus projects, like the Brown Corpus, were mostly monolingual. Although contrastive work emerged rather early, with pioneer work on a corpus of Serbo-Croatian translations of texts from the Brown Corpus (Filipović 1971), it was only in the early 1990s that seminal work by Johansson (Johansson/Hofland 1994) opened the way for further developments in the field (see Ebeling/Olsefjell Ebeling 2013 for an overview).

Parallel and comparable corpora have since been growing progressively, with different goals. Over the past three decades they have proved to be key training tools in machine translation and multilingual natural language processing, as well as essential elements in contrastive linguistics, translation studies and foreign language teaching. The burgeoning availability of multilingual parallel resources (different versions of the same text), for example within the EU, has stimulated increasing research on parallel corpora, especially with a view to corpus-based and corpus-driven approaches to translation (Saldanha 2009, Zanettin 2012, Laviosa 2015; see Doval/Sánchez Nieto 2019 for a recent overview). Comparable corpora, on the other hand, involve 'monolingual subcorpora designed using the same sampling frame' (McEnery/Xiao 2007: 132). These have provided an empirical basis for contrastive and cross-cultural studies (Johansson 2007), while drawing attention to the problems of assessing the comparability of their components, given the multiplicity of contextual factors in which texts are situated (Moreno 2008).

Using cross-cultural studies of Corporate Social Responsibility (CSR) reports as a case study, the chapter looks at how corpus tools (most notably keyness and concordances) offer different ways of integrating these lexical, semantic and functional-pragmatic perspectives in genre analysis, and how they can contribute to different, complementary paths of integration (bottom-up and top-down). It also shows that the integration of bottom-up procedures (from lexical units to semantics and functional-pragmatic units) and top-down procedures (from functional-pragmatic units to semantics and lexical units) can actually take place at different levels of textual structure.

The chapter is structured as follows. Section 2 deals with the background literature on cross-cultural approaches to CSR reporting. Section 3 presents problems of corpus compilation. Section 4 provides an analysis of different ways of looking at the structure of CSR reports and at some of their key components. Sections 5 and 6 look at keyness and concordances as tools for the analysis of the semantic and pragmatic features of the genre.

2. Background: cross-cultural analysis of CSR reports

The concept of CSR, first introduced by Bowen (1953), has been paid increasing attention. The European Commission has defined it as the responsibility of enterprises for their impact on society (COM 2011). The expression refers to the company's strategies, activities and practices that are relevant to its various stakeholder groups, covering the economic (e.g. shareholders, investors), environmental (e.g. local communities) and social dimension (e.g. employees). In the past twenty years, with globalization and the increasing role of the Web, CSR communication has proved a key tool for organizational communication.

CSR communication has also attracted great attention in applied language studies. An obvious focus has been the key role that CSR communication plays in impression management and identity creation. This has created intensive work on issues of legitimation (Breeze 2012, Fuoli 2012), repurposing and interdiscursivity (Catenaccio 2010, 2011, 2012), evaluative language use (Malavasi 2007, 2011, 2012, Lischinsky 2011, Fuoli 2012, Bondi 2016b) and modality (Aiezza 2015, Bondi 2016a). In a critical perspective, Aditi Bhatia (2012) has highlighted the interplay of three types of discourses: (a) the *discourse of promotion*, aiming at establishing credentials and building importance to (re)construct the corporate image; (b) the *discourse of good will*, aiming at demonstrating that the company cares for society and is committed to CSR principles and action; (c) the *discourse of self-justification*, used by companies to legitimize their practices emphasizing the constraints forced on the companies 'by external conditions' (Bhatia 2012: 235).

CSR reporting has rapidly grown into institutionalized practice in the world of corporate communication (Contrafatto 2014, Tang *et al.* 2015). This has led to the development of reporting guidelines and standards regulating what is otherwise in most countries voluntary practice (Bondi/Yu 2018b). The Global Reporting Initiative (GRI), for example, provides a flexible framework for creating standalone sustainability (non-financial) reports or integrated reports. National and supranational strategic documents – such as national action plans, the EU *2011 CSR strategy* and directive *95, 2014* – may also influence the structure of reports. Beyond coercitive and normative processes, however, what is most important is often 'mimetic isomorphism' (Bondi/Yu 2018a), that is, the tendency of an institution to imitate the structure or practice of more prestigious organizations (DiMaggio/Powell 1983).

Studies in this field often aim to understand how CSR is communicated to different stakeholders in different cultural and linguistic contexts (Williams/Aguilera 2008), highlighting elements of convergence and divergence. Scherer and Palazzo (2008) point at an interesting paradox in corporate reporting: corporate disclosure is clearly related to the global contexts and guidelines that influence the structure of reports, but it is also inevitably oriented to its immediate cultural context, that is, local orientations, business culture and corporate culture, rather than 'national culture' (see also Malavasi 2012).

On the one hand, it is true that companies all over the world are adopting the same standards and practices under the influence of globalization, converging national policies and international action (e.g. Fortanier *et al.* 2011, Tang *et al.* 2015). Many of the studies highlighting convergence focus on the themes and topics dealt with in reports, often drawing on the concept of legitimacy (e.g. Fortanier *et al.* 2011), that is, on the notion that the actions of an organization are only seen as appropriate within a socially constructed system of norms, values and beliefs (Suchman 1995: 574) and therefore tend to mirror them.

On the other hand, it is also possible to see the influence of specific cultural, social and political contexts (e.g. Bravo *et al.* 2013) with their values and norms. National cultural norms, organizational culture, professional culture and different types of stakeholders (communities, consumers, customers, regulators) may contribute to divergence patterns (Williams/Aguilera 2008, Tang *et al.* 2015). Bhatia (2012), for example, shows that US companies tend to articulate the discourse of goodwill in terms of company engagement with society, while

Chinese companies show more explicitly their caring and nurturing approach to the environment and society (Bhatia 2012: 232).

In line with what has been studied of globalizing and localizing trends in general, the two opposing forces may be seen to contribute to the coexistence of divergent local practices with convergent global trends (Einwiller *et al.* 2016, Kim *et al.* 2018) in forms of synergistic interaction that are often called forms of 'crossvergence' (Jamali/Neville 2011: 616, Conte *et al.* 2020: 9) or cross-cultural hybridity. A study of comparable corpora can help highlight these patterns from the point of view of cross-cultural genre analysis (Yu 2021).

3. Corpora and issues of corpus compilation

The analytical pathways discussed in the next sections are based on two different but related comparable corpora for a cross-cultural study of CSR reports. Both corpora were created for cross-cultural analysis of the genre and were used for different kinds of analyses.

3.1. The Ba-CSR corpus

The first corpus is a comparable corpus of CSR reports in the banking sector comprising reports in English and in Italian. When looking at these two languages from a cross-cultural perspective, a number of observations are in order. A major question lies obviously in the comparability of the two languages in terms of use, rather than in terms of the two language systems. This issue is linked to the question of the varieties of English to be considered and the status of different banks.

First of all, in fact, it will be obvious that Italian tends to address a basically national audience, whereas English may be thought of as also addressing an international audience. The different international status of the two languages is undeniable, but this difference may be more or less relevant in different contexts. In many fields of academic discourse, for example, it is a matter of language choice, and ultimately of different degrees of competitiveness of the contexts addressing a national and international audience. In corporate reporting, the readership issue ties in to the type of company: companies may operate more locally or more internationally and may therefore produce the same document in both languages with a national or international audience of stakeholders in mind (employees, investors, competitors, analysts, trading partners and activists). The CSR report is a high-stakes text anyway, for its role in communicating with stakeholders, as well as constructing and maintaining a positive corporate identity. This makes it a key document for smaller and large companies alike.

The choice of what varieties of English to consider is another important question. Rather than thinking of this in terms of native or non-native varieties, one could perhaps consider publication in English-speaking or non-English speaking contexts. Reports are often realized through different production processes, by national or multinational teams, but they are hardly ever the product of a single speaker and almost never of a definite speaker. This makes it difficult to establish systematically whether they were written by a native speaker, or by an international team, or rather translated or revised through language services, as there may be different production contexts globally and locally. In a way, from the point of view of professional communication in the field, the question is hardly relevant: the language variety that is relevant for professionals is primarily the English produced and disseminated by major companies in the field. It may thus be important to consider the use of English in an international context more generally, including both companies based in an English-speaking country, and companies based in non-English speaking countries.

The Ba-CSR corpus includes thirty standalone CSR reports from international banks who publish their reports in English and a 'comparable' corpus of thirty CSR reports in Italian from Italian banks, collected in the same time span of five years (before the introduction of integrated reports). The Ba-CSR-En component (Banking CSR in English) (about 855,000 words) consists of reports from six top international banks: three headquartered in the UK (Barclays, HSBC, Royal Bank of Scotland) and three headquartered in Spain, Germany and China, and thus more clearly representative of EIL (English as an International Language): Banco Santander, Deutsche Bank and ICBC. These are all major banks and, irrespective of the English-speaking or non-English speaking contexts, have a clear international standing, which makes their use of English representative of the English used in international banking communication. The Ba-CSR-It_Component (ca. 1.5 million words) comprises reports in Italian from six major Italian banks producing a standalone CSR report at the time: BNL, Cariparma, Monte dei Paschi di Siena, Banca Intesa SanPaolo, Unicredit, UBI. The range of banks is much wider here in terms of size and international orientation: two banks have an international standing (Unicredit and IntesaSanpaolo), two operate within the influence of French groups (Cariparma and BNL) and the other two are more local (see Bondi 2016b for more information).

There are therefore obvious limits in the comparability of the two language-specific components, in terms of the dimensions of the companies and of their potential international readership. Comparability, however, is hardly exempt from limits in contrastive linguistics. What is important is to be aware of these limits when setting research questions and interpreting the data. A corpus of this kind can still be used to highlight features of cross-cultural rhetoric, in that it allows comparison of textual structures and pragmatic choices. The internal variation of each component can also be further explored to study variation within the same language system. It is always extremely important, in fact, to avoid oversimplification in cultural contrast and appropriate awareness of corpus design principles can help.

3.2. The CSR-ICE Corpus

The CSR-ICE Corpus (Yu/Bondi 2017, 2019) (about 3 million tokens) comprises ninety CSR reports published by companies in the banking sector and in the energy sector in one financial year. Rather than trying to trace diachronic development over a time span, a corpus of this kind takes a picture of a point in time but offers a wider picture in terms of companies involved (ninety altogether, though with the same number of CSR reports per language, i.e. thirty). Having more than one sector of course introduced more variables, but this was regarded as a plus when trying to study the structure of the genre, as it avoided the risk of describing a specific case and treating it as a general case.

The CSR-ICE also offers a wider language span, in that it involves three languages: Italian, Chinese and English. The choice of three languages was deliberately taken in order to illuminate more clearly convergences and divergences of the three components, beyond easy oppositions (especially in terms of East and West). It was also interesting to have languages belonging to different families, so as to allow for a wider perspective when looking at more specific features.

Language and culture variation within the components was once again an issue: when looking for a definition of the generic structure of CSR reports (Yu/Bondi 2017), for example, it was important to consider a wide range of varieties and therefore we included British, American and Canadian companies. When interpreting the data, on the other hand, it may be important to keep in mind the different specific contexts and there may be different national influences in terms of legislation. Similarly, when looking at specific language questions, there may be norms that hold in one variety and do not hold in another. In quite a number of cases, working with sub-corpora also allows for more fine-tuning on these issues.

A combination of perspectives – working with the full corpus and with comparable subcorpora – is also often necessary for different reasons. When manually annotating a corpus in terms of rhetorical units or pragmatic functions, it is often expedient to reduce the scope of the analysis, while keeping the larger corpus as the appropriate tool for studying the frequency of occurrence of language features: a subcorpus of eighteen annotated reports (six per language) was thus created for the purpose. When the need is felt to have cultural homogeneity in the corpus from English-speaking contexts, it is also possible to select a homogenous subcorpus: Bondi/Yu (2018c), for example, used a subcorpus of twenty reports from China, Italy and the United States.

4. Exploring top-down pathways: Generic structure

The analysis of the rhetorical structure of reports is based on the tools of genre analysis (e.g. Swales 1990, Bhatia 1993, 2004). With longer documents like CSR reports, this may be done in different ways and stages. Bondi (2016b), for example, looks at the BA-CSR corpus trying to identify the highly complex nature of the whole document. The main report is introduced by a Preamble, consisting of part-genres like the front cover, the table of contents, the CEO's letter etc. and followed by a Corollary including guidelines, indicators, appendices etc. Borrowing the terminology from Parodi (2010), the complexity of these extended documents is characterized by a recursive structure that can be defined as a 'colony-in-loops', which appears to be based on the topics identified as relevant by the international guidelines of the GRI-Index. The structure also highlights two main sections aimed at self-presentation (with general issues of company history, corporate identity, governance etc.) and performance reporting (with a specific focus on economic, social and environmental performance) (Bondi 2016b: 177). The overall analysis highlights a homogeneous thematic structure across cultural contexts and marked repetitive patterns, with functional sequences repeated for each new topic and similar thematic organization. The organization of the report seems to be largely influenced by international standards, which lead to convergence in the nucleus of the macro-structure. There is variation in the satellites, however: Italian reports, for example, show a marked preference for including a conspicuous amount of facts and figures in the Corollary, with no explicit explanation for the lay reader.

A closer study of the CSR-ICE corpus also highlights both patterns of convergence and divergence. Bondi and Yu (2018a: 186) confirm that there is substantial variation in the way the Preamble and Corollary are organized. Italian reports show a marked inclination for placing a lot of the quantitative information and methodological statements in supplements, but an obvious lack of interest in feedback sections. Chinese companies have higher frequency of management statements, as well as feedback sections and glossaries. Reports in English are marked by a decided presence of cautionary statements. All this may reflect the legal context – possibly requiring cautionary statements or management statements – or the perceived readership – as with the marked preference for placing quantitative data in the Corollary, which seems to address a distinct kind of reader.

Closer move analysis (Yu/Bondi 2017) is based on a subcorpus of CSR-ICE consisting of eighteen reports (six per language), which was manually annotated (with Notetab) for the main moves used in CSR reports. Starting from Catenaccio's (2012) four-macro-move structure (presenting the company, with a focus on its role as responsible social actor; presenting the company's CSR strategy, reporting the company's activities and performance, situating the context), the study developed a model with fifteen moves, which were in turn analysed into steps/strategies used to realize them. The results certainly contributed to highlighting remarkable similarities in the general organization of the document and its main moves, while also confirming peculiarities, such as an Italian emphasis on performance reporting and a Chinese preference for presenting individual cases.

What is most relevant here, however, is that the process of manual annotation for rhetorical categories leads researchers to an exploration of the complexity of textual processes, as well as to the need for reliability checks. The identification of moves requires attention to lexico-grammatical, semantic and pragmatic features of the verbal and visual text, with a view to matching linguistic signals and units defined by content and function (see also Moreno/Swales 2018 for an overview of the problems).

Rhetorical tagging requires a number of steps for the identification of moves (see Yu/Bondi 2017: 277–81 for a more specific account of the annotation procedures). It is important to begin from the communicative purposes of the genre, but also to devise a procedure for segmenting the text into appropriate units. We aimed at defining the elements that influenced the inductive and cognitive process of move identification: the 'distinct linguistic boundaries that can be objectively analysed' mentioned by Biber *et al.* (2007: 24). In particular, we made use of formal realizations and elements related to the hallidayan metafunctions of language (ideational, interpersonal and textual, see e.g. Halliday 1985). By formal realizations we meant both elements of the verbal text (e.g. presence of future markers for the move 'Previewing future performance') and elements of the non-verbal text (e.g. paragraphing, highlighting, initial position etc.). A consideration of the metafunctions also helped us define units by a combination of their communicative purpose (e.g. presenting) and content-related themes (e.g. performance, values etc.). We also felt that in some cases it was important to grant the status of move to units that had a major textual function, like 'Introducing an aspect of CSR performance' (usually leading to 'Presenting performance' or 'Communicating strategies/methods/practices').

Identifying the moves first allowed measuring their extensiveness, showing for example what percentage of the report is actually devoted to a move. Chinese reports are characterized by greater extensiveness of moves showing commitment to CSR values, Italian reports by presenting performance moves and reports in English by presenting strategies/methods/practices (Yu/Bondi 2017: 282). The identification of moves and steps also helps to show typical sequences of moves or steps. For example, in the Ba-CSR corpus, where the English component shows a tendency to move from 'Identifying elements of vision/value' to 'Specifying strategy' and 'Stating strategies/methods/practices', as in Example 1, the Italian corpus shows a tendency to proceed from strategy to values, as in Example 2.

1. Good governance. HSBC's governance structure is focused on delivering sustainable value to our shareholders. The strategy and risk appetite for HSBC is set by the Board, which delegates the day-to-day running of the business to the Group Management Board. Global businesses and functions have established operating, financial reporting and management reporting standards for application throughout HSBC. (HSBC)

2. I VALORI. Intesa Sanpaolo ha adottato nel luglio 2007 il Codice Etico, carta valoriale che esprime in primo luogo l'identità della Banca, quello che vuole essere e i principi che adotta nelle relazioni con i propri stakeholder. Il Codice di Intesa Sanpaolo è imperniato sul concetto di responsabilità e richiede, non solo ai singoli ma anche a ogni funzione aziendale, di garantire il proprio impegno perché le attività siano sempre coerenti con i valori dichiarati. (IntesaSanpaolo) ['OUR VALUES. In July 2007 Intesa Sanpaolo adopted the Code of Ethics, a charter of values that first of all

expresses the Bank's identity, what it seeks to be and the principles it adopts in relations with stakeholders. The Intesa Sanpaolo Code of Ethics focuses on the concept of responsibility and requires that not only individuals but also every corporate department guarantee their commitment to ensuring that business activities remain consistent with the values stated']

Finally, and most importantly, the identification of components of the text (whether sections or moves), allows further lexico-grammatical, semantic and pragmatic study. One can for example focus on the lexico-grammatical features of a specific move, beyond the constitutive elements that defined it or in terms of the specific patterns that characterized the constitutive elements. Yu and Bondi (2019), for example, focus on forward-looking statements in 'Previewing future performance' moves, by looking first at the moves and steps that characterize the two corpora and then at the language features that characterize the move. Looking at the frequency and distribution of moves helps to identify elements of convergence such as the constitutive steps of the move ('Committing to future actions' and 'Predicting future actions and results') and the predominance of commitment, while also showing cross-cultural divergences in the extensiveness of prediction, which is highest in English and lowest in Chinese. Looking at the language features that characterize the move, on the other hand, allows a study of the key role played by words of 'change' in the move and, conversely, the preference of words of 'change' for a semantics of futurity in their immediate context.

The next two sections look more closely at how to explore the language of CSR reports in relation to their functions and purposes.

5. Bottom-up pathways: Starting from frequency data

A preliminary analysis of frequency data can help illuminate new aspects or confirm previous hypotheses. This might mean looking at complete frequency lists or at selected frequencies that highlight what characterizes a text or a corpus. The study of Keywords, for example (as elaborated by *WS Tools*, Scott 2020) is the study of word forms whose frequency varies significantly across two corpora. With similar principles (and a tagged corpus) one can calculate the frequencies of the tags. *WMatrix* (Rayson 2009), for example, is a tool for corpus analysis and comparison that extends the keywords method to key grammatical categories and key semantic domains.

A study of keywords can be very useful in highlighting the peculiarities of the two main sections of the report. Using a version of Ba-CSR that separates the SP (Self-Presentation) section and the PR (Performance Reporting) section, the wordlist of the SP section can be contrasted with the one of the PR section in both languages (and vice versa, of course). The contrast produces a list of the words that are distinctively more frequent or less frequent.

The number and nature of words may vary according to the parameters used: basic frequency of each word, number of texts in which it is found etc. While an analysis of the whole set of lexical elements is obviously advisable (see Gabrielatos/Marchi 2011, 2012, Gabrielatos 2018), a brief overview of the top keywords can still provide a picture of the words that characterize each section. Table 3.1 reports the top fifty words characterizing the Italian SP section (using BIC as the key ordering principle, and arbitrarily restricting the words to those present in 40 per cent of the reports, in order to focus on the words that are used across a substantial range of reports). With these settings we obtain 573 word forms, 226 of which are positively key, that is, they occur more often than would be expected by chance in comparison with the reference corpus, while 347 are negative keywords, that is, they occur less frequently. The top fifty are all positive.

Table 3.1 Top fifty keywords in Italian

Keyword	Freq.	%	Texts	RC. Freq.	Rc. %
Consiglio	902	0.31%	29	188	0.02%
Controllo	595	0.21%	29	288	0.03%
Comitato	528	0.18%	29	231	0.02%
Sorveglianza	364	0.13%	15	71	n/a
President	390	0.14%	25	94	n/a
Governance	342	0.12%	30	85	n/a
Stakeholder	521	0.18%	28	336	0.03%
Consigliere	258	0.09%	15	69	n/a
Direzione	410	0.14%	29	283	0.03%
Rischi	571	0.20%	30	553	0.06%
Amministrazione	354	0.12%	29	218	0.02%
Delegato	225	0.08%	27	61	n/a
Funzioni	315	0.11%	30	189	0.02%
Consiglieri	151	0.05%	17	13	n/a
Controlli	228	0.08%	26	105	0.01%
Codice	342	0.12%	29	279	0.03%
Governo	230	0.08%	28	115	0.01%
Compliance	215	0.07%	25	104	0.01%
Direttore	158	0.06%	27	41	n/a
Carica	117	0.04%	20	9	n/a
Statuto	146	0.05%	21	36	n/a

Keyword	Freq.	%	Texts	RC. Freq.	Rc. %
Amministratore	110	0.04%	19	10	n/a
Vice	128	0.04%	20	24	n/a
CSR	237	0.08%	19	178	0.02%
Audit	134	0.05%	21	43	n/a
Piena	165	0.06%	21	79	n/a
Reputazione	150	0.05%	21	69	n/a
Responsabilità	299	0.10%	20	341	0.03%
Collegio	103	0.04%	20	32	n/a
Funzione	256	0.09%	27	267	0.03%
Generale	261	0.09%	29	291	0.03%
Soci	226	0.08%	23	231	0.02%
Controllate	97	0.03%	21	35	n/a
Societario	88	0.03%	23	27	n/a
Vigilanza	149	0.05%	26	108	0.01%
Nomina	90	0.03%	21	33	n/a
Presidio	153	0.05%	23	121	0.01%
Sindacale	114	0.04%	19	68	n/a
Supervision	73	0.03%	21	19	n/a
Incarichi	78	0.03%	19	25	n/a
Sportelli	150	0.05%	19	126	0.01%
PIL	56	0.02%	13	6	n/a
Nomine	56	0.02%	16	6	n/a
Organi	119	0.04%	26	80	n/a
Esecutivo	63	0.02%	19	13	n/a
Interno	177	0.06%	30	182	0.02%
Sostenibilità	194	0.07%	16	217	0.02%
Nominato	58	0.02%	20	11	n/a
Comitati	122	0.04%	26	93	n/a
Amministratori	95	0.03%	16	58	n/a

If these words are grouped around relevant lexico-semantic fields, such as mission and vision, company history and description, stakeholder consultation etc., we may be able to see that the Italian SP section is largely dominated by the lexis of corporate governance – *consiglio* ('Board'), *controllo* ('control'), *comitato* ('Committee'), *president* ('President'), *governance*, *consigliere* ('Councillor'), *direzione* ('management'), *delegato* ('delegate', 'Chief officer'), *amministrazione* ('administration') etc. – with great emphasis on control functions – *controllo* ('control'), *sorveglianza* ('supervision'), *rischi* ('risks'), *controlli* ('controls'), *audit*, *vigilanza* ('surveillance'), *supervisione* ('supervision') – whereas the role of 'mission and vision' is relatively reduced – *codice* ('code'), *compliance*, *CSR*, *reputazione* ('reputation'), *responsabilità* ('responsibility'), *sostenibilità* ('sustainability') – and the role of stakeholders is very limited and generically identified – *stakeholders*.

If we look at the same list for English, the picture is more varied, even if the list of positive keywords is much smaller – it is limited to fifty-five items. The lexis of corporate governance is obviously present there too, but not so largely dominant as in the Italian corpus. The list shows greater attention to depicting stakeholders and their engagement, as well as a clear focus on banking services – for example, *deposits, equity, dividends* – and the presence of a number of metadiscursive nouns – for example, *issues, report, disclosure* – that highlight the previewing function of the first section of the report, pointing to various textual units.

Table 3.2 groups the fifty-five word forms (listed in decreasing order) according to topic or function areas.

The table shows there is much greater attention to describing financial issues in the English corpus than in the Italian one, an impression which is confirmed by looking at the whole list of 226 word forms that characterize the self-presentation section in Italian. In Italian reports the terms from the world of finance and economics are limited to a couple of references to financial services offered by the bank – *sportelli* ('branches'), *leasing, factoring* – and to the general economic context – *economie* ('economies'), *PIL* ('GDP').

The arbitrariness of thematic categorizations is obvious, but it can be countered by adopting specific principles of selection: in this case, for example, the choice was made with a view to the typical thematic elements identified in the functional analysis of SP sections of reports. It is also obvious that there are many cases where the attribution of lexical words to semantic areas necessarily requires looking at concordances: anything to do with accounting, for example, could relate both to the governance of the bank itself and to the services provided.

Table 3.2 Positive keywords in the English corpus

Groupings	Word forms
Corporate governance	*committee, board, directors, governance, executive, director, audit, chairman, regulators, meeting, committees, rules*
Vision	*responsibility, CSR, citizenship, citizen, reputation, integrity, vision*
Stakeholders	*stakeholders, stakeholder, shareholders, engagement, dialogue, engage, investor, views, surveys, media, opinion, discussions*
Bank history or general description	*founded, strength, owned, presence, limited*
Financial services	*tax, profit, remuneration, profits, deposits, profitable, ratio, profitability, equity, stability, dividends*
Labelling nouns	*issues, report, disclosure, page, highlights*
Function words	*You, what, before*

Negative keywords complete the picture, as they point at what is typically missing in this section when compared to the actual performance reporting. The most marked case in both components of the corpus is that of figures, representing 3.96 per cent of the tokens in the SP section vs 4.95 per cent in the PF section of the English corpus, and 4.94 per cent vs 5.93 per cent respectively in the Italian corpus. The data confirm the general structure of the genre, with the vast majority of quantitative data referring to CSR activities rather than to the bank in general; it also confirms a tendency of Italian reports to provide more figures overall.

Other negative keywords refer to specific sectors of CSR activity, with their practices – for example, *energy, programme, project, training, housing, electricity, art, service, cooperation, emissions; energia* ('energy'), *progetto/I* ('project/s'), *emissioni* ('emissions'), *formazione* ('training'), *iniziative* ('initiatives'), *ricerca* ('research') – and actions – *launched, help, support, reduce, continue, providing, supported; sostegno* ('support'), *riduzione* ('reduction'), *ridurre* ('reduce'), *realizzato* ('realized'), *contribuito* ('contributed') – as well as their specific stakeholders – *teachers, universities, youth, schools, children, students, employees; giovani* ('young'), *donne* ('women'), *clienti* ('clients'), *lavoratori* ('workers'), *fornitori* ('suppliers').

The convergence on topics is thus very strong. Divergences, on the other hand, appear to be mostly linked to well-known tendencies of writing in the two cultural contexts, with more frequent verbal elements in English and more frequent nominalizations in Italian. The most remarkable difference in English is shown by verbs – for example, *launched*, with fifty-two occurrences (0.04 per cent) in SP vs 533 (0.09 per cent) in PR – whereas in Italian it is represented by nominalizations of actions – for example, *sostegno* ('support', noun), with the same normalized figures, that is, 555 occurrences (0.04 per cent) vs 900 (0.09 per cent).

What is most important to notice, however, is that function words also deserve attention. Rather than pointing at the topics of the text, they point at other stylistic traits, such as the typical need to use specific structures, which can in turn be related to the meanings and functions of the text.

The most obvious function word in our list of positive keywords in the English corpus appears to be the use of *you*. This is often studied as a marker of establishing dialogue with the reader. What is interesting to notice here, however, is that in this case it does not manifest a higher degree of personalization in the SP section of the report. The higher incidence of the pronoun is rather due to a very high number of occurrences in a series of interviews reported by a single bank

(DB). The vast majority of the examples are either direct interview questions, or exclusive pronouns that refer impersonally to the activity of economic and financial agents, rather than the reader, for example:

(3) [Q:] Do you think that a focus on pure commerce and profit can achieve scale faster than a hybrid approach that combines commerce with a social mission?
[A:] While interest rates matter to poor people, access to money is far more important to them. Because so many poor need money, it is true that they will accept higher interest rates. At the same time, I can't agree that you can grow fast only with a purely commercial approach that allows you to charge whatever interest you can. I don't think this will yield good results. (DB)

Rather than pointing at the reader-friendly nature of the section, the pronoun seems to point at the different uses that reports can make of a multiplicity of voices (cfr. Bondi/Yu 2017, Bondi/Yu 2018c).

Similarly, the presence of *before* might suggest a key role of the temporal dimension in the company history. A look at the concordances shows however that 27/66 occurrences are in fact part of the financial expression *before tax*, thus leaving a more limited role to the temporal dimension of the company history or the economic context.

The presence of *what* is much more interesting in terms of qualifying the SP section. The expression is mostly used here as interrogative pronoun (66/127 occurrences), rather than a nominal relative pronoun (61/127). In the brief preview of issues that is usually offered in the SP section, direct and indirect questions can play an important cataphoric, introductory function by marking transition from one topic to the other. About a third of the total occurrences are topic-setting headings in the form of indirect questions – *What we do; What citizenship means to Barclays* (12/127) – or topic-setting direct questions – *What areas show social deficits? What would a road-map look like? What are the most important issues that HSBC's sustainability reporting should address?* (27/127). All the other indirect interrogative *what*-clauses (24/127) are found in passages that typically introduce elements of CSR by identifying an area to be explored. These dependent interrogatives introduce a new issue, often specified in the lines that follow, much in the same way as direct questions:

(4) HSBC's Global People Survey helps us to measure employee engagement in order to understand **what** actions are needed to increase business performance and to benchmark our progress both internally and externally.

> In 2011, 81 per cent of our employees responded and employee engagement rose one percentage point to 69 per cent. We report the main findings of the survey on page 22. (HSBC)

On the whole, the presence of these occurrences, combined with that of metadiscursive labelling nouns, would be largely interpretable in terms of the often-observed tendency of English writing to use more explicit forms of guiding the reader through the text.

Keyword analysis can then suggest items and groups of items for more focused analysis. The need to look at concordances in a lexico-grammatical perspective indeed remains the key contribution of corpus linguistics to cross-cultural genre analysis.

6. From the lexico-grammar to semantics and pragmatics

Concordance analysis is the key tool that allows, through the study of co-text, the integration of lexico-grammatical, semantic and pragmatic perspectives. Adopting Sinclair's extended-units-of-meaning model, the node word(s) can be studied by looking at collocation, colligation, semantic preference and semantic prosody. The exploration of context with a view to lexico-grammatical patterns and combinations of meanings also allows the study of local grammars (context-specific terminologies meant to analyse specific pragmatic or discourse acts (e.g. Sinclair/Hunston 2000, Su/Wei 2018) or semantic sequences (sequences of semantic elements that may reveal patterning even in contexts of formal variation, Hunston 2008). These can help reconstruct pragmatic functions and sequences.

Looking in particular at evaluative phraseology (Hunston 2011), Bondi (2016b) uses markers of importance to illustrate the procedure starting from a lexical set. The study shows that, when looking at syntactic patterns or patterns of semantic preference around markers of importance in claims, they can mostly be related to three main types of statements:

1. quality-attributing statements: for example, *è per noi di importanza cruciale* ('it is of crucial importance for us') /.. *is of fundamental importance*
2. statements involving mental processes (showing awareness of commitment to particular aspects): *essere consapevoli/convinti dell'importanza* ('to be aware of the importance'); *recognize/realize the importance etc.*;

3. more explicit references to verbal/argumentative processes: *ribadire/ sottolineare l'importanza* ('to reaffirm/underline the importance'); *highlight/underscore the importance*.

The three types can be illustrated in the terms adopted by Sinclair and Hunston's local grammar of evaluation. Table 3.3 provides an example (see Bondi 2016b for the full argument).

We can exemplify a similar procedure with a focus on the lexis used to refer to stakeholders, starting from the most general term (*stakeholder*) in the SP section of the report. Looking at collocation and colligation easily leads to semantic preference.

A preliminary overview of collocates of English *stakeholders* (228 occurrences, 1.7 ptw) shows that the top ten lexical words are: *key, business, engagement, dialogue, shareholders, various, important, interest, engage, range*. The top ten grammatical words, on the other hand, are: *our, and, the, with, its, are, for, that, all, from*.

The immediate co-text in the concordance of *stakeholders* clearly shows that the node word is typically identified by a possessive – *our* (65) or *its* (17) in L1 position – or qualified by importance – *key* (13), *important* (3) – and range of

Table 3.3 Statements of understanding/belief ('Vision statements')

Evaluation framework		Entity/process evaluated
Evaluator 'WE' + expression of awareness/belief	Evaluation IM – Importance marker	Element of 'Vision'
We place	great importance	on activities that stimulate economic growth (RBS)
The Bank has been attaching	great importance	to communication with shareholders (ICBC)
Siamo consapevoli ('We are aware')	dell'importanza ('of the importance')	di avere una chiara visione a supporto della gestione dei contributi a favore del territorio (Cariparma) ('of a clear vision for the management of contributions to the local community')
UniCredit è convinta ('UniCredit Group is fully aware')	dell'importanza ('of the importance')	della lotta ai fenomeni del riciclaggio e del finanziamento del terrorismo (Unicredit) ('of combating money laundering and terrorist financing')

Source: M. Bondi, 'CSR Reports in English and Italian' (Newcastle. Cambridge Scholars 2016b: 187).

the stakeholders – *various* (9), *different* (3), but also *broad/wider range of* (7). It is also often found in the vicinity of words referring to other, more specific categories – *customers* (8), *shareholders* (11), *clients* (5), *investors* (5) – and preceded by prepositions which in turn are related to various nominal, adjectival or verbal forms expressing either the notion of engagement – *engage with* (28), *dialogue with* (12), *listening to* (14) – or of relevance – *important* (11), *matter most to* (7), *of interest to* (9). The co-text on the right is perhaps less marked by dominant patterns, but a few trends emerge: for one thing, the word form is often found in collocations like *stakeholders' expectations* and *stakeholders' interests*; moreover, the expression is often followed by *and*, and often listed with *shareholders*; similarly, it is often followed by *are*, and different forms of the verb *include* (in turn followed by types of stakeholders).

It soon becomes evident that it is possible to subdivide all the occurrences, irrespective of the specific forms used, into three main types of semantic preference: forms of engagement/communication between the bank and its stakeholders (97/226, 43 per cent), expressions of relevance/concern on the part of stakeholders (93/226, 41 per cent), identification of types of stakeholders (37/226, 26 per cent).

If we look at *stakeholder* (plural) in Italian, excluding the loan expression *stakeholder engagement* (twenty-nine occurrences), we have 471 occurrences (1.6 ptw), quite similar in normalized frequency to the English form. A preliminary overview of collocates shows that the top lexical words are: *coinvolgimento* ('engagement'), *tutti* ('all'), *dialogo* ('dialogue'), *gruppo* ('group'), *aspettative* ('expectations'), *interessi* ('interests'), *attività* ('activities'), *relazioni* ('relations'). The top grammatical words, on the other hand, are: *degli (dei/l/lla/lle)* ('of the'), *gli* ('the'), *con* ('with'), *per* ('for'/ 'to'), *nostri* ('our'), *che* ('that'/ 'which'), *propri* ('own'), *nei (nel)* ('in the'), *una* ('a'/ 'an'), *agli(/lla)* ('to the').

Looking at patterns of collocation, colligation and semantic preference in the concordance of *stakeholder* in Italian, the co-text shows that the node word is typically identified by articles, but also by possessives – *nostri* ('our') (66), *propri* ('own') (15) and *suoi* ('their') (7) – and quantifiers and adjectives highlighting the range of stakeholders – *tutti* ('all') (42), *altri* ('other') (12), *diversi* ('several') (12), *vari* ('various') (4) – or their importance – *principali* ('main') (8), *chiave* ('key') (4). The figures confirm a limited use of personal reference and greater attention to generic identification of stakeholders in Italian. The node word is indeed found in the vicinity of words referring to more specific categories, but with markedly lower frequency than in the English corpus – *clienti* ('clients') (15), *azionisti* ('shareholders') (6). The node word is also preceded by prepositions related to expressions of 'engagement' – *coinvolgimento degli stakeholder* ('engagement') (52), *dialogo con gli stakeholder* ('dialogue with') (29), *relazione con gli stakeholder* ('relations') (9) – or 'relevance' – *aspettative degli stakeholder* ('expectations') (12), *interessi di tutti gli stakeholder* ('interests') (12), *valore per tutti gli stakeholder* ('value') (5). When looking at semantic preference altogether, the approximate ratio of occurrences associated to what the bank does to engage the stakeholders is largely dominant in Italian reports (67 per cent of the occurrences), whereas both stakeholder identities and expectations/values are rather limited (around 16 per cent each).

Aiming to move towards larger patterns, it is possible to highlight recurrent combinations of meanings and thus identify the main functions of the sentences in which the expression is used. This points at functional units of the text which may correspond to the 'steps' in move-step analysis. In particular, in this case, they can be associated with steps that contribute to moves such as 'Stating values and beliefs', 'Stating strategies, methods, practices' or 'Showing commitment' to materiality assessment (i.e. identifying CSR priorities on the basis of stakeholders' interests).

Roughly speaking, when the node word is associated to specific references to stakeholders through linking verbs, expressions of inclusion and attributive complement constructions, we are often facing steps such as 'Identifying the nature/range of stakeholders':

(5) *'Stakeholders' are* groups and individuals who have an interest in, and may be affected by, our business activities. (RBS)

(6) *Riconosciamo come stakeholder* i soggetti portatori di un interesse rilevante rispetto all'attività della Banca, *quali* gli azionisti/soci, i dipendenti, la clientela, […]. ['We see stakeholders as holders of relevant interests in relation to the bank's business activities, like shareholders/partners, employees, our clientele, […]'] (MPS)

The step 'Presenting general methodological strategies' adopted by the company to establish contact with stakeholders is usually introduced by general verbs (*be/have*) attributed to the report or the company, verbs of reporting, expressions of intent or expressions of engagement:

(7) The Group's approach *is to work with* stakeholders to share knowledge and expertise. (HSBC)

(8) *Our engagement with s*takeholders serves to inform and advise our decision-making process across our operations. *We are committed to developing*

constructive relationships with all groups impacted by our business as we progress though our five-year restructuring programme.

(9) *L'iniziativa* il Circolo di Sostenibilità di Bank Austria *organizza incontri frequenti* con stakeholder, ONG, mondo scientifico e pubblica amministrazione su temi come [...] ['The UniCredit Bank Austria Sustainability Circle initiative organizes frequent meetings with stakeholders, NGOs, scientists and public administrators on topics such as [...]'] (Unicredit)

(10) È stato attivato un *percorso di coinvolgimento* degli stakeholder che [...] dà luogo alla costituzione di cantieri/laboratori permanenti che consentiranno di *integrare* in maniera sistematica il *punto di vista* degli stakeholder nelle attività aziendali [...] nel quadro di un percorso *condiviso*. ['A structured stakeholder involvement program has been launched [...]; this program will result in the constitution of permanent laboratories that will work on systematically integrating the points of view of the stakeholders in the Group's activities [...] within the framework of a shared project'] (IntesaSanpaolo)

The combination of *stakeholders* with expressions of 'relevance' and reference to 'issues' characterizes steps 'Introducing material issues':

(11) the table below provides an overview of the engagement mechanisms and *key issues* for our main stakeholders at a Group-level. (RBS)

(12) Il risultato è un grafico di *materialità* multi-stakeholder che rappresenta i vari livelli di *rilevanza* che i nostri stakeholder (clienti, dipendenti e collettività) attribuiscono ai differenti *temi*. ['The result is the multi-stakeholder materiality chart that represents the varying levels of importance that our stakeholders (customers, employees and communities) place on different topics'] (Unicredit)

Looking at words in combination thus brings us back to potential functional contexts in which preferred combinations occur.

7. Conclusions

The chapter has explored the potential of corpus tools in cross-cultural genre studies, focusing on a cross-cultural analysis of CSR reports. Starting from a discussion of problems of corpus compilation, the chapter has provided examples of two main pathways in looking at the intersection of schematic structures of the genre and their lexico-grammatical realizations, a long-standing key question in genre studies (Biber *et al.* 2007, Flowerdew/Forest 2009). First we have adopted a top-down perspective looking at the structure of CSR reports and at some of their key components. Then we have adopted a bottom-up perspective, starting from keyness and concordances as tools for the analysis of the semantic and pragmatic features of the text.

The top-down functional analysis has highlighted a homogeneous thematic structure across cultural contexts and a common set of basic moves; variation has been noticed in the organization of the corollary of the main report and in the sequences of steps. This perspective also helps analyse lexico-grammatical features building up the moves (Bondi 2016b, Bondi/Yu 2017, Yu/Bondi 2017). In more general methodological terms, I hope to have shown that a reliable identification of moves requires attention to definitions that include communicative purpose, topic, textual function, lexico-grammatical features and elements of the non-verbal text (Yu/Bondi 2017). Once the functional units have been identified, they can be more thoroughly described in terms of recurrent lexico-grammatical patterns and recurrent semantic patterns (Yu/Bondi 2019).

The bottom-up lexico-grammatical study presented here has focused on the distinctive features of the self-presentation section of the reports when compared to the performance-reporting section. Starting from keywords obtained with similar parameters in the two language components of the corpus, the preliminary overview grouped lexical word forms around relevant lexico-semantic fields and looked at how function words could be related to textual or interpersonal elements, to typical meanings and functions of the text. Common elements manifested convergent thematic, textual and interpersonal features of the report, together with peculiarities of the two cultural contexts – closer attention to metadiscourse and to presenting financial issues and banking services in the English corpus vs greater attention to normative regulation and quantification in the Italian corpus.

Similarly, starting from individual words or lexical sets, it is possible to reconstruct their common lexico-grammatical associations (collocation, colligation, patterns) as well as their semantic and pragmatic associations (semantic preference and semantic or discourse prosody). This once again highlights both patterns of convergence – for example, the presence of common areas of semantic preference and of the same communicative functions around the node expressions – and patterns of divergence – for example, fewer personal patterns in identifying stakeholders and greater attention to what the bank does to engage the stakeholders in Italian reports vs greater attention to different types of stakeholders, and equal attention to stakeholder engagement and stakeholder expectations in the English corpus.

The distinction between the two pathways illustrated here is mostly heuristic. The movement can often be cyclically combined. The complexity of texts suggests the need for an integration of both perspectives, as well as of the different levels of analysis involved: lexico-grammatical, semantic, pragmatic.

References

Aiezza, M. C. (2015), '"We May Face the Risks" … "Risks that Could Adversely Affect Our Face". A Corpus-assisted Discourse Analysis of Modality Markers in CSR Reports', *Studies in Communication Sciences*, 15 (1): 68–76.

Berkenkotter, C. and T. N. Huckin (1994), *Genre Knowledge in Disciplinary Communication: Cognition/Culture/Power*, London: Routledge.

Bhatia, A. (2012), 'The Corporate Social Responsibility Report: The Hybridization of a "Confused" Genre (2007–2011)', *IEEE Transactions on Professional Communication*, 55 (3): 221–38.

Bhatia, V. K. (1993), *Analysing Genre: Language Use in Professional Settings*, Harlow: Longman.

Bhatia, V. K. (2004), *Worlds of Written Discourse: A Genre-based View*, London: Continuum.

Biber, D., U. Connor and T. A. Upton (2007), *Discourse on the Move: Using Corpus Analysis to Describe Discourse Structure*, Amsterdam: John Benjamins.

Bondi, M. (2016a), 'The Future in Reports: Prediction, Commitment and Legitimization in CSR', *Pragmatics and Society, Special issue on the Pragmatics of Professional Discourse*, 7 (1): 57–81.

Bondi, M. (2016b), 'CSR Reports in English and Italian: Focus on Generic Structure and Importance Markers', in G. Garzone, D. Heaney and G. Riboni (eds), *Language for Specific Purposes. Research and Translation across Cultures and Media*, 168–99, Newcastle: Cambridge Scholars.

Bondi, M. and D. Yu (2017), '"I Highly Commend Its Efforts to Ensure Power Supply": Exploring the Pragmatics of Textual Voices in Chinese and English CSR Reports', in M. Janebová, E. Lapshinova-Koltunski and M. Martinková (eds), *Contrasting English and Other Languages through Corpora*, 218–47, Newcastle: Cambridge Scholars.

Bondi, M. and D. Yu (2018a), 'The Generic Structure of CSR Reports: Dynamicity, Multimodality, Complexity and Recursivity', in W. Giordano and G. Garzone (eds), *Discourse Communication and the Enterprise: When Business Meets Language*, 176–205, Newcastle: Cambridge Scholars.

Bondi, M. and D. Yu (2018b), 'CSR between Guidelines and Voluntary Commitments', in G. Tessuto, V. K. Bhatia and J. Engberg (eds), *Frameworks for Discursive Contexts and Practices for the Law*, 40–68, Newcastle: Cambridge Scholars.

Bondi, M. and D. Yu (2018c), 'Textual Voices in Corporate Reporting: A Cross-cultural Analysis of Italian, Chinese and English CSR Reports', *International Journal of Business Communication*. Available online: https://doi.org/10.1177/2329488418784690 (accessed 6 June 2021).

Bowen, H. R. (1953), *Social Responsibility of the Businessman*, New York: Harper & Row.

Bravo, R., L. D. Chernatony, J. Matute and J. Pina (2013), 'Projecting Banks' Identities through Corporate Websites: A Comparative Analysis of Spain and the United Kingdom', *Journal of Brand Management*, 20 (7): 533–57.

Breeze, R. (2012), 'Legitimation in Corporate Discourse: Oil Corporations after Deepwater Horizon', *Discourse & Society*, 23 (1): 3–18.

Catenaccio, P. (2010), 'Representations of Corporate Philanthropy. A Linguistic Approach', in P. Evangelisti Allori and G. Garzone (eds), *Discourse, Identities and Genres in Corporate Communication*, 121–42, Bern: Peter Lang.

Catenaccio, P. (2011), 'Green Advertising and Corporate CSR Communication: Hybrid Discourses, Mutant Genres', in S. Sarangi, V. Polese and G. Caliendo (eds), *Genre(s) on the Move. Hybridization and Discourse Change in Specialized Communication*, 353–72, Napoli: ESI.

Catenaccio, P. (2012), *Understanding CSR Discourse. Insights from Linguistics and Discourse Analysis*, Milano: Arcipelago.

Christie, F., J. R. Martin, eds (1997), *Genre and Institutions: Social Processes in the Workplace and School*, London: Cassell.

COM 2011. Communication from the Commission to the European Parliament, the Council, the European Economic and Social Committee and the Committee of the Regions. A Renewed EU strategy 2011–14 for Corporate Social Responsibility, COM/2011/0681. Available online: https://eur-lex.europa.eu/LexUriServ/LexUriServ.do?uri=COM:2011:0681:FIN:en:PDF (accessed 6 June 2021).

Conte, F., A. Vollero, C. Covucci and A. Siano (2020), 'Corporate Social Responsibility Penetration, Explicitness, and Symbolic Communication Practices in Asia: A National Business System Exploration of Leading Firms in Sustainability', *Corporate Social Responsibility and Environmental Management*, 27 (3): 1425–35.

Contrafatto, M. (2014), 'The Institutionalization of Social and Environmental Reporting: An Italian Narrative', *Accounting, Organizations and Society*, 39 (6): 414–32.

DiMaggio, P. J. and W. W. Powell (1983), 'The Iron Cage Revisited: Institutional Isomorphism and Collective Rationality in Organizational Fields', *American Sociological Review*, 48 (2): 147–60.

Doval, I. and M. T. Sánchez Nieto, eds (2019), *Parallel Corpora for Contrastive and Translation Studies: New Resources and Applications*, Amsterdam and Philadelphia: John Benjamins.

Ebeling, J. and S. Oksefjell Ebeling (2013), *Patterns in Contrast*, Amsterdam and Philadelphia: John Benjamins.

Einwiller, S., C. Ruppel and A. Schnauber (2016), 'Harmonization and Differences in CSR Reporting of US and German Companies', *Corporate Communications: An International Journal*, 21 (2), 230–45.

Filipović, R. (1971), 'The Yugoslav Serbo-Croatian-English Contrastive Project', in G. Nickel (ed.), *Papers in Contrastive Linguistics*, 107–14, Cambridge: CUP.

Flowerdew, J. and R. W. Forest (2009), 'Schematic Structure and Lexico-Grammatical Realization in Corpus-based Genre Analysis: The Case of Research in the Phd Literature Review', in M. Charles, S. Hunston and D. Pecorari (eds), *Academic Writing: At the Interface of Corpus and Discourse*, 15–36, London: Continuum.

Fortanier, F., A. Kolk and J. Pinkse (2011), 'Harmonization in CSR Reporting: MNEs and Global CSR Standards', *Management International Review*, 51: 665–96.

Fuoli, M. (2012), 'Assessing Social Responsibility: A Quantitative Analysis of Appraisal in BP's and IKEA's Social Reports', *Discourse & Communication*, 6 (1): 55–81.

Gabrielatos, C. (2018), 'Keyness Analysis: Nature, Metrics and Techniques', in C. Taylor and A. Marchi (eds), *Corpus Approaches to Discourse: A Critical Review*, 225–56, Oxford: Routledge.

Gabrielatos, C. and A. Marchi (2011), 'Keyness: Matching Metrics to Definitions', *Theoretical-Methodological Challenges in Corpus Approaches to Discourse Studies - and Some Ways of Addressing Them*. Available online: http://eprints.lancs.ac.uk/51449 (accessed 6 June 2021).

Gabrielatos, C. and A. Marchi (2012), 'Keywords: Appropriate Metrics and Practical Issues', *CADS International Conference, Bologna, Italy, 13–15 September 2012*. Available online: https://repository.edgehill.ac.uk/4196 (accessed 6 June 2021).

Halliday, M. A. K. (1985), *An Introduction to Functional Grammar*, 1st edn, London: Edward Arnold.

Hunston, S. (2008), 'Starting with the Small Words: Patterns, Lexis and Semantic Sequences', *International Journal of Corpus Linguistics*, 13 (3): 271–95.

Hunston, S. (2011), *Corpus Approaches to Evaluation: Phraseology and Evaluative Language*, New York: Routledge.

Jamali, D. and B. Neville (2011), 'Convergence versus Divergence of CSR in Developing Countries: An Embedded Multi-layered Institutional Lens', *Journal of Business Ethics*, 102, 599–621.

Johansson, S. (2007), *Seeing through Multilingual Corpora*, Amsterdam: John Benjamins.

Johansson, S. and K. Hofland (1994), 'Towards an English-Norwegian Parallel Corpus', in U. Fries, G. Tottie and P. Schneider (eds), *Creating and Using English Language Corpora*, 25–37, Amsterdam: Rodopi.

Kim, C., J. Kim, R. Marshall and H. Afzali (2018), 'Stakeholder Influence, Institutional Duality, and CSR Involvement of MNC Subsidiaries', *Journal of Business Research*, 91: 40–7.

Laviosa, S. (2015), 'Corpora and Holistic Cultural Translation', in M. T. Sánchez Nieto (ed.), *Corpus-based Translation and Interpreting Studies: From Description to Application*, 31–51, Berlin: Frank & Timme.

Lischinsky, A. (2011), 'In Times of Crisis: A Corpus Approach to the Construction of the Global Financial Crisis in Annual Reports', *Critical Discourse Studies*, 8: 153–68.

Malavasi, D. (2007), *Promotion in Banks' Annual Reports: An Integrated Analysis of Genre, Evaluative Lexis and Institutional Identity*, Modena: Il Fiorino.

Malavasi, D. (2011), '"Doing Well by Doing Good": A Comparative Analysis of Nokia's and Ericsson's Corporate Social Responsibility Reports', in G. Garzone and M. Gotti (eds), *Discourse, Communication and the Enterprise. Genres and Trends*, 193–212, Bern: Peter Lang.

Malavasi, D. (2012), 'The Necessary Balance between Sustainability and Economic Success: An Analysis of Fiat's and Toyota's Corporate Social Responsibility Reports', in P. Heynderickx, S. Dieltjens, J. Geert, P. Gillaerts and E. de Groot (eds), *The Language Factor in International Business. New Perspectives on Research, Teaching and Practice*, 247–64, Bern: Peter Lang.

McEnery, T. and R. Xiao (2007), 'Parallel and Comparable Corpora: The State of Play', in Y. Kawaguchi, T. Takagaki, N. Tomimori and Y. Tsuruga (eds), *Corpus-based Perspectives in Linguistics*, 131–45, Amsterdam: John Benjamins.

Moreno, A. I. (2008), 'The Importance of Comparable Corpora in Cross-cultural Studies', in U. Connor, E. Nagelhout and W. Rozycki (eds), *Contrastive Rhetoric: Reaching to Intercultural Rhetoric*, 25–41, Amsterdam: John Benjamins.

Moreno, A. I. and J. M. Swales (2018), 'Strengthening Move Analysis Methodology towards Bridging the Function-form Gap', *English for Specific Purposes*, 50: 40–63.

Parodi, G., ed. (2010), *Academic and Professional Discourse Genres in Spanish*, Amsterdam: John Benjamins.

Rayson, P. (2009), *Wmatrix: A Web-based Corpus Processing Environment*. Available online: http://ucrel.lancs.ac.uk/wmatrix/ (accessed 6 June 2021).

Saldanha, G. (2009), 'Principles of Corpus Linguistics and Their Application to Translation Studies Research', *Tradumàtica: traducció i tecnologies de la informació i la comunicació*, 7. Available online: https://www.raco.cat/index.php/Tradumatica/article/view/154828 (accessed 6 June 2021).

Scott, M. (2020), *WordSmith Tools Version 8*, Liverpool: Lexical Analysis Software.

Scherer, A. and G. Palazzo (2008), 'Globalization and Corporate Social Responsibility', in A. Crane, A. McWilliams, D. Matten, J. Moon and D. Siegel (eds), *The Oxford Handbook of Corporate Social Responsibility*, 413–31, Oxford: Oxford University Press.

Sinclair, J. (1991), *Corpus, Concordance, Collocation*, Oxford: Oxford University Press.

Sinclair, J. (1996), 'The Search for Units of Meaning', *Textus*, 9: 75–106.

Sinclair, J. (1998), 'The Lexical Item', in E. Weigand (ed.), *Contrastive Lexical Semantics*, 1–24, Amsterdam: John Benjamins.

Sinclair, J. and S. Hunston (2000), 'A Local Grammar of Evaluation', in S. Hunston and G. Thompson (eds), *Evaluation in Text: Authorial Stance and the Construction of Discourse*, 74–101, Oxford: Oxford University Press.

Stubbs, M. (2001), *Words and Phrases*, Oxford: Blackwell.

Stubbs, M. (2007), 'Quantitative Data on Multi-word Sequences in English: The Case of the Word *World*', in M. Hoey, M. Mahlberg, M. Stubbs and W. Teubert (eds), *Text, Discourse and Corpora*, 163–89, London: Continuum.

Stubbs, M. (2013), 'Sequence and Order: The Neo-Firthian Tradition of Corpus Semantics', in H. Hasselgård, J. Ebeling and S. Ebeling (eds), *Corpus Perspectives on Patterns of Lexis*, 13–33, Amsterdam: John Benjamins.

Su, H. and N. Wei (2018), '"I'm Really Sorry about What I Said": A Local Grammar of Apology', *Pragmatics*, 28 (3): 439–62.

Suchmann, M. (1995), 'Managing Legitimacy: Strategic and Institutional Approaches', *Academy of Management Review*, 20, 571–611.

Swales, J. (1990), *Genre Analysis: English in Academic and Research Settings*, Cambridge: Cambridge University Press.

Tang, L., C. C. Gallagher and B. Bie (2015), 'Corporate Social Responsibility Communication through Corporate Websites: A Comparison of Leading Corporations in the United States and China', *International Journal of Business Communication*, 52 (2): 205–27.

Williams, C. A. and R. V. Aguilera (2008), 'Corporate Social Responsibility in a Comparative Perspective', in A. Crane, A. McWilliams, D. Matten, J. Moon and D. Siegel (eds), *The Oxford Handbook of Corporate Social Responsibility*, 452–72, Oxford: Oxford University Press.

Yu, D. (2021), *Cross-Cultural Genre Analysis: Investigating Chines, Italian and English CSR Reports*, London: Routledge.

Yu, D. and M. Bondi (2017), 'The Generic Structure of CSR Reports in Italian, Chinese, and English: A Corpus-based Analysis', *IEEE Transactions on Professional Communication*, 60 (3): 273–91.

Yu, D. and M. Bondi (2019), 'A Genre-Based Analysis of Forward-Looking Statements in Corporate Social Responsibility Reports', *Written Communication*, 36 (3): 379–409.

Zanettin, F. (2012), *Translation-driven Corpora. Corpus Resources in Descriptive and Applied Translation Studies*, Manchester: St. Jerome.

4

Applying a corpus-driven approach in linguistic analyses: The case of lexical bundles and phrase frames

Miguel Fuster-Márquez

1. Introduction

The term 'lexical bundles' (LBs) has been used in the last two decades to refer to multiword sequences frequently found in all sorts of discourse (for example, *in the heart of, one of the most, will be happy to* found in the discourse of hotel websites, see Fuster–Márquez 2014, Fuster-Márquez and Pennock-Speck 2015), since it was first introduced in Biber *et al.*'s *Longman Grammar of Spoken and Written English* (1999), a groundbreaking corpus-based grammar where the authors devoted a whole section to the identification of such sequences in academic and conversational registers. These sequences are identified by means of some quantitative parameters which are decided beforehand by the researcher, and crucially require a corpus methodology – the most relevant factor being their corpus frequency. Evidence of interest in LBs is supported by the plethora of corpus research that has been published in the last two decades, most particularly inspired by Biber *et al.*'s work.

The major driving force that has motivated a large amount of contributions on LBs has been and still is pedagogical. For example, Römer (2010: 96) encourages linguists to identify and create 'phraseological profiles' (i.e. inventories of phraseological items) for different text types. In her view, such profiles should be obtained through the empirical methodology afforded by corpus-driven analysis. In this line of research, authors hope to obtain relevant lists of sequences which should be prioritized in second language acquisition (SLA) teaching contexts (see, for example, Simpson-Vlach and Ellis 2010). A good number of LB studies are located in what Granger (2015) calls *Contrastive*

Interlanguage Analysis (CIA), which involves quantitative and qualitative comparisons between L1s and different varieties of L2/L3 data, or between learners with different L1s. In this line of research, authors home in on contrasts between the phraseological repertoires of L1 and L2 speakers, or between the production of novel and/or expert writers in their L1. This kind of research (see, for example, Ädel and Erman 2012, Chen and Baker 2010, Chen and Baker 2016, Cortes 2004, Csomay 2013, De Cock 2004, Fuster-Márquez and Fernandez-Domínguez 2020, Granger 2014, 2018, Hyland 2008a, Hyland 2008b, Hyland 2012, Luzón Marco 2010, Pan *et al.* 2016) is often related to issues of learners' proficiency in academic prose and specialized discourses (EAP). Research has also been undertaken on the phraseology of a number of specialized domains such as accounting and business (see Binon *et al.* 2001, Cohen 1986, Verlinde *et al.* 1993–2003), computing and the Internet (e.g. DicoInfo), the environment (e.g. Buendía and Faber 2012), advertising of hotel websites (Fuster-Márquez 2014), pharmacy (see Grabowski 2018) or historical linguistics (Kopaczyk 2012), among others. It is impossible to do proper justice in this chapter to the plethora of papers published in this burgeoning area in current corpus-linguistics. Even though the application of a corpus-driven methodology is a sine qua non in this kind of analysis, recent research carried out by Pan *et al.* (2020) suggests that corpus design, for example the number and size of texts, can influence the results.

By drawing on current research, the aim of this contribution is to review the literature on LBs by considering different angles of it, namely their place in phraseological studies (psycholinguistic, linguistic, and applied linguistic approaches), their empirical extraction by means of corpus techniques, structural and functional analysis and quantification approaches within the digital humanities domain. The concluding remarks highlight some pending questions and pedagogical challenges for this kind of research.

2. The formulaic status of lexical bundles

Biber *et al.* (2004) and Forchini and Murphy (2010) claim that attested frequency in usage, quantifiable through corpus techniques, is a crucial aspect in the identification of LBs as core phraseological items:

> Frequency data have additional importance for the study of multi-word sequences because they are one reflection of the extent to which a sequence

of words is stored and used as a prefabricated chunk, with higher frequency sequences more likely to be stored as unanalysed chunks than lower frequency sequences.

(Biber *et al.* 2004: 376)

Various studies have addressed lexical bundles as potential candidates of formulaic status, namely, by referring to the psycholinguistic issues of storage, processing and retrieval by native speakers. Wray and Perkins (2000: 1) define *formulaic sequence* as follows:

> a sequence, continuous or discontinuous, of words or other meaning elements, which is, or appears to be, prefabricated: that is, stored and retrieved whole from memory at the time of use, rather than being subject to generation or analysis by the language grammar.

For Wray and Perkins, opaque and immutable strings like *by and large*, but also far more transparent and less rigid ones containing variable slots which can be filled with different words, as is the case of the frame *NP be-TENSE sorry to keep-TENSE you waiting* (see Pawley and Syder 1983: 210), deserve to be considered as formulaic. According to Wray, formulaic expressions should be treated as morpheme equivalent units (MEUs) since they are 'processed like a morpheme, that is, without recourse to any form-meaning matching of any sub-parts it may have' (Wray 2008: 12). In other words, the grammatical make-up of formulaic expressions is only accessed by native speakers if called for 'as predicted by the Needs Only Analysis' (Wray 2008). To what extent would it be possible to consider as formulaic, for example, discourse organizing bundles like *if you look at, going to talk about, what I want to,* mentioned by Biber *et al.* (2004: 386) in Classroom Teaching? Should they be classified as holistic units on an equal footing with English idioms like *kick the bucket*? Be that as it may, Carrol and Conklin (2020: 96) cite a number of contributions which suggest that frequency of occurrence contributes to faster processing. Likewise, Gablasova *et al.* (2017: 156) cite research in SLA which proves that alongside other formulaic units, LBs are linked to the fluency and native-like language production.

For Wray (2008: 11), formulaic expressions should be accounted for at three different levels: (1) language, (2) groups and (3) individuals. Thus, she considers that not all native speakers possess the same formulaic sequences in their 'mental lexicon'. Consequently, differences in the formulaic stock between native speakers would result from their own socio-linguistic or personal experiences. In Wray's view (2008), the fact that a word sequence is associated with a specific situation and/or register may be an indication of formulaicity. Hence, for example, bundles with a referential function like *as a result of, on the basis of, in the absence of, the extent to which,* typically found in the context of academic prose (see Biber *et al.* 2004), would be part and parcel of the academic repertoire of individuals who participate in that environment. Indeed, familiarity with LBs like the ones cited above in academic settings is gained through exposure to research papers, teaching materials and disciplinary discourses. Hyland (2008a, 2008b; also Hyland and Feng 2018) claims that, given that knowledge is socially constructed, academic writers develop a pragmatic competence by means of which they construct for themselves and their work a credible representation. Such representation would imply that the linguistic choices of writers would be shaped or constrained by their social alignment with the communities they belong to.

Less strong claims about the formulaic status of LBs can be found in the work of a number of authors. For Schmitt (2005: 36) it remains questionable whether LBs are stored holistically, although he cites empirical evidence which suggests that some are. Hyland (2012: 150) considers that LBs are no strictly formulaic, although he argues that they 'are nevertheless glued together in everyday discourse'. Somewhat earlier, Altenberg (1998: 120–1) referred to 'recurrent word-combinations' as conventionalized expressions, 'preferred ways of saying', 'conventionalized building blocks that are used as convenient routines in language production'. Reference to LBs as was put forward by Altenberg, will be encountered again and again in the literature on LBs. Hence, more recently, Granger (2018) also refers to LBs as 'the building blocks' of fluent spoken and written discourse which learners need to acquire to become truly fluent in their L2.

3. The phraseological approach vs the distributional approach

A useful distinction has been made between two kinds of approach (see Ebeling and Hasselgård 2015, Granger and Paquot 2008, Groom 2017, Nesselhauf 2005) which are referred to as (1) the classical *phraseological approach* and (2) the *distributional* (or frequency-based, probabilistic or statistical) *approach*.

The *phraseological approach* (Nesselhauf 2005) is mostly concerned with distinguishing phraseological types proposed beforehand, for example, pure idioms, figurative idioms and restricted collocations, among others (see Cowie 1998, Gläser 1986). In this approach, linguists would need to judge the acceptability of pre-selected phraseological expressions according to arguments like their opacity/

transparency, fixedness or fossilization. According to Stubbs (2007), reference grammars of English have made use of classical taxonomic arguments in their phraseological description.

On the other hand, *the distributional* or *probabilistic approach* is associated with the work of Sinclair and his followers at the University of Birmingham (Groom 2017). These are scholars with a Firthian linguistic background, who conceive phraseology as a core characteristic of language. According to Sinclair (1991: 110; see also Erman and Warren 2000), two principles operate in language: the idiom principle and the open choice principle. The idiom (or phraseological) principle indicates that speakers make use of pre-constructed multiword combinations. By contrast, the open choice principle would assume that for each slot in a phrase or clause native speakers have a free lexical choice. In Sinclair's view, the idiom principle is the default principle; thus, implying that the phraseological load in our native lexicons is far more important than previously thought, although it is hard to quantify very precisely. Hunston (2002: 137) adheres to Sinclair's approach, by highlighting that words have a tendency to co-occur, 'not randomly, or even in accordance with grammatical rules only, but in preferred sequences'. Indeed, the observation of large amounts of texts and language in corpora has proved that the open choice principle, espoused earlier in linguistics, is much less relevant in language use than Sinclair's idiom principle.

Followers of the probabilistic approach have had little interest in distinguishing phraseological types. The main reason is that for them 'phraseological items, whatever their nature, take precedence over single words' (Granger and Paquot 2008: 29). Also, methodologically, while the classical phraseological approach is top-down, followers of the probabilistic approach have identified sequences through an inductive bottom-up approach in the hope of unveiling typical usage.

Regrettably, in the probabilistic approach one comes across a variety of rubrics to refer to fairly similar word sequences (Vilkaitė 2016): *clusters, collocations, colligations, ngrams, lexical bundles, grammatical patterns, recurrent sequences, units of meaning, semantic sequences,* etc. For Groom (2019: 309), although the eclectic use of terms makes comparisons across empirical studies difficult, it proves the dominant vigour of phraseology as an emerging field of linguistic research. However, Biber and Barbieri (2007: 264) consider that this apparent messiness is understandable because researchers use different criteria; so they provide us with 'different perspectives on the use of multi-word sequences'.

Regarding methodology, followers of the probabilistic approach rely entirely on corpus techniques. In fact, the different names used to call it refer to aspects of such methodology: it is 'probabilistic', relies on 'frequencies' and 'distribution' patterns. As to their findings, although it has been argued that Sinclair's 'idiom principle' lies at the heart of this approach, it does not imply that the sequences they come across lack compositionality, as is the case of classical 'idioms'. Rather, what counts as idiomatic is simply phraseological native-like production as described by Pawley and Syder (1983). Biber *et al.*'s (1999) work on LBs is in all likelihood one of the main proponents of the probabilistic approach. In their corpus-based grammar, they showed that idioms like *a piece of cake, not on your face* are either very rare or not common at all in English usage (1999: 989, 1025). Hence, they recommend to redirect their focus to LBs, which prove to have far higher frequency in usage.

This new focus which comes from extensive research on the distributional phraseological approach is also having important consequences in current ESL and EFL studies. Thus, for example, the results obtained from a large number of corpus-based contributions in ESL (see Granger 2018), have led Paquot (2018) to advocate for a change in teaching and testing the phraseological competence of EFL learners. In her view, language testers should adopt linguistic indices which include this statistically frequent phraseology revealed by numerous corpus-based analyses.

4. The identification and analysis of Lexical Bundles

As in the case of most studies that have adopted the distributional approach, there is also a lack of widely accepted terminology to refer to LBs. Stubbs (2007) has found the following terms as having very close meanings: *clusters, chains, lexical bundles, multi-word sequences, recurrent word combinations, sentence stems* or *statistical phrases*. However, the term *lexical bundle* seems to have gained greater acceptance than any other term. Most of the defining features of LBs are outlined in Biber *et al.* (1999, Chapter 13). However, acknowledgement is given to Altenberg (1993, 1998) for the methodology and identification of these sequences (see Cortes 2015: 197). The identification and features found in this section are based on Biber *et al.* (1999) and later research (see, for example, Biber and Conrad 1999, Biber *et al.* 2004, Biber 2006, Biber and Barbieri 2007, Hyland 2008a, Hyland 2008b), and echoed in most recent research on LBs.

Most published research on LBs refers to the core features shown in Table 4.1 above. These studies describe the corpus methodology required for their extraction and the resulting list of LBs, also refer to the structural, semantic and

Table 4.1 Features of Lexical Bundles

Lexical bundles as collocations	• They show a statistical tendency to co-occur. • They are extended collocations.
Methodological parameters set by researchers when extracting LBs with dedicated software	• Variable length, minimum of three-word forms. • Dispersion thresholds: Occurring at least in five different texts per million words.
Syntactic & semantic features	• Most of them are structurally incomplete: cross the boundaries of grammatical categories. • Typically unidiomatic and not fixed.
Pragmatics/discourse functions	• The most typical in a register. • Discernible functions in register. • The building blocks of discourse.

pragmatic features of bundles. Also, they may establish subsequent comparisons between different registers and corpora, refer more or less extensively to methodological discussions, or to pedagogical implication as drivers for their research. Section 5 below discusses in detail some of central methodological parameters in the extraction of LBs. As shown in Table 4.1, LBs are conceived as extended collocations (see Biber *et al.* 1999, Biber and Conrad 1999, Conrad and Biber 2004, Biber 2009, Hyland 2008a, Hyland 2012, Hyland and Jiang 2018: 383); that is, LBs are syntagmatic associations that occur more frequently than would be expected by chance across a given range of texts.

A general observation in the literature on LBs is that they are incomplete syntactic clauses and phrases, as in, for example, *the size of the*, *what I want to*. As Biber *et al.* (2004: 377) note in their research on academic registers, the number of complete structural units among LBs in conversation was as low as 15 per cent, and in academic prose even lower, 5 per cent. Biber *et al.* (1999) propose a structural description of bundles that has also become widely accepted in the literature. These authors establish a broad division into three grammatical types: Noun Phrase-based (NP-based), Prepositional Phrase-based (PP-based) and Verb Phrase-based (VP-based) bundles, with more detailed distinctions of subtypes. They highlight preferences for specific structural types in the two registers they examined, observing that while academic prose relies on NP-based, for example, *the nature of the*, and PP-based phrases, for example, *on the other hand*, conversation contained a considerable number of LBs with a pronominal subject followed by a verb phrase, for example, *I don't know what*.

Attention is also paid to the analysis and discussion of the discourse and/or pragmatic functions that bundles perform in discourse. LBs are judged as being widely used in discourse, co-occurring in a register, the 'building blocks' of discourse, where they carry out discernible functions. For Stubbs (2002: 230) 'chains', as he calls these multiword sequences, contribute to cohesiveness in texts, and 'provide evidence about units of language use'. However, Schmitt (2005: 36) remarks that three-word LBs like *you know what* and *the fact that*, which occur frequently in English, are semantically or functionally ambiguous. Nevertheless, it appears that ambiguity is mitigated when attention is turned to the function of bundles in specific discourses or registers, instead of looking at a language as a whole. In this regard, Biber *et al.* (2004: 377) observe that different registers make use of different lexical bundles. For example, the multiword sequence *in the heart of* (see Fuster-Márquez 2014) is identified as the most frequent four-word bundle in hotel websites, where it performs a crucial referential function of location.

Biber *et al.* (2004), and a large number of researchers after them, propose to analyse the pragmatic/discourse functions of LBs by breaking them down into three groups, namely: reference (e.g. *a wide range of*), stance markers (e.g. *I don't think so*) and discourse organizers (e.g. *on the one hand, as I was saying*). Briefly, according to these authors:

> Stance bundles express attitudes or assessments that frame some other proposition. Discourse organizers reflect relationships between prior and coming discourse. Referential bundles make direct reference to physical or abstract entities, or to the textual context itself, either to identify the entity or to single out some particular attribute of the entity as especially important.
>
> (Biber *et al.* 2004: 384)

This tripartite distinction is further divided into subtypes to allow for more fine-grained linguistic analyses. For example, Fuster-Márquez (2014) classified the four-word bundles *you would like to, make the most of* as expressing obligation/directives or desire and *we reserve the right, would be delighted to* as bundles that express intention or prediction within the larger category of stance bundles. Further, Hyland (2008a: 18) has suggested a finer subdivision of Biber's stance expressions and distinguishes between (1) *stance*, which he defines as 'the ways writers explicitly intrude into the discourse to convey epistemic and affective judgements, evaluations and degrees of commitment to what they say'; and (2) *engagement*, which involves writers intervening 'to actively address readers as participants in the unfolding discourse'.

Nevertheless, it should be noted that LBs can fulfil overlapping pragmatic functions within the same kind of discourse or register, as shown in Fuster-Márquez (2014), who argues that the four-word bundle *the perfect venue to* classified as referential, indicating quality specification, also embodies highly positive evaluation in the discourse of hotel websites.

5. Lexical bundles: extraction and operationalization

Sinclair and Renouf (1988) encouraged the use of computers for the identification of recurrent phraseology in corpora. In their view, unlike human beings, if properly instructed computers miss nothing. The methodology for the identification of LBs follows this recommendation, hence it is empirical (not intuitive), inductive (or bottom-up) and also corpus-driven (see Tognini-Bonelli 2001). In other words, LBs are identified automatically by means of adequate corpus software (see also Römer 2010, Cortes 2015). Consequently, automatic corpus extraction takes priority before arriving at any generalizations about the particular presence of multiword sequences in any kind of discourse. Most corpus software can perform these functions, for example, any version of *Wordsmith tools*, *AntConc*, *SketchEngine* or more recently *AntGram*. All these programmes feature an in-built n-gram or cluster tool to generate n-grams (i.e. uninterrupted sequences of n words) out of a selected corpus.

In her review of publications on bundles in SLA literature, Granger (2018) distinguishes two main operational approaches: (1) Frequency-defined bundles and (2) Association-defined bundles. In particular, the former relies on: quantitative criteria (bundle size, frequency threshold, dispersion, other criteria), structural categories and discursive functions. The latter relies on different quantitative criteria than Frequency-defined bundles (namely span size, frequency threshold, dispersion and statistical association measures (such as MI, t-score, etc., statistical association thresholds, and other criteria), as well as on structural categories and on discursive functions.

In these two operational approaches, the identification of lexical bundles follows the same initial route.

According to Granger (2018), bundle size, frequency threshold and dispersion are the principal criteria that underlie the operationalization of LBs. It is important to note that LBs rely on sequences of 'word forms', not 'lemmas'. Also, most work on LBs adopts frequency thresholds that range between ten and forty times per million words; however, cut off frequencies will depend on the size of the sequence. The longer the sequence, the lower the threshold to be applied (Biber *et al.* 1999: 990). Additionally, relative frequencies are usually recorded per million words for sake of later comparisons across corpora containing different registers.

The standard size of LBs is three to five, following the recommendation of Biber *et al.* (1999) and Altenberg (1998: 101). However, most research on LBs to date has focused on four-word bundles. For Csomay (2013), shorter sequences, as for example three-word bundles, are too prevalent and hard to interpret. Similarly, Hyland (2008a: 8) argues that three-word bundles do not offer a clear range of structures and functions. The overlap of bundles of different sizes is also a common observation: shorter bundles often being embedded in longer ones. In such cases, researchers need to give reasons for choosing a specific size.

To ensure the validity of the resulting list of bundles, thresholds on dispersion (i.e. the number of texts in which bundles are found in the corpus) should be established so that the idiosyncratic influence which might stem from particular texts in the corpus can be prevented. This will have the effect of obtaining more robust results, truly representative of the register under scrutiny (Biber and Barbieri 2007: 268). Biber and his colleagues suggest that an LB should appear in a minimum of five different texts per million words (Biber *et al.* 2004, Biber 2006, Biber and Barbieri 2007).

The *association-defined approach* is a development of the frequency-defined approach. The only difference is that it relies on additional statistical measures. The association measures which are proposed in this approach are those we have seen as being regularly used to gauge the strength of collocations, namely MI or *t*-score. The main difference between these two is that MI gives prominence to word pairs which are less common but often found together, *t*-score emphasizes very frequent collocations. Granger (2018) advocates for the use of association measures in order to get more precise results about the relevant bundles. More recently, Chen (2019) has suggested the introduction of Delta P, a directional collocation measure (see Gries 2013) to assess 'formulaicity arising from either strong forward-directed or backward directed lexical associations' (Chen 2019: 444). Given the fact that corpus linguistics is comparative in essence, various other statistics may be added. In order to do that, relative (normalized) frequencies, typically per million words, are used for the comparison among corpora. For example, Fuster-Márquez (2014) also used the non-parametric Mann-Whitney U test, since a non-parametric test was implemented as the normality of the distribution in the data could not be assumed in the comparison between the corpus of hotel websites he analysed and the data in the BNC spoken and written subcorpora which were used as reference corpora.

Other criteria in both approaches necessarily entail at the very least a manual removal of highly idiosyncratic or uninteresting LBs, sequences, for example, sequences that cross punctuation boundaries, repeated material in bundles of different sizes or, in the case of non-native production, prefabricated material copied from the essay prompt, among others (see Fuster-Márquez and Fernández-Domínguez 2020, Wray 2002: 26).

6. Concluding remarks

Until recently, phraseology was poorly known or even neglected, being considered peripheral in most linguistic treatments. Systematic empirical research has showed, particularly after Sinclair's work, that phraseology should occupy a central place in linguistic research. Lexical bundles are the result of a newer statistical approach to phraseology, requiring a corpus approach. A large amount of corpus research on LBs in recent times has ensued from the publication of Biber *et al.* (1999). However, according to scholars (see Granger 2018: 231), the corpus methodology to identify lexical bundles would require some refinement in the future, perhaps through the introduction of new association measures and also of triangulation methods.

Some authors (Römer 2010, Granger 2018) have pointed out that the lack of consensus in the methodology may lead to problems in terms of comparability or replicability of results. However, this is hardly avoidable. Major or minor discrepancies are related to researchers' own decisions on various matters, concerning, for example, the nature and features of their study corpus, the register they wish to explore, the internal variety or size of texts (Wray 2002: 26). In addition, as Byrd and Coxhead (2010: 32) remark, researchers apply cut-off points in the light of 'what seems reasonable given the volume of data'.

There are also other pending challenges. For example, it has been noted that LBs can be subject to internal variation (Schmitt 2005). An important rival pattern is a multiword sequence called Phrase Frame (P-Frame), which is similar to an LB except for the fact that some of its words admit variation. Thus, in their study of these sequences in a corpus of hotel websites (Fuster-Márquez 2014, Fuster-Márquez and Pennock-Speck 2015) they found that some LBs were quite fixed, others appeared to be extremely variable and could not be classified as LBs, for example, the four-word sequence *hotel is * in*, had an overall frequency of twenty-five tokens. Also, Fuster-Marquez (2017) discusses the kind of variation which is associated with the extensions of LBs by some optional elements, for example, the wording of the LB sequence *in the heart of*, is occasionally found as *in the very heart of* in the discourse of hotel websites, without losing its main pragmatic function. If we admit the existence of these two kinds of variation as part of the phraseological picture in the analysis of discourses, then the overall frequency of these closely parallel corpus-driven multiword sequences would also increase.

Finally, applied linguistics, and most particularly SLA, is an area that has benefitted enormously from research on LBs. However, some authors cast doubts as to the learnability and teachability of this native phraseology in an EFL context. For Schmitt (2005: 37), the form-meaning relationship of LBs is not sufficiently transparent. Also, in Wray's view (2019), LBs are certainly useful to learn, although relatively invisible to native speakers, and if there was direct instruction, they would require the assistance from teachers. In the same line, Cortes (2004: 417–20) has pointed out that learners' exposure to texts that contain bundles does not guarantee their acquisition or even that they will be noticed.

Acknowledgement

This research has been granted with grant PID2019-110863GB-I00, funded by MCIN/AEI/10.13039/501100011033.

References

Ädel, A. and B. Erman (2012), 'Recurrent Word Combinations in Academic Writing by Native and Non-native Speakers of English: A Lexical Bundles Approach', *English for Specific Purposes*, 31: 81–92.

Altenberg, B. (1993), 'Recurrent Word Combinations in Spoken English', in J. D'Arcy (ed.), *Proceedings of the Fifth Nordic Association for English Studies Conference*, 17–27, Reykjavik: University of Iceland.

Altenberg, B. (1998), 'On the Phraseology of Spoken English: The Evidence of Recurrent Word Combinations', in A. P. Cowie (ed.), *Phraseology: Theory, Analysis and Applications*, 101–22, Oxford: Oxford University Press.

Anthony, L. (2019a), *AntConc (Version 3.5.8)* [Computer Software], Tokyo, Japan: Waseda University.

Anthony, L. (2019b), *AntGram (Version 1.2.2)* [Computer Software], Tokyo, Japan: Waseda University.

Biber, D. (2006), *University Language: A Corpus-based Study of Spoken and Written Registers*, Philadelphia: John Benjamins.
Biber, D. (2009), 'A Corpus-driven Approach to Formulaic Language in English: Multi-word Patterns in Speech and Writing', *International Journal of Corpus Linguistics*, 14 (3): 275–311.
Biber, D. and S. Conrad (1999), 'Lexical Bundles in Conversation and Academic Prose', in H. Hasselgård and S. Oksefjell (eds), *Out of Corpora: Studies in Honour of Stig Johansson*, 181–90, Amsterdam: Rodopi.
Biber, D., S. Johansson, G. Leech, S. Conrad and E. Finegan (1999), *Longman Grammar of Spoken and Written English*, Harlow: Pearson.
Biber, D., S. Conrad and V. Cortes (2004), '"If You Look at …": Lexical Bundles in University Teaching and Textbooks', *Applied Linguistics*, 25 (3): 371–405.
Biber, D. and F. Barbieri (2007), 'Lexical Bundles in University Spoken and Written Registers', *English for Specific Purposes*, 26: 263–86.
Binon, J., S. Verlinde, J. van Dyck and A. Bertels (2001), *Dictionnaire d'apprentissage du français des affaires. Dictionnaire de compréhension et de production de la langue des affaires*, Paris: Didier.
Buendía, M. and P. Faber (2012), 'EcoLexicon: Algo más que un tesauro sobre el Medio Ambiente', in J. L. Martí Ferriol and A. Muñoz Miquel (eds), *Estudios de traducción e interpretación. Entornos de especialidad*, vol. 2, 59–72, Castelló: Publicacions de la Universitat Jaume I.
Byrd, P. and A. Coxhead (2010), 'On the Other Hand. Lexical Bundles in Academic Writing and in the Teaching of EAP', *University of Sydney Paper in TESOL*, 5: 31–64.
Carrol, G. and K. Conklin (2020), 'Is All Formulaic Language Created Equal? Unpacking the Processing Advantage for Different Types of Formulaic Sequences', *Language and Speech*, 63 (1): 95–122.
Chen, A. C. H. (2019), 'Assessing Phraseological Development in Word Sequences of Variable Lengths in Second Language Texts Using Directional Association Measures', *Language Learning*, 69 (2): 440–77.
Chen, Y. H. and P. Baker (2010), 'Lexical Bundles in L1 and L2 Academic Writing', *Language Learning and Technology*, 14 (2): 30–49.
Chen, Y. H. and P. Baker (2016), 'Investigating Criterial Discourse Features across Second Language Development: Lexical Bundles in Rated Learner Essays, CEFR B1, B2 and C1', *Applied Linguistics*, 37 (6): 849–80.
Cohen, B. (1986), *Lexique de cooccurrents: Bourse-conjoncture économique*, Montreal: Linguatech.
Conrad, S. and D. Biber (2004), 'The Frequency and Use of Lexical Bundles in Conversation and Academic Prose', *Lexicographica*, 20: 56–71.
Cortes, V. (2004), 'Lexical Bundles in Published and Student Disciplinary Writing: Examples from History and Biology', *English for Specific Purposes*, 23 (4): 397–423.
Cortes, V. (2015), 'Situating Lexical Bundles in the Formulaic Language Spectrum: Origins and Functional Analysis Developments', in V. Cortes and E. Csomay (eds),

Corpus-bases Research in Applied Linguistics: Studies in Honor of Doug Biber, 197–216, Amsterdam: John Benjamins.

Cowie, A. P., ed. (1998), *Phraseology: Theory, Analysis, and Applications*, Oxford: Clarendon Press.

Csomay, E. (2013), 'Lexical Bundles in Discourse Structure: A Corpus-based Study of Classroom Discourse', *Applied Linguistics*, 34 (3): 369–88.

De Cock, S. (2004), 'Preferred Sequences of Words in NS and NNS Speech', *Belgian Journal of English Language and Literatures (BELL)*, 2 (1): 225–46.

Ebeling, S. O. and H. Hasselgard (2015), 'Learner Corpora and Phraseology', in S. Granger, G. Gilquin and F. Meunier (eds), *The Cambridge Handbook of Learner Corpus Research*, 207–30, Cambridge: Cambridge University Press.

Erman, B. and B. Warren (2000), 'The Idiom Principle and the Open Choice Principle', *Text. Interdisciplinary Journal for the Study of Discourse*, 20: 29–62.

Forchini, P. and A. Murphy (2010), 'N-grams in Comparable Specialized Corpora', in U. Römer and R. Schulze (eds), *Patterns, Meaningful Units and Specialized Discourses*, 87–103, Amsterdam: John Benjamins.

Fuster-Márquez, M. (2014), 'Lexical Bundles and Phrase Frames in the Language of Hotel Websites', *English Text Construction*, 7 (1): 84–121.

Fuster-Marquez, M. (2017), 'The Discourse of US Hotel Websites: Variation through the Interruptibility of Lexical Bundles', in M. Gotti, S. Maci and M. Sala (eds), *Ways of Seeing, Ways of Being: Representing the Voices of Tourism*, 401–20, Bern: Peter Lang.

Fuster-Marquez, M. and B. Pennock-Speck (2015), 'Target Frames in British Hotel Websites', *International Journal of English Studies*, 15 (1): 51–69.

Fuster-Márquez, M. and J. Fernández-Domínguez (2020), 'Overused Bundles in the Written Academic English of Spanish EFL Students', in M. L. Carrió Pastor (ed.), *Corpus Analysis in Academic Discourse: Discourse Markers, English for Specific Purposes and Learner Corpora*, 282–99, London and New York: Routledge.

Gablasova, D., V. Brezina and T. McEnery (2017), 'Collocations in Corpus-based Language Learning Research: Identifying, Comparing, and Interpreting the Evidence', *Language Learning*, 67 (1): 155–79.

Gläser, R. (1986), *Phraseologie der englischen Sprache*, Berlin: Walter de Gruyter.

Grabowski, Ł. (2018), 'Fine-tuning Lexical Bundles: A Methodological Reflection in the Context of Describing Drug-Drug Interactions', in J. Kopaczyk and J. Tyrkkö (eds), *Applications of Pattern-driven Methods in Corpus Linguistics*, 57–80, Amsterdam: John Benjamins.

Granger, S. (2014), 'A Lexical Bundle Approach to Comparing Languages: Stems in English and French', *Languages in Contrast*, 14 (1): 58–72.

Granger, S. (2015), 'Contrastive Interlanguage Analysis: A Reappraisal', *International Journal of Learner Corpus Research*, 1 (1): 7–24.

Granger, S. (2018), 'Formulaic Sequences in Learner Corpora: Collocations and Lexical Bundles', in A. Siyanova-Chanturia and A. Pellicer-Sanchez (eds), *Understanding Formulaic Language: A Second Language Acquisition Perspective*, 228–47, Oxford: Routledge.

Granger, S. and M. Paquot (2008), 'Disentangling the Phraseological Web', in S. Granger and F. Meunier (eds), *Phraseology: An Interdisciplinary Perspective*, 27–49, Amsterdam: John Benjamins.

Gries, S. T. (2013), '50-something Years of Work on Collocations. What Is or Should be Next', *International Journal of Corpus Linguistics*, 18 (1): 137–65.

Groom, N. (2017), 'Phraseology: A Critical Reassessment', Invited talk, Idiomaticity Workshop, University of Oslo, Norway, 2 September 2017.

Groom, N. (2019), 'Construction Grammar and the Corpus-based Analysis of Discourses: The Case of the WAY IN WHICH Construction', *International Journal of Corpus Linguistics*, 24 (3): 335–67.

Hunston, S. (2002), 'Using a Corpus to Investigate Stance Quantitatively and Qualitatively', in R. Englebretson (ed.), *Stancetaking in Discourse: Subjectivity, Evaluation, Interaction*, 27–48, Amsterdam: John Benjamins.

Hyland, K. (2008a), 'As Can Be Seen: Lexical Bundles and Disciplinary Variation', *English for Specific Purposes*, 27 (1): 4–21.

Hyland, K. (2008b), 'Academic Clusters: Text Patterning in Published and Postgraduate Writing', *International Journal of Applied Linguistics*, 18 (1): 41–62.

Hyland, K. (2012), 'Bundles in Academy Discourse', *Annual Review of Applied Linguistics*, 32: 150–69.

Hyland, K. and F. Jiang (2018), 'Academic Lexical Bundles How Are They Changing?' *International Journal of Corpus Linguistics*, 23 (4): 383–407.

Kopaczyk, J. (2012), 'Applications of the Lexical Bundles Method in Historical Corpus Research', in P. Pęzik (ed.), *Corpus Data across Languages and Disciplines*, 83–95, Bern: Peter Lang.

Luzón Marco, M. J. (2010), 'Analysis of Organizing and Rhetorical Items in a Learner Corpus of Technical Writing', in M. C. Campoy, B. Bellés Fortuño and M. L. Gea-Valor (eds), *Corpus-based Approaches to English Language Teaching*, 79–94, London: Continuum.

Nesselhauf, N. (2005), *Collocations in a Learner Corpus*, Amsterdam: John Benjamins.

Pan, F., R. Reppen and D. Biber (2016), 'Comparing Patterns of L1 versus L2 English Academic Professionals: Lexical Bundles in Telecommunications Research Journals', *Journal of English for Academic Purposes*, 21: 60–71.

Pan, F., R. Reppen, Randi and D. Biber (2020), 'Methodological Issues in Contrastive Lexical Bundle Research: The Influence of Corpus Design on Bundle Identification', *International Journal of Corpus Linguistics*, 25 (2): 215–29.

Paquot, M. (2018), 'Phraseological Competence: A Missing Component in University Entrance Language Tests? Insights from a Study of EFL Learners' Use of Statistical Collocations', *Language Assessment Quarterly*, 15 (1): 29–43.

Pawley, A. and F. H. Syder (1983), 'Two Puzzles for Linguistic Theory', in J. C. Richards and R. W. Schmidt (eds), *Language and Communication*, 191–227, London: Longman.

Römer, U. (2010), 'Establishing the Phraseological Profile of a Text Type: The Construction of Meaning in Academic Book Reviews', *English Text Construction*, 3 (1): 95–119.

Schmitt, N. (2005), 'Formulaic Language: Fixed and Varied', *ELIA*, 6: 13–39.
Scott, M. (1997), *WordSmith Tools Manual*, Oxford: Oxford University Press.
Sinclair, J. (1991), *Corpus, Concordance, Collocation*, Oxford: Oxford University Press.
Sinclair, J. and A. Renouf (1988), 'A Lexical Syllabus for Language Learning', in R. Carter and M. McCarthy (eds), *Vocabulary and Language Teaching*, 140–58, London: Longman.
Simpson-Vlach, R. and N. C. Ellis (2010), 'An Academic Formula List: New Methods in Phraseology Research', *Applied Linguistics*, 31 (4): 487–512.
Stubbs, M. (2002), 'Two Quantitative Methods of Studying Phraseology in English', *International Journal of Corpus Linguistics*, 7 (2): 215–44.
Stubbs, M. (2007), 'An Example of Frequent English Phraseology: Distribution, Structures and Functions', in R. Facchinetti (ed.), *Corpus Linguistics 25 Years on*, 89–105, Amsterdam: Rodopi.
Tognini-Bonelli, E. (2001), *Corpus Linguistics at Work*, Amsterdam: John Benjamins.
Verlinde, S., J. Folon, J. Binon and J. van Dyck (1993–2003), *Dictionnaire contextuel du français économique* (*4 Tomes*), Antwerp: Garant.
Vilkaitė, L. (2016), 'Formulaic Language Is Not All the Same: Comparing the Frequency of Idiomatic Phrases, Collocations, Lexical Bundles, and Phrasal Verbs', *Taikomoji kalbotyra*, 8: 28–54.
Wray, A. (2002), *Formulaic Language and the Lexicon*, Cambridge: Cambridge University Press.
Wray, A. (2008), *Formulaic Language: Pushing the Boundaries*, Oxford: Oxford University Press.
Wray, A. (2019), 'Concluding Question: Why Don't Second Language Learners More Proactively Target Formulaic Sequences?', in A. Siyanova-Chanturia and A. Pellicer-Sánchez (eds), *Understanding Formulaic Language: A Second Language Acquisition perspective*, 248–69, London: Routledge.
Wray, A. and M. R. Perkins (2000), 'The Functions of Formulaic Language: An Integrated Model', *Language & Communication*, 20 (1): 1–28.

5

Data triangulation using Sketch Engine and WMatrix: Ketogenic diet on *Twitter*

Stefania M. Maci

1. Introduction

When corpora are collected from the Net and form digital archives, they are sometimes underused by academics (Hedstrom 1997, Borgman 1999, Eshet 2004, Bell *et al.* 2009, Ge 2010, Griffin/Hayler 2016). Indeed, the analysis of these digital libraries requires the academic researcher not only to read digital data, but also to have 'access to both the data themselves, [...] and access to the software required to support the analyses to be undertaken' (Griffin/Hayler 2016: ebook), which requires consistently and regularly updating digital skills consistently and regularly. All this shows that the investigation of digital data is a very dynamic process, which can sometimes benefit from interesting methodological approaches.

The aim of this chapter is to show how two research methods can be applied in digital discourse analysis to provide more in-depth insights into the data collected, offering triangulation of data interpretation when such topics as medical problems are dealt with by lay users on the Web, the place where, as claimed by Hawn (2009: 361), the way doctors and patients interact is being reengineered, but also where illnesses and healthcare are communicated outside doctor-patient interaction (Demjén/Semino 2017).

In recent times, Web 2.0 has played a significant role in the construction of *e-health* (i.e. the transfer of medical knowledge through digital platforms). On social media (Dynell 2014), in particular, people turn to *e-health* mainly for support, for sharing and checking relevant factual information (Lamberg 2003) and, above all, for receiving and expressing empathy (Rheingold 1993).

Many studies have investigated the role of digital and social media in the dissemination of medical discourse (Vicentini 2012, Grego/Vicentini 2015, Luzón 2015, Tessuto 2015, Turnbull 2015, 2016, Mattiello 2017). Cavalieri (2020) carried out socio-semiotic and discourse analysis research on the use of YouTube to enhance health literacy with particular emphasis on the ketogenic diet (KD). KD is a high-fat, low-carbohydrate nutritional treatment used in refractory treatment for epilepsy, migraine and obesity. Although in the UK and the United States this treatment is quite popular, in Italy, knowledge about KD is scarce. Given that the author of this contribution suffers from chronic migraines and has found relief thanks to KD and medical and personal support on social media, the purpose of this chapter is to analyze how the medical discourse of KD is transferred to Twitter. Drawing on corpus linguistics, two methodological approaches will simultaneously be adopted and data triangulation will be achieved by using Sketch Engine and WMatrix4.

In order to carry out this study, some background information and a literature review supporting medical and linguistics studies about KD will be given in Section 2, where the aims of this research can be found, followed by the methodological approaches adopted for this investigation in Section 3. Data description and interpretation will be found in Section 4, while conclusions will be drawn in Section 5.

2. Literature review

The Ketogenic Diet (KD), which developed in the 1920s, is rich in fat and low in carbohydrates, and this correlates with a reduction in the number of epileptic seizures for people suffering from this condition. In the 1960s, KD was found to be a sound treatment for obesity (Bueno *et al.* 2013, Paoli *et al.* 2013). It then became popular in the United States and the UK in the 1980s, thanks to two foundations, the *Charlie Foundation* (http://charliefoundation.org/) in the United States, and the *Matthew's Friends Foundation* (www.matthewsfriends.org) in the UK, which helped parents to make more autonomous choices, based on doctors' decisions, as to children treatments, particularly in the case of epilepsy (Freedman *et al.* 2006). For this reason, in the 1990s, the KD rejuvenated the treatment of child epilepsy and other neurological diseases (Kossoff *et al.* 2016, Rho 2017, Falcicchia *et al.* 2018), migraine (Barbanti *et al.* 2017), pain (Masino and Ruskin 2013) and other neurological disorders (Kossoff 2013).

From a medical perspective, KD is defined in various ways according to the treatment it is required for. Paoli *et al.* (2013: 789) emphasize how KD can be useful for weight loss, because it can help to control hunger and 'improve fat oxidative metabolism and therefore reduce body weight' (Paoli 2014: 2101) due to a 'reduction in carbohydrates (usually to less than 50 g/day) and relative increases in the proportions of proteins and fat'. Barbanti *et al.* (2017: S111), instead, explain that it is useful for 'refractory paediatric epilepsy and a promising therapy for diverse neurological diseases'.

From an applied linguistics perspective, extensive investigations into health literacy and KD, in particular for the treatment of such chronic diseases as autism, epilepsy or other neurological diseases, and the communication of dietary requirements, have been carried out. Cavalieri (2020), for instance, examines the role of YouTube in making KD information cognitively accessible to lay people. Attention is also paid to the strategies (Cavalieri 2019) and discursive practices (Cavalieri/Diani 2019) employed for the dissemination of medical knowledge to caregivers through Web-based materials, in particular with reference to KD for the treatment of refractory epilepsy (Cavalieri 2019). Informative booklets on KD in the Italian context have also been investigated (Cavalieri *et al.* 2019). Diani (2019) focuses her attention on web pages created by parents whose children suffer from neurological diseases, written in collaboration with medical experts. Lazzaretti and Poppi (2019) focus their analysis on Web texts dealing with neurological diseases, while Sezzi and Bondi (2019) explore the popularization strategies employed by the *Matthew's Friends Foundation* and the *Charlie Foundation* to disseminate KD information. These studies show how the Web can become a source of information and communication of health knowledge. Moreover, they confirm that doctor-patient interaction has been rapidly changing with the advent of Web-based social media (Hawn 2009), which has also contributed to modifying the process of medical knowledge transference (e-health) (Dynell 2014). Indeed, e-health is increasingly communicated via blogs, video chat and social networks, such as Facebook and Twitter, as confirmed by recent research investigating the role of digital media in the dissemination and transfer of medical knowledge (Vicentini 2012, Grego/Vicentini 2015, Luzón 2015, Tessuto 2015, Turnbull 2015, 2016, Mattiello 2017). Nevertheless, online medical knowledge of KD is still scarce and, most of the time, adequate information is difficult to find. As Mazzi (2020, 2018) claims, on the one hand, there is the deeply held conviction that KD should be given proper consideration in epilepsy refractory cases; on the other hand, the idea according to which KD has no medical efficacy is also quite commonly held – and this has given rise to an emotional as well as dialectical debate around KD.

Anecdotally speaking, we have experienced the same debate in Italy in the case of KD as a treatment for chronic migraine. While the author of this contribution has found information about KD as a treatment for chronic migraine in a Facebook group and was directed to KD thanks to the group's neurologist, more 'conservative' neurologists tend to treat chronic migraine with drugs only – which does not solve the problem of daily migraine fits – because KD is considered to be unbalanced when compared to the so-called 'Mediterranean' diet. Given this personal experience and considering that, to the best of our knowledge, no empirical research has been conducted on the role of social media to promote KD to boost health literacy, it is also the aim of this contribution to describe how the discourse around the KD debate develops on Twitter. More precisely, the research questions posed in this chapter are:

1. How is KD presented/described on Twitter?
2. Can Twitter be a *locus* where (e-)health literacy can be developed?

To answer these questions, two research methods will be applied to offer an in-depth insight of the data collected. The materials under investigation and the methodological guidelines will be presented in the next section.

3. Methodological approach

The study is based on a corpus of tweets collected from around the world and exported from 14–22 April and 9–17 May, 2018, from Socialbearing.com. Socialbearing.com is a free Twitter analytics application, which searches for tweets, timelines and twitter maps for a period up to nine days. The keyword inserted in the Socialbearing search engine was keto*, with the wildcard standing for any suffix that can be added to the stem keto-. Furthermore, the following hashtags were searched: #keto; #ketodiet; #ketodietapp; #ketofam; #ketofood; #ketogenic; #ketogenicdiet; #ketolife; #ketolifestyle; #ketorecipes; #ketosis; #ketoweightloss. From the general corpus, a small corpus formed by tweets written only in English has been considered for the present investigation, comprising 4,592 tweets (83,189 tokens; 59,471 types), as will be explained in detail in the Results section.

Permission to download tweets is granted by Twitter Terms of Agreement[1] and any sensitive data from Twitter users have been erased from collected posts.

For the purpose of the research, only verbal elements were collected from tweets, given that any visual aspect of tweets, if present, is not relevant for this study.

From a methodological point of view, the study consisted of two main stages. The first was a quantitative-based analysis with Sketch Engine (https://www.sketchengine.eu/). Sketch Engine is an online tool to search and analyze corpora in order to instantly identify typical linguistic characteristics for that corpus, defined by Sketch Engine as *word sketches*, or sequences of words. Following Sinclair (1991) sequences of words identify extended units of meaning in terms of collocational profiles (lexical realization), colligational profiles (grammatical realization), common semantic fields (semantic preference) and pragmatic realizations (semantic prosody). In addition, *word sketches* help to identify words' concordance lines, as well as *sketch grammar*, or the grammatical relation present for the word under consideration in that corpus. A word sketch, and in particular an *n-gram*, processes a lexical bundle, or a sequence of words 'that occur most frequently in particular genres, regardless of whether or not they constitute[d] idioms or structurally complete units' (Breeze 2013: 230), and which, as Mazzi (2018) underlines, play a fundamental role in corpus linguistics because they 'are important for the production and comprehension of texts' (Biber 2006: 155). The collocational profile of each item under investigation in this study is therefore seen in the lexical bundle identified as an *n-gram* by Sketch Engine.

The second step was a quantitative-based analysis of the semantic domains of which the corpus is formed. Since the investigation of semantic preferences could not be carried out with Sketch Engine, this was completed with WMatrix4. A semantic analysis of all tweets was then realized. The purpose of the second step of investigation was to have a more comprehensive account of the key themes of the data collected in relation to the online discourse of KD. WMatrix4 is a web-based tool for corpus analysis elaborated by Lancaster University, UK.

Through its web interface, WMatrix4 offers tools for Constituent Likelihood Automatic Word-tagging System (CLAWS) and UCREL Semantic Analysis System (USAS) corpus annotation, besides standard corpus-linguistic methodologies, such as frequency lists, keyword lists, collocations and concordances. When key semantic domains are analyzed, what is taken into consideration is the context of the semantic prosody of words grouped under the semantic fields forming the corpus under investigation, achieved by collating all items detected within the semantic domain, rather than single keywords in context. A semantic domain can be defined as a cluster of terms and texts that have a high level of lexical coherence. Key semantic domains are such because they are identified with keyness computation. WMatrix4 detects key semantic domains through the Lancaster University Centre for Computer Corpus Research on Language's (UCREL's) semantic analysis system (USAS), on the basis of Tom McArthur's Longman Lexicon of Contemporary English (McArthur 1981). The USAS semantic tagset 'has a multi-tier structure with 21 major discourse fields [...], subdivided, and with the possibility of further fine-grained subdivision in certain cases' for a total tagset of 363 semantic fields (http://ucrel.lancs.ac.uk/usas/ [12/8/2020]; cf. also Rayson 2008).

Each key semantic domain (SemTag) was detected by comparing the corpus against the (spoken Sampler) British National Corpus (BNC) (990,704 words).[2] For $p \leq 0.01$ and 1 degree of freedom (1 d.f. is when two corpora are compared), the resulting cut-off point for the log-likelihood statistics is 6.63. The number of key semantic fields thus detected (186) granted a more comprehensive account of the key themes of the data collected, necessary to answer the research questions posed in the previous section.

Qualitative analysis accompanied the description of the findings and in the next sections this will be exemplified by the most relevant excerpts analyzed in this contribution with the purpose of identifying KD discursive practices on Twitter.

4. Results

As indicated above, the use of Socialbearing.com allowed the scraping of 22,242 English tweets about KD by using the keywords and hashtags indicated in Section 3.

The sentiment analysis carried out by SocialBearing.com on all the tweets gives a general idea of the attitudes people have towards KD, as can be seen in the histogram reproduced in Figure 5.1.

As can be seen, overall, the sentiment analysis suggests that 19 per cent of the tweets have a negative attitude, 21 per cent a positive one and 60 per cent a neutral stance towards KD. The positive and negative polarities, therefore, are somewhat balanced.

However, as can be seen in Figure 5.2, tweets are collected and classified by Socialbearing.com in more typologies of texts that are not always relevant for this study, namely retweets (that is sharing the same tweet), replies to a tweet, mentions (the mention of a Twitter user), pictures, videos and links.

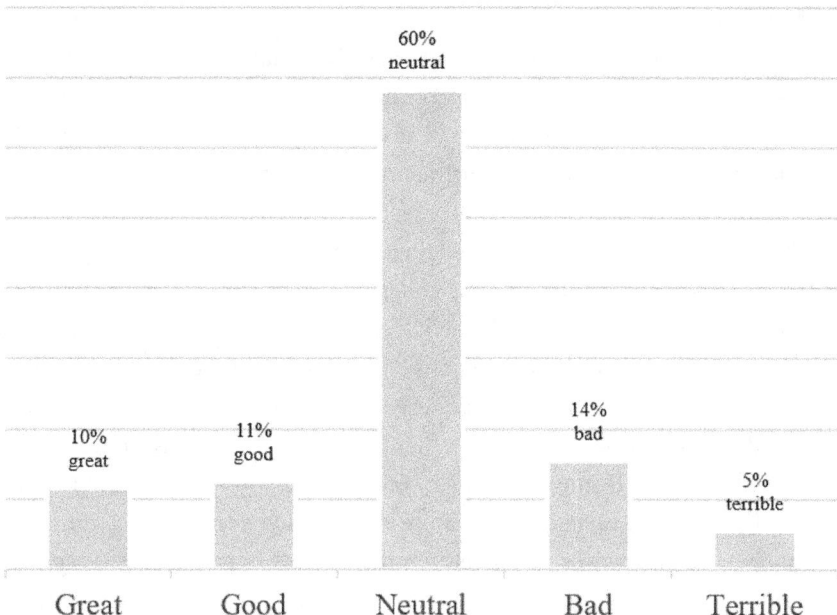

Figure 5.1 Tweet by sentiment

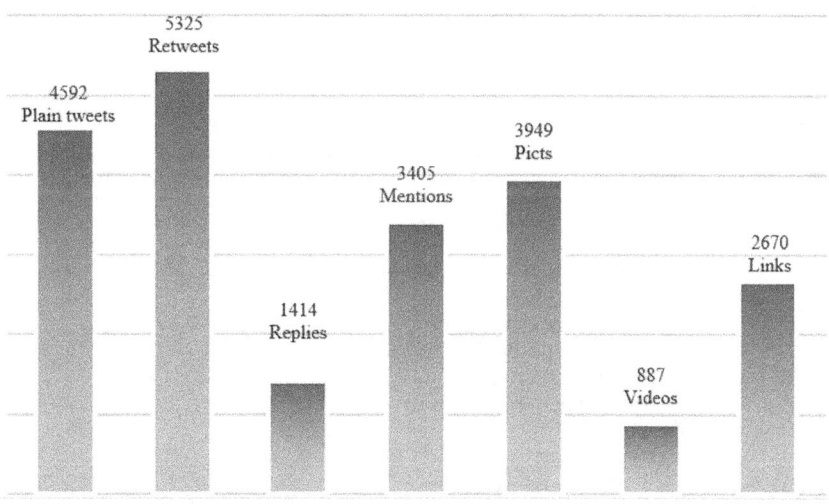

Figure 5.2 Corpus breakdown

As explained in Section 3, this study is based only on the verbal elements of tweets. Therefore, only *plain* tweets have been taken into consideration, giving a total of 4,592 tweets (83,189 running words; 59,471 types). We will therefore concentrate on these small texts, for which we have no specific sentiment analysis – since the sentiment overview seen above applies to all tweet types.

The investigation with Sketch Engine began by searching for *n-grams* of *keto**. After uploading the corpus of collected tweets onto Sketch Engine, the item *keto** was introduced into the search engine to search all items containing the stem *keto-*, given that the wildcard '*' stands for any suffix to be applied to the item, so that, for instance, the words *ketone, ketogenic, ketodiet, ketolife* etc. could be found together with other accompanying words or sequences of words *–keto_N-Grams*. In Sketch Engine, an *n-gram*, or a multiword unit (MWU), is a sequence of a number (*n*) of items (*gram*) that can refer to numbers, digits, words, letters etc. In the context of text corpora, *n-grams* typically refer to sequences of words next to each other. *N-grams* differ from collocations because the latter are words with a statistical relation between them, but not necessarily next to each other.

The first fifty *keto*_3-4n-grams* by frequency yield some interesting results, as can be seen in Table 5.1.

Table 5.1 Breakdown of the top 50 *keto*_3-4n-grams* by frequency

#	Item	Freq.
1	Ketogenic Diet and Ketosis	163
2	Ketogenic Diet And	163
3	Diet and Ketosis	163
4	Diet and Ketosis Motivation	74
5	Diet and Ketosis Inspiration	74
6	And Ketosis Motivation	74
7	And Ketosis Inspiration	74
8	the ketogenic diet	39
9	the keto diet	36
10	a ketogenic diet	35
11	the Keto diet	29
12	I don't	23
13	Of Ketogenic Carnivore	22
14	Health Benefits of Ketogenic	22
15	Health Benefits Of	22
16	Benefits of Ketogenic Carnivore	22
17	Benefits of Ketogenic	22

#	Item	Freq.
18	I can't	19
19	to lose weight	18
20	on the Keto	16
21	on the keto	15
22	keto diet for	14
23	a keto diet	14
24	the Keto diet	13
25	one of the	13
26	a lot of	13
27	Of Ketogenic Carnivore Diet	13
28	Low-Carb High-Fat Ketogenic Diet	13
29	Low-Carb High-Fat Ketogenic	13
30	Ketogenic Carnivore Diet	13
31	High-Fat Ketogenic Diet	13
32	on the keto diet	12
33	ketogenic diet is	12
34	the Ketogenic Diet	11
35	on the Keto Diet	11
36	easy to make	11
37	you don't	10
38	The ketogenic diet	10
39	The Ketogenic Diet	10
40	loss is available here	10
41	loss is available	9
42	keto diet for fat	9
43	is available here	9
44	for fat loss is	9
45	for fat loss	9
46	fat loss is available	9
47	fat loss is	9
48	diet for fat loss	9
49	diet for fat	9
50	This is a	9

Skimming the various entries and without reading their context, by simply reading the *n-grams* in Table 5.1, what emerges from the tweets is that the *keto* or *ketogenic diet is low carb-high fat/carnivore/easy to make diet for weight loss*. So, the main notions behind this diet are that the keto(genic) diet 'is' something specific and that the keto(genic) diet 'is for' a given purpose. We therefore checked the concordance lines for the following:

1. *keto diet is*
2. *keto diet for*
3. *ketogenic diet is*
4. *ketogenic diet for*

4.1. The keto diet

When checking the concordance lines for the phrase *keto diet is* (eleven concordance lines overall) the results indicate that Twitter users define the diet mainly in terms of a *low carb diet* and try to explain how it works:

(1) The keto diet is a *very low carb diet* that makes the body think it is fasting.

(2) (b) BEGINNERS GUIDE TO KETO DIET. The ketogenic or keto diet is a *diet low in carbohydrates*, consisting mainly of high-fat foods.

(3) The keto diet is *chemically starving your cells*.

In a few cases (three occurrences), the diet is regarded as negative, but no reasons are offered as to why this diet should be avoided:

(4) I'm sorry, but I think the keto diet is kinda ridiculous.

(5) The keto diet is actually REALLY bad for you. No wonder all Keto guys enjoy coffee

When looking at the reasons why the *keto diet* is used (twenty-four concordance lines), Twitter users' motivations can be grouped as indicated in the concordances shown below:

- keto diet for *fat loss* (nine hits)
- keto diet for losing weight (one hit)
- keto diet for cancer/diabetes/bipolar disorder (four hits overall)

The keto diet is indeed seen as a diet for losing weight or fat and, though less frequently, as a medical treatment for certain diseases. In some cases, the preposition *for* refers to the length of time a person can be on a diet (three occurrences), as in 'I've been on a keto diet for 18 months'. In others, it refers to people being on a diet who either have knowledge or not about the diet as a lifestyle as in the expression – which is also the title of a book – 'Keto Diet for Beginners' (seven occurrences).

4.2. The ketogenic diet

The concordance lines of *ketogenic diet is* (fifteen occurrences) reveal that a different definition is offered for the diet when compared to the expression *keto diet*. Indeed, as can be seen in the excerpts below, the *ketogenic diet* is not only 'a very low-carb diet which can help you burn fact more effectively' (6), but also a medical treatment (seven occurrences):

>   (6) A keto or ketogenic diet is a very low-carb diet, which can help you burn fat more effectively.
>
>   (7) A ketogenic diet is more powerful than any drug I've ever prescribed to treat diabetes (T2DM).
>
>   (8) The #ketogenic diet is sometimes recommended for children whose seizures have not responded to medication.
>
>   (9) The ketogenic diet is an intervention that the physician, patient, & dietitian all need to be on.

Unlike the case of *keto diet*, when people use the expression *ketogenic diet*, they are referring to a medical dietary treatment used to cure diabetes and epilepsy. The Twitter *ketogenic diet* definition already contains or points to the reasons why this diet can be prescribed as a medical treatment.

When we come to the investigation of the concordance lines of the phrase *ketogenic diet for* (thirteen occurrences), we can see that Twitter users tend to use it with the following group concordances:

- ketogenic diet for cancer/diabetes/pregnancy diabetes/clinical therapy/type II bipolar disorder (seven hits)
- keto diet for weight loss (two hits)

Some examples can be found in the excerpts below:

>   (10) My neurosurgeon who is one of the best in the country told me about it when we were discussing my choice to use the ketogenic diet for clinical therapy.
>
>   (11) Update on Ketogenic Diet for Obesity, Diabetes, and Metabolic Syndrome has been published on fitnhealthy.com.

In three cases the preposition *for* shows the length of time people are/have been on diet, while in one case it simply indicates whom the diet is for, in the title of a book:

>   (12) Ketogenic Diet for Beginners: Your Essential Guide to Living the Keto Lifestyle.

4.3. Keto vs ketogenic diet

Given that the *n-gram* results for *keto diet* and *ketogenic diet* seem to yield precise results, whereby *keto* is apparently used whenever people are speaking about a diet for weight loss and *ketogenic diet* when speaking of a medical treatment, we checked the concordances of *keto diet* vs *ketogenic diet* in the whole corpus. Findings indicate that *ketogenic diet* is used to refer to the diet as a medical treatment in forty-seven concordances out of 385 (12.2 per cent), whereas the expression *keto diet* with the meaning of medical treatment is employed in four (0.18 per cent) concordances out of 2,151 – as we have already seen in the section above. Statistical significance cannot be computed as the *p*-value is too small to measure[3] ($p = 0.0000000$).

When neither *ketogenic* nor *keto diet* is used in the medical sense as a dietary treatment to treat some serious disease, such as cancer, diabetes or bipolar disorder, they are expressions employed to exalt one's success in losing weight, to eulogize keto recipes for food or to promote keto products, as shown in excerpts (13) to (15), below:

(13) Try Keto. That's how I lost my weight so fast.

(14) These almond butter cups are the bomb 💣 The #fatbomb 💣 Being on a #ketogenic diet doesn't mean you have to do without the flavors that you love. It just means letting your creativity …

(15) Thanks for trying Slimfast Keto.

As claimed by Cavalieri (2020), health literacy should start from new knowledge to be integrated with existing knowledge in order to make appropriate decisions as to whether to adopt a new treatment. This should also involve any decisions in relation to KD. However, when speaking about KD, the use of *keto* and *ketogenic* does not seem to depend on personal stylistic choice or preference. In other words, *keto* is not always a truncated form of *ketogenic*, as it may appear in a context where space constraint is relevant, as on Twitter. It seems, in contrast, that laypersons are beginning to use either *keto* or *ketogenic* in semantically different domains. Indeed, when the diet is referred to as a medical treatment, that is meant to cure specific conditions, it is *ketogenic*; when the diet is referred to as an aesthetic treatment for well-being purposes, it is *keto*. We will see, below, what the key semantic domains are that form the context in which both *keto* and *ketogenic* are used.

4.4. WMatrix and *keto** semantic domains

The key semantic domains (also known as SemTags) have been detected by WMatrix 4 with the USAS tool by comparing the whole corpus against the BNC oral sampler Corpus. The cut-off point of 6.62 has been determined by default with $p \leq 0.01$ and one degree of freedom (d.f.), set when two corpora are compared. The resulting list of 186 key semantic domains statistically significant for this investigation is shown in the Table 5.2 found in the *Appendix*, below.

The analysis of SemTags around KD did not reveal any unexpected type of discourse: they range from *medical* treatment to *dietary* treatment, the types of scientific *studies* about this diet – thus confirming the trend evidenced with Sketch Engine as illustrated above. In addition, the SemTags also show the *length* of the diet, when one can *begin* the diet, the type of *food* allowed on this diet or the *absolute absence* of *drinks* (alcohol) when on the diet, the *quantity* of *food* and the fact that the diet is *healthy* and how *energetic* one can feel despite being on it. SemtTags are also related to *weight gain* and *rapid weight loss*. These two aspects, in particular, were indicated by a SemTag that apparently had nothing to do with the notion of being on a diet: *I1.2 Money: Debts*, which includes 121 items (keyness value 0.23). This required a manual check of all concordance lines, revealing that all items were related to weight *loss*, as shown in (16), below (our emphasis here and there):

(16) A ketogenic diet is not a weight *loss* diet, it is a body composition normalization diet.

Linked to this, there was also the SemTag *X9.2- Failure* (ninety-six items; keyness value: 0.18): it actually indicated *loss of weight* in a short time ('Try keto. That's how I lost my weight so fast').

Other SemTags showed a different meaning thanks to the manual check of concordance lines. This different interpretation from the one given by default in WMatrix 4 is due to the context. Although the accuracy of WMatrix semantic tagging by USAS is around 91 per cent (Rayson *et al.* 2004), WMatrix tags general discourse in a top-down process on the basis of pre-assigned semantic categories. This might be a WMatrix 4 limitation in consideration of the fact that words are polysemous. The need for manual tagging is also confirmed by Rayson (2008: 529), who underlines the necessity of being aware of 'possible tagging errors', not only because the tagging is automatic, but also because the tagging is 'coarse-grained and may not match [sense distinctions] required in specific studies'.

Therefore, manual tagging was necessary for the following SemTags:

1. *S9 Religion and the supernatural* (108 items; keyness value: 0.20);
2. *S6- No obligation or necessity* (thirty-eight items; keyness value: 0.07);
3. *S1.2.4+ Polite* (thirty-one items; keyness value: 0.06);
4. *W1 The universe* (thirty-one items; keyness value: 0.06);
5. *W2- Darkness* (seven items; keyness value: 0.01);
6. *A5.1- Evaluation: Bad* (seven items; keyness value: 0.01).

The SemTag *S9 Religion and supernatural* refers to the fact that the diet is regarded as a *divinity* or something *god-sent,* and keto products are *magic*:

(17) KETO IS THE ONE TRUE *GOD*!

(18) Keto *magic* bar, no flour!

On the other hand, the ketogenic diet is also associated to *myths* surrounding it, which need to be dissipated:

(19) When it comes to keto, I hear the same questions time and time again from so many of you, from my clients and family members, as well I am constantly observing a general overabundance of rumors and *myths.*

The SemTag *S6 No obligation or necessity* is linked to the possibility of having either sugar/flour *free* products/recipes, or *free* sample products, if one decides to buy from certain e-shops:

(20) This #sugar*free* treat can be made in just 5 minutes.

(21) Keto and wheat *free* lifestyles steadily on the rise.

(22) Get The BRAND NEW eBOOK Simply Tasty Ketogenic Cookbook 100% *FREE.*

Politeness is apparently the main topic of SemTag *S1.2.4+ Polite*. In this group, people actually are grateful for the support they are getting for KD:

(23) Wow, *grateful* for the support!

(24) *Thanks* again for what you do!

These people are living a new lifestyle in a keto *world,* as the SemTag *W1 The universe* reveals:

(25) The #keto world will thank you!!!

And where there is any reference to *planet*, this is actually a reference to a gym:

(26) #methirsty #postworkout @*Planet* Fitness

The corpus reveals that this is a world where *darkness* (*SemTag W2- Darkness*) refers to a type of chocolate:

(27) Luxurious *dark* chocolate is fine on keto.

and where any apparently negative attitude (SemTag A5.1 – *Evaluation: Bad*) is linked to the difficulty of overcoming the desire for sweet food during the first weeks of KD:

(28) that second week is the *worst*! To stave off the sweet cravings, make yourself some iced tea and fat bombs with granulated erythritol to sweeten it up, and there's also a ketone supplement that helps get you into ketosis faster. Best of luck on your keto journey!

The empathy and support between people on KD are evident in excerpt (28) above, where one would not expect it, given the *Evaluation: Bad* SemTag. This positive support is, of course, also found in the SemTag A5.1+++ *Evaluation: Good* (162 items; keyness value: 0.30). The items contained in this SemTag are:

- good (seventy-seven hits, keyness value 0.14);
- great (sixty-nine hits, keyness value 0.13);
- well (twenty-three hits, keyness value 0.04)
- super (sixteen hits, keyness value 0.03);
- positive (fourteen hits, keyness value 0.03);
- improve (ten hits, keyness value 0.02).

These items are centred around positive clusters: people are wished 'Good luck' with KD or, if given a suggestion, they reply by acknowledging that it was 'great!' or a 'great idea!'. Keto recipes are 'great!' or 'super easy' and 'super fast' and the very existence of the KD is 'great' because it 'improves one's metabolism, health, and even athletic performance'.

5. Concluding remarks

The analysis carried out in this chapter has shown how two methodological approaches can be combined in order to offer a better interpretation of the data collected, particularly when sensitive issues such as those related to health are dealt with on social media, the place where healthcare interaction is being re-engineered. The approaches also offer data triangulation and allow answering the research questions posed in the introduction, namely: How is KD presented/described on Twitter? Can Twitter be a *locus* where (e-)health literacy can be developed?

First of all, by using Sketch Engine, we have seen that amongst the *keto* n-grams* the expression *keto(genic)is/keto(genic) for* respectively offers a definition and a reason for KD. The concordance lines for *keto* and *ketogenic*, however, have shown that the two terms are not used interchangeably. In fact, in both cases on Twitter, KD is mainly presented as a diet low in carbohydrates. Yet, in tweet narratives, the *ketogenic diet* can refer to the diet used as a medical treatment, whereas the *keto diet* refers to the diet used as an aesthetic treatment for well-being purposes.

Second, the key semantic fields found with Wmatrix 4 are those compatible with medical treatments and dietary treatments, the latter being particularly for losing weight, confirming what has been evidenced in Sketch Engine. WMatrix 4 is still a program that requires manual tagging to better contextualize SemTags. Indeed, some SemTags are apparently unexpected, since they are those related to evaluation (*worst* vs *good/extremely good*), religion (*magic/god-like*) or even money (*loss*). When reading the concordance lines of the manually checked SemTags, the analysis shows that the context is diet-related: for instance, bad *Evaluation* refers to the difficulty one faces at the beginning of the diet, *Money* refers to the loss of weight and *Religion* to the metaphoric magic or prodigious properties the diet has.

In a final step of investigation, the quantitative analysis has effectively achieved deeper insights in the investigation with the two methodological approaches. On the one hand, corpus findings not only confirmed the importance that lexical bundles play in Twitter discourse, because they helped us to identify the definition and reason for KD, but also highlighted a trend in terms of different usage related to the lexico-semantic function of *keto* vs *ketogenic* within the very same lexical bundle. The triangulation with WMatrix 4 has confirmed what has been highlighted by Sketch Engine. However, the fact that information about the KD as a medical treatment is found only in limited data (ca. 13 per cent) suggests that Twitter is apparently a *locus* where (e-)health literacy still needs to be developed.

This investigation can clearly open up paths for further research on dimensions only briefly mentioned in this contribution. For example, it would be stimulating to concentrate on that part of the corpus specifically dealing with KD as a medical treatment. Data could thus provide evidence on how e-health can be constructed on the basis of the discourse of those Twitter users who have found relief in KD, in comparison to those who have been treated with conventional medicines or drugs.

Appendix

Table 5.2 presents the list of the key semantic domains generated against the spoken Sampler of the BNC, the British National Corpus (990,704 words. For $p \leq 0.01$ and one degree of freedom (1 d.f. is when two corpora are compared), the resulting cut-off point for log-likelihood statistics is 6.63. Each Semantic

Table 5.2 Key semantic domains generated against the spoken sampler of the BNC

Item	O1	%1	O2	%2		LL	Log Ratio	SemTag
Z99	14076	26.31	5684	0.58	+	60325.18	5.51	Unmatched
F1	3001	5.61	3914	0.40	+	8738.13	3.82	Food
O1	398	0.74	362	0.04	+	1345.66	4.34	Substances and materials generally
N3.5	213	0.40	195	0.02	+	718.42	4.33	Measurement: Weight
X3.1+	81	0.15	0	0.00	+	480.13	11.54	Tasty
N3.7-	106	0.20	104	0.01	+	348.24	4.23	Short and narrow
A2.2	349	0.65	1891	0.19	+	330.92	1.76	Cause & Effect/Connection
B2+	100	0.19	106	0.01	+	318.59	4.12	Healthy
A5.1+++	162	0.30	428	0.04	+	312.08	2.80	Evaluation: Good
B2-	234	0.44	959	0.10	+	307.61	2.16	Disease
S8+	332	0.62	2020	0.21	+	267.28	1.59	Helping
N3.6-	49	0.09	7	0.00	+	248.99	7.01	Measurement: Area
B1	464	0.87	3703	0.38	+	231.60	1.20	Anatomy and physiology
F2	204	0.38	1022	0.10	+	213.86	1.87	Drinks and alcohol
X9.2-	96	0.18	207	0.02	+	212.57	3.09	Failure
X3.1	72	0.13	105	0.01	+	198.73	3.66	Sensory: Tasty
A12+	113	0.21	347	0.04	+	193.69	2.58	Easy
B3	194	0.36	1024	0.10	+	190.38	1.80	Medicines and medical treatment
B2	72	0.13	148	0.02	+	164.29	3.16	Health and disease

N3	25	0.05	2	0.00	+	134.14	7.84	Measurement
F1-	39	0.07	47	0.00	+	117.68	3.93	Lack of food
L3	108	0.20	564	0.06	+	107.46	1.81	Plants
X5.2+	109	0.20	612	0.06	+	98.49	1.71	Interested/excited/energetic
L2	210	0.39	1727	0.18	+	98.35	1.16	Living creatures: animals, birds, etc.
S1.2.1+	39	0.07	78	0.01	+	90.50	3.20	Informal/Friendly
L1+	33	0.06	51	0.01	+	88.45	3.57	Alive
N3.7+	72	0.13	320	0.03	+	86.80	2.05	Long tall and wide
X2.4	127	0.24	889	0.09	+	81.44	1.39	Investigate, examine, test, search
X2	19	0.04	12	0.00	+	72.51	4.86	Mental action and processes
S6-	38	0.07	106	0.01	+	70.28	2.72	No obligation or necessity
E2+++	24	0.04	47	0.00	+	56.40	3.23	Like
O2	352	0.66	4156	0.42	+	56.11	0.64	Objects generally
N3.7	56	0.10	292	0.03	+	55.83	1.82	Measurement: Length & height
Y1	68	0.13	415	0.04	+	54.49	1.59	Science and technology in general
A13	9	0.02	0	0.00	+	53.35	8.37	Degree
K5.1	112	0.21	914	0.09	+	53.33	1.17	Sports
T2+	149	0.28	1386	0.14	+	52.05	0.98	Time: Beginning
S1.2.4+	31	0.06	103	0.01	+	49.71	2.47	Polite
N3.1	54	0.10	308	0.03	+	47.74	1.69	Measurement: General
W2	8	0.01	0	0.00	+	47.42	8.20	Light
E4.2+	39	0.07	178	0.02	+	45.64	2.01	Content
N5++	225	0.42	2514	0.26	+	44.55	0.72	Quantities: many/much
N3.2+	116	0.22	1046	0.11	+	43.87	1.03	Size: Big
N5---	15	0.03	20	0.00	+	43.23	3.78	Quantities: little
I1.2	121	0.23	1117	0.11	+	43.11	0.99	Money: Debts
W2-	7	0.01	0	0.00	+	41.49	8.01	Darkness
A6.2+	114	0.21	1087	0.11	+	37.28	0.95	Comparing: Usual
A2.1+	180	0.34	2031	0.21	+	34.36	0.70	Change
A15-	30	0.06	140	0.01	+	34.23	1.98	Danger

A1.5.1	118	0.22	1213	0.12	+	30.99	0.84	Using
N5.1+++	5	0.01	0	0.00	+	29.64	7.52	Entire: maximum
X9.2+	70	0.13	603	0.06	+	29.54	1.09	Success
N3.3	40	0.07	260	0.03	+	29.06	1.50	Measurement: Distance
N3.8-	22	0.04	90	0.01	+	28.97	2.17	Speed: Slow
S9	108	0.20	1106	0.11	+	28.70	0.84	Religion and the supernatural
N6-	33	0.06	205	0.02	+	25.74	1.56	Infrequent
O1.2	76	0.14	732	0.07	+	24.17	0.93	Substance and materials: Liquid
A1.8+	54	0.10	457	0.05	+	23.73	1.12	Inclusion
S1.2.5+	23	0.04	119	0.01	+	23.16	1.83	Tough/strong
S1.1.1	75	0.14	746	0.08	+	21.76	0.89	Social actions, states and processes
N3.8+	79	0.15	819	0.08	+	20.21	0.83	Speed: Fast
Y2	53	0.10	480	0.05	+	19.83	1.02	Information technology and computing
X2.6-	12	0.02	39	0.00	+	19.61	2.50	Unexpected
N3.7--	5	0.01	3	0.00	+	19.37	4.94	Short and narrow
T1.1	11	0.02	35	0.00	+	18.31	2.53	Time: General
N5--	16	0.03	75	0.01	+	18.16	1.97	Quantities: little
T3---	23	0.04	143	0.01	+	17.92	1.56	Time: New and young
B2+++	3	0.01	0	0.00	+	17.78	6.78	Healthy
B2++	5	0.01	4	0.00	+	17.70	4.52	Healthy
X8+	104	0.19	1213	0.12	+	17.44	0.66	Trying hard
S8-	33	0.06	260	0.03	+	16.91	1.22	Hindering
X2.6+	33	0.06	261	0.03	+	16.78	1.22	Expected
A5.2+	53	0.10	513	0.05	+	16.63	0.92	Evaluation: True
A11.1++	5	0.01	5	0.00	+	16.30	4.20	Important
P1	149	0.28	1928	0.20	+	15.39	0.51	Education in general
S1.2	8	0.01	22	0.00	+	14.96	2.74	Personality traits
T1.3	471	0.88	7171	0.73	+	14.77	0.27	Time: Period
F3	19	0.04	119	0.01	+	14.64	1.55	Smoking and non-medical drugs
A2.1-	14	0.03	72	0.01	+	14.20	1.84	No change
X3.4+	6	0.01	13	0.00	+	13.24	3.08	Seen

X2.3+	37	0.07	341	0.03	+	13.24	1.00	Learning
N3.8+++	5	0.01	8	0.00	+	13.16	3.52	Speed: Fast
A6.1	5	0.01	9	0.00	+	12.34	3.35	Comparing: Similar/different
X2.2+++	2	0.00	0	0.00	+	11.86	6.20	Knowledgeable
A12+++	5	0.01	10	0.00	+	11.60	3.20	Easy
W1	31	0.06	300	0.03	+	9.73	0.92	The universe
O4.1	72	0.13	890	0.09	+	9.36	0.57	General appearance, physical properties
A5.1---	7	0.01	29	0.00	+	9.10	2.15	Evaluation: Bad
I1.3---	4	0.01	9	0.00	+	8.62	3.03	Cheap
T2+++	7	0.01	31	0.00	+	8.47	2.05	Time: Beginning
A13.2	79	0.15	1015	0.10	+	8.47	0.52	Degree: Maximizers
S5+++	2	0.00	1	0.00	+	8.14	5.20	Belonging to a group
S1.1.4+	5	0.01	17	0.00	+	7.86	2.43	Deserving
X2.2	7	0.01	34	0.00	+	7.62	1.92	Knowledge
Q4.1	52	0.10	635	0.06	+	7.15	0.59	The Media: Books

Domain is indicated with a Semantic Tag (first column), which is expanded in the ninth column. For each semantic domain, the frequencies observed in the corpus (O1, second column) and in the reference corpus (O2, fourth column) are indicated, as well as their relative frequencies in the text (fourth and fifth columns, respectively). The positive overuse of a semantic domain compared to the reference corpus is shown in the sixth column. Log-likelihood statistics (cf. https://ucrel-wmatrix4.lancaster.ac.uk/wmatrix4.html) are indicated in the seventh column. In the eighth column, LogRatio is an effect size and represents how 'big' the difference between two corpora is for a particular keyword statistic (http://cass.lancs.ac.uk/log-ratio-an-informal-introduction/ [14/8/2020].

Notes

1 Cf. https://developer.twitter.com/en/developer-terms/agreement.
2 See http://ucrel.lancs.ac.uk/bnc2sampler/sampler.htm [12/8/2020].
3 We computed the significance of p-value with three different statistical tests: for log likelihood, p-value is 0.0000000; for Chi-squared test, p-value = 1.063626×10^{-52}; for a Fisher exact test, p-value is 3.854612×10^{-35}.

References

Barbanti, P., L. Fofi, C. Aurilia, G. Egeo and M. Caprio (2017), 'Ketogenic Diet in Migraine: Rationale, Findings and Perspectives', *Neurological Science*, 38 (1): 111–15.

Bell, G. C., T. Hey and A. S. Szalay (2009), 'Beyond the Data Deluge', *Science*, 323 (5919): 1297–8.

Biber, D. (2006), *University Language: A Corpus-based Study of Spoken and Written Registers*, Amsterdam: John Benjamins.

Borgman, C. L. (1999), 'What Are Digital Libraries? Competing Visions', *Information Processing Management*, 35 (3): 227–43.

Breeze, R. (2013), 'Lexical Bundles across Four Legal Genres', *International Journal of Corpus Linguistics* 18 (2): 229–53.

Bueno, N. B., I. S. V. de Melo, S. L de Oliveira and T. Da Rocha Ataide (2013), 'Very-low-carbohydrate Ketogenic Diet v. Low-fat Diet for Long-term Weight Loss: A Meta-analysis of Randomised Controlled Trials', *British Journal of Nutrition*, 110 (7): 1178–87.

Cavalieri, S. (2020), 'Broadcasting Medical Discourse: The Dissemination of Dietary Treatments for Refractory Epilepsy through YouTube', in M. Gotti, S. Maci and M. Sala (eds), *Scholarly Pathways. Knowledge Transfer and Knowledge Exchange in Academia*, 429–46, Bern: Peter Lang.

Cavalieri, S. (2019), 'The Dissemination of Dietary Treatments for Refractory Epilepsy. A Preliminary Analysis of Web-based Discourse on the Ketogenic Diet', in M. Bondi, S. Cacchiani and S. Cavalieri (eds), *Communicating Specialized Knowledge: Old Genres and New Media*, 52–68, Newcastle: Cambridge Scholar Publishing.

Cavalieri, S. and G. Diani (2019), 'Exploring Health Literacy. Web-based Genres in Disseminating Specialised Knowledge to Caregivers: The Case of Pediatric Neurological Disorders', in G. Garzone, M. C. Paganoni and M. Reisigl (eds), *Discursive Representations of Controversial Issues in Medicine and Health*. Special issue of *Lingue, Culture, Mediazione / Languages, Cultures, Mediation*, 6 (1): 89–106.

Cavalieri, S., M. Marchiò, M. Bondi and G. Biagini (2019), 'Assessing Caregiver Informative Materials on the Ketogenic Diet in Italy: A Textual Ethnographic Approach', in M. Bondi and F. Poppi (eds), *Exploring Health Literacy*. Special issue of *TOKEN: A Journal of English Linguistics*, 9: 87–118.

Demjén, Z. and E. Semino, eds (2017), *The Routledge Handbook of Metaphor and Language*, London: Routledge.

Diani, G. (2019), 'Metadiscourse in Web-based Health Communication to Paediatric Patients and Their Caregivers', in M. Bondi and F. Poppi (eds), *Exploring Health Literacy*. Special issue of *TOKEN: A Journal of English Linguistics*, 9: 12–34.

Dynel, M. (2014), 'Participation Framework Underlying YouTube Interaction', *Journal of Pragmatics*, 73: 37–52

Eshet-Alkalai, Y. (2004), 'Digital Literacy: A Conceptual Framework for Survival Skills in the Digital Era', *Journal of Educational Multimedia and Hypermedia*, 13 (1): 93–106.

Falcicchia, C., M. Simonato and G. Verlengia (2018), 'New Tools for Epilepsy Therapy', *Frontiers in Cellular Neuroscience*, 12: 147.

Friedman, J. R. L., E. A. Thiele, D. Wang, K. B. Levine, E. K. Cloherty, H. H. Pfeifer, D. C. De Vivo, A. Carruthers and M. R. Natowicz (2006), 'Atypical GLUT1 Deficiency with Prominent Movement Disorder Responsive to Ketogenic Diet', *Movement Disorder*, 21 (2): 241–5.

Ge, X. (2010), 'Information-seeking Behavior in the Digital Age: A Multidisciplinary Study of Academic Researchers', *College and Research Libraries*, 71 (5): 435–55.

Grego, K. and A. Vicentini (2015), 'English and Multilingual Communication in Lombardy's Public Healthcare Websites', in M. Gotti, S. Maci and M. Sala (eds), *The Language of Medicine: Science, Practice and Academia*, 255–75, Bergamo: CERLIS SERIES.

Griffin, G. and M. Hayler (2016), *Research Methods for Reading Digital Data in the Digital Humanities*, Edinburgh: Edinburgh University Press.

Hawn, C. (2009), 'Take Two Aspirin and Tweet Me in the Morning: How Twitter, Facebook, and Other Social Media Are Reshaping Health Care', *Health Affairs*, 28 (2): 361–8.

Hedstrom, M. (1997), 'Digital Preservation: A Time Bomb for Digital Libraries', *Computers and the Humanities*, 31 (8): 189–202.

Kossoff, E. H. (2013), 'The Evolution of Dietary Therapy for Neurological Disorders', *Journal of Child Neurology*, 28 (8): 969.

Kossoff, E. H., S. C. Doerrer, S. P. Winesett, Z. Turner, B. J. Henry, S. Bessone, A. Stanfield and C. Mackenzie Cervenka (2016), 'Diet Redux: Outcomes from Reattempting Dietary Therapy for Epilepsy', *Journal of Child Neurology*, 31 (8): 1052–6.

Lamberg, L. (2003), 'Online Empathy for Mood Disorders: Patients Turn to Internet Support Groups', *Journal of American Medical Association*, 280: 3073–7.

Lazzeretti, C. and F. Poppi (2019), 'Children with Autism or Autistic Children? Indexicality in the Websites for Parents of Children with Neurological Conditions', in M. Bondi and F. Poppi (eds), *Exploring Health Literacy*. Special issue of *TOKEN: A Journal of English Linguistics*, 9: 35–58.

Luzón, M. J. (2015), 'Recontextualizing Expert Discourse in Weblogs: Strategies to Communicate Health Research to Experts and the Interested Public', in M. Gotti, S. Maci and M. Sala (eds), *Insights into Medical Communication*, 331–52, Bern: Peter Lang.

Masino, S. A. and D. N. Ruskin (2013), 'Ketogenic Diets and Pain', *Journal of Child Neurology*, 28 (8): 993–1001.

Mattiello, E. (2017), 'The Popularisation of Science via TED Talks', *International Journal of Language Studies*, 11: 77–106.

Mazzi, D. (2020), '"... through Hell and Back": Emotionality and Argument in the UK and Irish Discourse on the Ketogenic Diet', in M. Gotti, S. Maci and M. Sala (eds), *Scholarly Pathways. Knowledge Transfer and Knowledge Exchange in Academia*, 385–405, Bern: Peter Lang.

Mazzi, D. (2018), '"The Diet Is not Suitable for All ...": On the British and Irish Web-based Discourse on the Ketogenic Diet', *Lingue, Culture, Mediazioni / Languages, Cultures, Mediation*, 5 (1): 37–56.

McArthur, T. (1981), *Longman Lexicon of Contemporary English*, Harlow: Longman.

Paoli, A. (2014), 'Ketogenic Diet for Obesity: Friend or Foe', *International Journal of Environmental Research and Public Health*, 11: 2092–107.

Paoli, A., A. Rubini, J. S. Volek and K. A. Grimaldi (2013), 'Beyond Weight Loss: A Review of the Therapeutic Uses of Very-low-carbohydrate (Ketogenic) Diets', *European Journal of Clinical Nutrition*, 67: 789.

Rayson, P. (2008), 'From Key-words to Key Semantic Domains', *International Journal of Corpus Linguistics*, 13 (4): 519–49.

Rayson, P., D. Berridge and B. Francis (2004), 'Extending the Cochran Rule for the Comparison of Word Frequencies between Corpora', *Les poids des mots: Actes des 7es journées internationales d'Analyse statistique des données textuelles (JADT)*, Louvain-la-Neuve, Belgium, 10–12 Mar, 926–36.

Rheingold, H. (1993), *The Virtual Community: Homesteading on the Electronic Frontier*, Reading, MA: Addison-Wesley.

Rho, J. M. (2017), 'How Does the Ketogenic Diet Induce Anti-Seizure Effects?' *Neuroscience Letters*, 637: 4–10.

Sezzi, A. and M. Bondi (2019), '"I Am Going on a Ketogenic Diet." Engaging Different Audiences in Communicating Dietary Requirements for Pediatric Patients', in M. Bondi and F. Poppi (eds), *Exploring Health Literacy*. Special issue of *TOKEN: A Journal of English Linguistics*, 9: 59–85.

Sinclair, J. (1991), *Corpus Concordance Collocation*, Oxford: Oxford University Press.

Socialbearing.com. Permanent link available onlineat https://socialbearing.com/

Tessuto, G. (2015), 'Empowering Patients to Self-care in Web-mediated Communication: A Multimodal Discourse Analysis', in M. Gotti, S. Maci and M. Sala (eds), *Insights into Medical Communication*, 213–46, Bern: Peter Lang.

Turnbull, J. (2015), 'Living with Diabetes: The Discourse of Medical Information on the Internet for Young People', in M. Gotti, S. Maci and M. Sala (eds), *Insights into Medical Communication*, 247–68, Bern: Peter Lang.

Turnbull, J. (2016), 'Knowledge Dissemination Online: The Case of Health Information', in M. Bondi, S. Cacchiani and D. Mazzi (eds), *Discourse in and through the Media. Recontextualizing and Reconceptualzing Expert Discourse*, 290–314, Newcastle: Cambridge Scholars.

USAS, 'UCREL Semantic Analysis System (University of Lancaster)'. Available online: http://ucrel.lancs.ac.uk/usas/ (accessed 6 June 2021).

Vicentini, A. (2012), 'Institutional Healthcare E-Brochures and Multilingualism Issues in the Recent Immigration Era in Italy (2007–2010)', in S. Campagna, G. Garzone and C. Ilie (eds), *Evolving Genres in Web-mediated Communication*, 53–76, Bern: Peter Lang.

WMatrix4 (Corpus analysis and comparison software tool). Available online: https://ucrel-wmatrix4.lancaster.ac.uk/wmatrix4.html (accessed 6 June 2021).

Part Two

Translation for digital humanities: Research methods and applications

6

The legal translator as a digital humanist: On the use of digital corpora in professional legal translation

Patrizia Anesa

1. On legal translation, corpora and digital humanities

From an ontological and operational perspective, legal translation practice has evolved noticeably in the last few decades. The implementation of digital tools, such as corpora and the related corpus linguistics applications, has to some extent challenged traditional epistemic structures. The role of translators has evolved, emphasizing their need to act within interoperable professional networks and collaborating communities.

This study is situated within an area of research which is generated by a dynamic connection between three main fields, namely: (1) legilinguistics, which is itself the result of the complex and mutually constructive interaction between linguistics and law; (2) translation studies, with specific reference to legal translation; and (3) corpus linguistics, with a focus on specialized legal corpora.

These three areas can be seen as developing within the overarching concept of digital humanities. Most of the attempts to define its contours are simplistically subject either to outright acceptance or to unreflective rejection; yet, this concept requires a constant problematization, and any definition may seem to disregard the complex nuances that the phenomenon entails.

The locution 'digital humanities' implies using 'digital' as an apparently equivocal modifier which may refer both to a tool and an object of analysis. However, neither of these two interpretations should be discarded *a priori* in that digital humanities inherently encourage a multiperspectival and transdisciplinary approach. Thus, when referring to the expression 'digital humanities', the focus should be placed on its inclusiveness rather than on its potential ambiguity. In this regard, the porousness of the boundaries of the idea of digital humanities itself may be seen as one of its greatest values. Indeed, following a well-established tradition, the term 'humanities', thanks to its plural form, emphasizes its polycentric nature and its essential heterogeneity and complexity.

The approaches pertaining to digital humanities are, to some extent, intrinsically transdisciplinary (or even postdisciplinary), but can also be viewed as transhistorical, transnational, transcultural and transmedia. Thus, such approaches do not derive merely from the addition, the merging or the fusion of different frameworks for the fulfilment of a given objective; nor are they the result of a fight for legitimacy between divergent theoretical and methodological agendas. Instead, digital humanities are based on the productive development of innovative frameworks and constitute a dynamic multifaceted construct. Consequently, digital humanities cannot be molded into static forms or fixed models in that what is under discussion is ultimately a productive, organic and living concept.

Working in this context often implies an attempt to critically position new theories and methods in relation to the complexity of contemporary societal changes. In this regard, we can reason with Burdick *et al.* that digital humanities have contributed to expanding 'the potential power and reach of the humanities disciplines, both within the academy, and, just as importantly, outside its walls' (2012: 4).

The key role played by digital humanities in professional contexts emerges visibly within specialized translation, which involves a vast array of subjects, not necessarily operating within academia. Indeed, the application of this framework to translation brings with it the expansion of consolidated semiotic and representational translation practices and such expansion inevitably develops in a collaborative space. In particular, significant advancements of knowledge in the field are generated by the intertwinement of diverse, but complementary, key aspects such as computational proficiency, translation capacity and scholarly expertise.

Thanks to digital technologies, the ways in which we can understand, access and query texts varies profoundly, generating new questions, issues and challenges. This clearly holds true for the application of digital tools to legal translation and, more specifically, for the use of legal corpora. Hereof, some of the salient questions to be posed include: How do we detect hermeneutically valuable translation patterns throughout the data offered by corpora? How do we navigate the deluge of metadata available? How do we account for the specificities of local legal systems that go beyond the macro scale?

As its founding postulation this chapter takes the view that the translation of legal texts through the assistance of sophisticated computational tools is not in contrast to the traditional hermeneutic and operational goals of professionals and researchers operating in the field, but can actually serve the very same purposes.

Thus, digital humanities do not imply the (rather apocryphal) risk of a demise of traditional approaches to translation. Quite the opposite, they represent a new way of contributing knowledge construction and communication by drawing on, and building upon, tradition, thanks to the opportunities offered by new digital means.

From a broader perspective, digitally savvy translators are not to be seen as digital humanists only because they operate in the field of digital humanities, but because they incarnate the spirit of digital humanism. This view implies a paradigmatic shift from technology-focused people to people-focused technology, and consequently from a mechanistic view (which tends to equate the implementation of digital tools with the replacement of a human capital) to a digital culture which has an anthropocentric character and serves humans' needs.

2. The evolving relationship between corpora and specialized legal translation

The law is generally considered to be a field that is highly conservative and unresponsive to change from a discursive perspective. However, that is not always the case, in that the law inexorably evolves together with societal changes. Legal translation practices are also required to adapt to such variations and evolutions and, thus, the need for flexible tools is fundamental in order to guarantee efficacy and accuracy in this type of specialized translation. As a consequence, rapidly updating processes need to be implemented in order to ensure that legal translations are consistent with the changes that languages inevitably undergo.

One tool which can be employed to optimize translation processes is represented by corpora. They have long proven to be particularly relevant in legal translation, and their use in professional practice has increased substantially in recent years. Corpus-based translation studies (CBTS) developed considerably in the 1990s and have gradually contributed to shifting the focus from the relation between source text (ST) and target text (TT) to the TT and its independence (see, *inter alia*, Biel 2010), acknowledging that the TT may 'function on its own in the new situation without necessary recourse to the source text' (Engberg 2002: 382).

Corpus-based and corpus-driven approaches in legal translation have evolved substantially (see Biel *et al.* 2019), and the complexity of translation dynamics requires a constant flow of contributions to the debate. While traditional descriptive translation studies focus predominantly on the regularities of translation behaviours, recent approaches have undergone a paradigmatic shift towards broader dynamics of culture, which, in the case of legal translation, include social, political, jurisprudential, historical and linguistic factors (see Martìn Ruano 2019).

Although, initially, legal corpora could not comply with the principle of representativeness in terms of size, they could provide valuable information, especially from a contrastive perspective.[1] As happened with general corpora, at first legal corpora were used in translation studies mainly as a tool to compare the language of translation versus non-translated language. Subsequently, their application spread significantly and they started to be employed in translation evaluation, and in research on style and ideology, a trend which was clearly in line with the developments previously undergone by general corpora (Baker 2000, Bowker 2000).

The use of corpora legal linguistics has proven to be significant in different contexts (judiciary, legislative, academic, etc.) (Vogel/Hamann/Gauer 2018). Only relatively recently, however, has the importance of these tools received formal recognition as various courts have stated that corpus linguistics may contribute to disambiguating interpretive issues in the law (see Mouritsen 2011, 2017). In this respect, even formal legal circles have acknowledged the value of corpus linguistics in hermeneutic practice. For example, in *People v. Harris* [2016] the Michigan Supreme Court's majority stated that '[l]inguists call this type of analysis corpus linguistics, but the idea is consistent with how courts have understood statutory interpretation' (Vogel/Hamann/Gauer 2018). The affirmation of the usefulness of corpora in textual interpretation in turn demonstrates that they can assist the legal translator as an interpretive method. Thus, while corpus analyses cannot automatically replace the theory of legal interpretation, in that complex theoretical and practical issues often arise, their usage is becoming an accepted complementary instrument.

The specific use of electronic corpora in legal translation may be intended as a particular application of computer-assisted legal linguistics (see the notion of

CAL discussed in Vogel/Hamann/Gauer 2018), which focuses on the computer-assisted analysis and processing of legal texts from different perspectives (Hamann/Vogel/Gauer 2016). Legal corpora may indeed be consulted with an exploratory approach (corpus-driven) as well as with an inferential one (corpus-based) (see Vogel/Hamann/Gauer 2018).

A large number of legal corpora have been made available over time and, as will be shown, their sophistication and the range of their potential applications have evolved considerably. The next sections aim to offer reflections on the nature of different legal corpora and to discuss how they can be employed for translation purposes. Their features, potential applications and limitations will be illustrated, along with the awareness that corpus-powered translation methods present both fascinating opportunities and new complications for legal translators.

Corpora can serve translators well, but the mechanical application of corpus linguistics tools to translation practices may be criticized as overreaching or based on an inappropriate understanding of the interpretive translation process. Against this backdrop, new corpus methods are not meant to substitute existing approaches; instead, they can essentially represent not only a valuable tool from an operational perspective, but also an opportunity to revitalize current approaches (Dobson 2019).

3. Investigating legal corpora

Legal corpora may display varying degrees of heterogeneity in terms of genre. Indeed, legal discourses subsume a vast range of text types, which may imply different translation approaches. At the same time, however, such genres strongly interact and reciprocally influence and create interdependent complexes which have been defined as systems (Bazerman 1994), chains (Fairclough 2003: 216), constellations (Swales 2004: 12), networks (Fairclough 2006: 34) or colonies (Bhatia 2004: 57) of genres. It is now a truism that translation strategies have to be implemented according to the communicative functions of a given text type (Göpferich 1995: 322).

Along these lines, in their seminal work, Hatim and Mason (1990) describe genre as a key driver in translation choices given that genre structures imply specific cultural, pragmatic and rhetorical functions. Corpora inherently display noticeable sensitivity to generic features in that corpus design is often highly genre-based. In this respect, corpora can also contribute to making the most suitable choices thanks to the authenticity of the genres available (Biel 2018b).

3.1. Definitional issues

Before discussing the types of legal corpora available, some clarifications will be offered regarding the definitions adopted in this chapter. The traditional distinction between parallel versus comparable corpora is particularly relevant for corpus-assisted translation. Parallel corpora typically include source texts and target texts, while comparable corpora include texts which do not depend on a translation process but which have a given level of comparability in relation to a set of criteria (theme, register, audience, design, etc.).

When discussing parallel corpora, a distinction has also been propounded between unidirectional and bidirectional ones (Olohan 2004). A unidirectional corpus contains 'source texts in language A and target texts in language B', whereas a bidirectional one includes 'source texts in language A and target texts in language B, and source texts in language B and their translation into language A' (Olohan 2004: 24). For the purpose of this study, one aspect which should be highlighted is that of alignment, which often characterizes parallel corpora.[2] Indeed, while aligned parallel corpora usually comply with specific criteria, comparable corpora are compiled on the basis of more general principles of similarity.

Following traditional definitions, comparable corpora are mainly suitable for observing, *inter alia*, cross-linguistic variation (e.g. Biel 2014), while parallel corpora are valuable in translation decision-making (e.g. Prieto Ramos/Guzmán 2018). Mixed corpora can integrate both aspects and offer interesting insights into cross-linguistic variation in terms of textual patterns.

The boundaries between the concepts of parallel and comparable corpora are often not as clear as might be expected (cf. Zanettin 2012: 149; Fantinuoli/Zanettin 2015). Firstly, there are several mixed texts in which translated sections are juxtaposed with ones which are more in line with the concept of comparability. In this respect, Fantinuoli and Zanettin (2015) cite news translation and text crowdsourcing[3] as examples of heterogeneous texts which are created via practices defined as 'transediting' (Stetting 1989) and often derive from different sources. Secondly, in a way that would seem contrary to the basic definitional premises, parallel corpora may contain texts which are not technically pure translations. For instance, multilingual parallel corpora, such as Europarl and Acquis Communautaire, contain texts which are, formally, original documents and it is not possible to identify immediately the source text and the target text *stricto sensu*. Finally, the level of comparability of the texts included in a comparable corpus may vary, thus implying a certain level of heterogeneity. On a practical note, it should also be pointed out that the term 'translation corpus' is at times used as a synonym for 'parallel corpus', while in other cases it assumes the function of an umbrella term covering both parallel and free translation corpora (Tognini-Bonelli 2001).[4]

The notion of parallel and comparable corpora remains essential for applicational and practical purposes. However, their conceptualization is understood in this work as referring mainly to the principles underpinning the corpus design rather than the process lying behind the production of the single texts included (cf. Fantinuoli/Zanettin 2015).

Another definitional aspect to be considered is that terms such as special corpora, special purpose corpora or specialized corpora are at times employed interchangeably although they may imply some differences. Special corpora are generally defined as those whose aim is to investigate distinct aspects that the compilers aim to focus on, rather than the language as a whole (Teubert/Cermakova 2004). This definition is to some extent in line with that offered by Pearson (1998: 48) when referring to a Special Purpose Corpus as 'a corpus whose composition is determined by the precise purpose for which it is to be used', but not necessarily based on LSP. Specialized corpora are traditionally described as those designed for specific purposes and are therefore, by their very nature, smaller than general reference corpora (Pearson 1998). In recent years, LSP corpora have proliferated and they refer specifically to an LSP area or subarea, such as legal discourse.

3.2. An overview of selected legal corpora

Detailed overviews of existing legal corpora can be found in Marín Pérez and Rea Rizzo (2012), Pontrandolfo (2012) and Goźdź-Roszkowski and Pontrandolfo (2015). An exhaustive description of all the legal text corpora in existence would go beyond the scope of this paper. Rather, the aim is to present some examples of selected corpora and to reflect on how they can be employed in legilinguistics and, more specifically, in legal translation. Given the large number of legal corpora available, this overview has been limited to selected English and Italian corpora.

Among the corpora focusing on the English language, we can find the following:

- The *Cambridge Legal English Corpus* (Cambridge University Press) is part of the *Cambridge English Corpus* (CEC), formerly known as *Cambridge*

International Corpus, and contains written and spoken data, both in British and American English. It includes books, journals and newspaper articles concerning legal discourse. The size is approximately 20 million tokens.
- The *House of Lords Judgments Corpus* (HOLJ) (University of Edinburgh) is a well-established corpus consisting exclusively of one genre, namely House of Lords' judgments.
- The *Proceedings of the Old Bailey*[5] allows diachronic research in that it comprises examples of judicial language from the Central Criminal Court in London dating from 1674 to 1913.
- The *British Law Report Corpus* (BLaRC) (2008–10) comprises law reports from Northern Ireland, Scotland, England and Wales (Marín Pérez 2014).
- The *American Law Corpus* (ALC) (Goźdź-Roszkowski 2011) includes different genres such as academic journals, textbooks, briefs, contracts, legislation and opinions.
- The *Corpus of US Supreme Court Opinions*[6] can be employed to access approximately 32,000 SCOTUS decisions dating from the 1790s to the present.
- The *Corpus of Historical English Law Reports* (CHELAR) is diachronic and contains material from 1535 to 1999.
- The *Hansard Corpus of British Parliament Speeches*[7] is a semi-legal corpus, covering the time span 1803–2005.

Among bilingual comparable corpora, we can list:

- The *Bononia Legal Corpus* (BoLC), a bilingual (English – Italian) corpus of legal language (see Favretti/Tamburini/Martelli 2007). Two comparable subcorpora have been compiled for the two languages, focusing on texts of a legislative, judicial and administrative nature.[8]
- CADIS (*Corpus of Academic English*), compiled at the University of Bergamo, which also includes a section about academic legal language (English and Italian) specifically composed of research articles (RA), abstracts (A), book reviews (B) and editorials (E) on legal topics.

Parallel resources prove to be valuable in translation practice and research as they can, in turn, contribute to the development of translation and text analysis applications. In particular, the European Union's multilingual parallel corpora represent an important source of data. Some of the core resources available in this context include the following:

- JRC-Acquis (Steinberger *et al.* 2006). The JRC Joint Research Centre made use of the EU's parallel text collections in order to create a twenty-two-language parallel corpus (JRC-Acquis) which was released in 2006. It paved the way for several other parallel corpora and remains a benchmark in its field.
- The EuroParl corpus contains proceedings of the European Parliament. It includes versions of such proceedings in twenty-one European languages, namely: French, Italian, Spanish, Portuguese, Romanian, English, Dutch, German, Danish, Swedish, Bulgarian, Czech, Polish, Slovak, Slovene, Finnish, Hungarian, Estonian, Latvian, Lithuanian and Greek (cf. Koehn 2005).
- The OPUS open parallel corpus collection (Tiedemann/Nygaard 2004; Tiedemann 2009) consists of translated texts from the Internet, including legal ones (e.g. the subcorpus Europarl).[9]
- The DCEP (*Digital Corpus of the European Parliament*) contains documents published on the European Parliament's website such as reports, adopted texts, written answers to questions, written questions, press releases, motions and minutes of plenary meetings. The DCEP includes full-text documents as well as sentence-aligned data (in plain-text format).

The highly practical and scientific value of corpora of EU documents derives from the fact that translations are generally carried out by experienced professionals and are subject to accurate revisions both from a linguistic and legal perspective, thus representing a reliable source.

On a practical note, it should be stressed that, by and large, legal corpora tend to be representative mainly of legislative texts. For instance, such texts can easily be accessed through large databases including:

- UK legislation: www.legislation.gov.uk;[10]
- US legislation: www.loc.gov/law/find/databases.php; and[11]
- EU legislation: eur-lex.europa.eu.[12]

Conversely, other legal texts, such as private legal documents, are not nearly as well represented for reasons related to confidentiality and privacy, *inter alia*

(Biel 2017; see also Prieto Ramos 2014: 265), and these limitations often lead to difficulty in accessing non-legislative genres.

4. Applications

4.1. Tools and processes

Corpora can be convenient for the translation process, especially when automatic or computer-assisted translation is involved. In particular, parallel corpora prove to be highly beneficial in professional translation practice using CAT (Computer-Assisted Translation) tools. These tools provide the translator with quick access to previous translations and term databases and thus contribute to increasing efficiency and productivity.

CAT tools include Translation Memories (TMs) with aligned segments of texts. Yet, for a long time, TMs in the field of legal language appeared to be less common than other types of language due to privacy and confidentiality limitations (Biel 2010). However, their usage has grown considerably in recent years, especially as a consequence of the diffusion of material developed within EU institutions. More specifically, the use of legal corpora is strictly linked to the development of TMs, which include Translation Units (TU) and their translations.[13] Among the main Translation Memories we can mention DGT-TM[14] (Steinberger et al. 2012), ECDC-TM and EAC-TM.

Given the relative ease of updating TMs, these tools have acquired growing popularity in legal translation, while other resources, such as specialized dictionaries, have been increasingly viewed as less flexible or able to be kept adequately up to date. TMs appear to display a high degree of precision in legal discourse as they are based on large collections of official documents and characterized by a high level of professionalism in terms of text production.

Besides TMs, other related resources prove to be fundamental in legal translation, especially within the EU context. These include the database of EU terminology, IATE37 and the multilingual thesaurus EuroVoc38. Such resources are also meant to work in combination with specialized corpora: for instance, JRC released the indexer software JEX (Steinberger/Ebrahim/Turchi 2012), which classifies texts according to the multilingual EuroVoc thesaurus. EU corpora can be used to train JEX, and similar software can be updated using EU corpora (Steinberger et al. 2014).

Translators can also make use of a vast range of tools available online, which are often based on corpora. For example, Linguee[15] is a widely employed website which can be consulted as a multilingual dictionary as well as a translation service. Through specialized web crawlers Linguee browses the Internet to identify relevant bilingual texts and provide parallel units. Linguee includes, *inter alia*, EU Parliament protocols and laws of the European Union available in several languages, and proves highly reliable in the translation of texts related to EU institutions. Although it may be less relevant for the translation of texts pertaining to specific areas of law, for example Contract Law, Linguee represents a key to legal translation, especially because of its ease of use and of access.

Legal translators can also benefit from databases such as Westlaw or Nexis, which are widely used for text retrieval, or other extensive collections of legal texts, for instance the Free Law Project,[16] which is regularly updated.

4.2. Translation practice

Legal corpora, especially of a bilingual or multilingual nature, may be adopted for different professional and research purposes, such as machine translation, comparative legilinguistics or the development of alignment algorithms. Moreover, not only does the use of corpora in translation imply specific applications in the target text (TT) production, but it also involves a series of practices which can be suitable for the translator at various levels of the translation practice. Such processes include: (technical) vocabulary extraction and comparison, analysis of the collocability of words and terms in different languages and specialist fields, raising awareness of stylistic issues and ultimately, from a broader perspective, the evaluation of legal concepts across languages, cultures and legal systems.

The use of corpora in legal investigation can also help us to understand the diachronic evolution of legal language, to define the frequency of specific words and expressions as well as to circumscribe their semantic value in specific legal contexts, and to observe the co-occurrence of words in order to make more appropriate terminological choices. In this respect, corpora can provide legal translators with information on the contexts of use from a terminological and phraseological perspective (see Lombardi 2004, Pontrandolfo 2015). This awareness also has an impact with regard to stylistics as the consultation of corpora can help professionals to produce texts which are stylistically appropriate given the specific context of use and genre-specific conventions.

Concerning lexical choices, parallel corpora can also provide information about equivalence, but also about non-equivalence when there is no equivalence between lexical units across languages (Zanettin 2002: 11). In this regard, it should be kept in mind that the convergence between ST and TT chiefly depends on whether intersystemic or intrasystemic translations are being dealt with. In addition, in the former case, on the level of divergence between those systems being considered (see Šarčević 1997: 232 on the system-dependent nature of legal terms).

As regards terminology, comparable corpora may serve to solve text production issues through terminology mining. The translator can verify potential equivalents and assess their appropriateness, employing these corpora in word disambiguation, especially in the case of near-synonyms (see Goźdź-Roszkowski 2013). Moreover, the analytical approach to lexical meanings offered by corpora goes beyond the synthetic approach offered by a dictionary, thanks to the presence of multiple contexts which can help the translator to derive meanings more accurately. From a broader angle, comparable corpora offer the advantage of being able to focus on general patterns, on the collocational environment of terms[17] and on textual organization, rather than exclusively on single lexical items (see Varantola 2002: 175).

In general terms, corpora can beneficially inform professionals, including translators, of the relations existing between language and law as corpus resources allow the translator to have access to more contextual information. However, it should not be assumed that this is necessarily sufficient to produce adequate translations. Indeed, legal terminology is so inherently culture-bound that complex translational issues often arise. For instance, even a common legal term may assume different meanings not only across different legal systems or languages, but also across countries which share the same language.

4.3. Translator training

Corpora can be particularly valuable in teaching translation theories and methods. Students and trainees can use corpora to develop their translation competence[18] by analysing source texts and target texts, by observing lexical choices as well as socio-cultural patterns, and by gaining hands-on experience of authentic translations. This approach can also enhance critical observations and awareness of process-oriented research.

More specifically, following the traditional definitions, comparable corpora can be helpful at the initial stage of translator training, in that they can generate awareness of the main linguistic, discursive and socio-pragmatic features of specific texts. Conversely, parallel corpora can be beneficial especially for more expert translators as they represent 'a repository of translators' strategies and choices' (Zanettin 2014).

Corpora are functional to the translation process itself, but they can also be used to gain a better understanding of other areas that the student needs to focus on while practicing legal translation. These include genre analysis, contrastive stylistics and specialized lexicography, among others (Laursen/Arinas Pellón 2014). Along the same lines, Biel (2017) argues that corpora can have two main complementary applications in training. Firstly, they can represent a practical decision-making aid.*** This utilization 'is oriented towards increasing the textual fit of trainees' translations by raising the awareness of target legal conventions, allowing for more nuanced terminology/phraseology work, reduced interference, and a selection of more familiar patternings' (Biel 2017: 316). Secondly, they can be employed to favour critical thinking about translation practices (Biel 2017).

In translator training, ad hoc corpora can also be compiled. As Scott (2012) notes, despite their lack of representativeness, these corpora can be functional in that they stimulate critical thinking about the language structures and legal terminology. The research-informed development of critical thinking skills (Biel 2017) through corpora can represent a tool for reflecting upon the translation process. From this perspective (which has a more critical, rather than instrumental, focus), corpora can be used in training to enhance experiential learning. Indeed, the consultation of corpora can foster 'the students' active involvement in the management of their own learning' (Monzó Nebot 2008: 247). This helps the learners not only to refine their practical skills but also to take a critical stance towards the different stages of the translation process.

On a final note, one may argue that the readiness and apparent ease with which translational solutions are made available via corpora may hamper the development of critical reflection upon the translation process. However, in order to prevent these dynamics, the usage of corpus resources should be preceded, or at least accompanied, by a certain degree of acquaintance with the legal translation process, and with the cultural specificities of the texts being translated (see Biel 2017).

5. Conclusions

The dynamic and heterogeneous nature of digital humanities as a cultural space is apparently one of its few uncontentious aspects. Confronted with the wide spectrum of roles, forms, functions and statuses of digital humanities, it was not the aim of this chapter to offer an uncontested definition of the area and its boundaries. Rather, it was aimed to problematize it within the legal translation landscape and the related communities of interest, which are increasingly hybrid and complex.

All too often, the transdisciplinary paradigm has to face disciplinary-bound entropic forces. However, what may appear an amorphous field represents a complex ecosystem of knowledge production characterized by multiple trajectories; its evolution and development depend on its ability to prevent disciplinary chasms by enhancing the reciprocal validation of practices originating from different areas.

Often labelled as traditional and static, legal translation has actually been in greater flux than is often assumed. In particular, the productive and polymorphous development of translation practices in the legal field has matured alongside digital advancements. This has generated not only different practical approaches, but novel conceptualizations of such practices too. Corpus linguistic practices, translation frameworks and new digital methods have reciprocally enriched and cross-fertilized the field, contributing to the evolution of legal translation.

Corpus-assisted translation capitalizes on IT opportunities and implies a shift from traditional foci towards multidisciplinary approaches to translation practice, which include cultural, pragmatic, applied and discursive aspects (Biel 2018a). Thus, corpus-assisted legal translation represents an inherently transdisciplinary area which is expected to witness a further rise in empirical approaches. Its cornerstone lies in the relationship between law, language, translation and computational studies, and these areas can benefit from mutual enrichment, not only from a theoretical perspective, but also from practical and applied ones too.

Legal and institutional translation draws on the use of corpora, for research purposes, in professional practice and in training (see e.g. Biel 2017) across languages and jurisdictions. In this respect, the integration of parallel and comparable corpora is a valued didactic tool to be implemented in translator training and deserves to be further explored.

It could be argued that the use of digital corpora may imperil or impoverish the translator's creative ability. Without neglecting the potential existence of this source of conflict, this study argues that professionals are not renouncing authority to make textual and discursive choices. Indeed, computational methods can assist translators, without replacing them, in making correlations, identifying trends and showing relationships. Also, the adoption of corpora in legal translation can contribute to creating a connection between the micro level of individual cases and the macro level related to the overall pattern in legal argumentation. It can thus represent a valuable instrument both from a quantitative and a qualitative viewpoint.

Some experts in the field could also claim that an overreliance on computational tools might be in contrast with the complexity of the hermeneutic process involved in legal translation. However, the use of computerized corpora does not imply that the intricacy of language patterns in law texts can be reduced to mere statistical correlations. Conversely, it provides an additional instrument with which the expert can be assisted in their translation choices. From this perspective, the use of corpora, or the implementation of computer-assisted processes in legal translation, is not to be considered as favouring acritical practices; on the contrary, the amount of information available through (and the range of processes favoured by) corpora can enhance a more reflexive and critical approach.

Notes

1 See, for instance, Schäffner (1998) as regards the information offered by corpora at large.
2 Alignment refers to the creation of correspondences between units of texts, which can take place at sentence, phrase or word level. Different criteria can be applied for assessing the evaluation of alignment methods, for example, management of embedded extra-linguistic data (SGML markers, anchor points etc.), performance success rate (at least at sentence level); reliability and speed of training or error correction mechanisms.
3 These include, for instance, Wikipedia articles available in different languages.
4 In this case, parallel corpora are typically aligned, while free translation corpora are not.
5 See https://www.oldbaileyonline.org/ (accessed 1 December 2019).
6 See corpus.byu.edu/scotus (accessed 10 January 2020).
7 See https://www.english-corpora.org/hansard/ (accessed 10 January 2020).
8 The English section includes: Acts of Parliament, Chancery Division, Court of Appeal, Family Division, House of Lords, Privy Council, Queen's Bench Division, Statutory Instruments. The Italian section includes: Costituzione, Codice Civile, Codice Penale, Codice di Procedura Civile, Codice di Procedura Penale, Decreti Legislativi, Leggi Costituzionali, Leggi Ordinarie, Sentenze Penali Corte di

Cassazione, Sentenze Civili Corte di Cassazione, Sentenze e Ordinanze della Consulta. For details see http://corpora.dslo.unibo.it/BOLCCorpQuery.html (accessed 20 January 2020).
9 See http://opus.nlpl.eu/ (accessed 1 July 2020).
10 It includes a vast collection of enacted legislation with accompanying explanatory documents (for the UK, Scotland, Wales and Northern Ireland).
11 The website contains databases and resources providing legal and legislative information not only for the United States but also of an international nature.
12 The website includes sections on EU law and EU case-law, as well as on national law and case-law.
13 TUs can be of different types and lengths (sentences, titles, paragraphs, captions, etc.).
14 In particular, DGT-TM was first released in 2007, and its new versions are based on automatic sentence alignment using Euramis. The DGT-TM is currently available in twenty-four languages.
15 See https://www.linguee.com/ (accessed 1 July 2020).
16 See https://free.law/ (accessed 10 January 2020).
17 This aspect is essential in legal language, which is always seen as fixed, conservative and formulaic (Biel 2014: 47).
18 It should be pointed out that different models have been developed over time to describe the competences that legal translators should possess, ranging from Šarčević's (1997) seminal model to Prieto Ramos' (2011) integrative process-oriented approach, from the PACTE group's framework emphasizing strategic competence (PACTE 2003) to Cao's model of legal translation competence (2014: 112–13), from the EMT (European Master's in Translation) competence framework to Scarpa and Orlando's integrative model (2017). Competences relating to the use of corpora are subsumed by most of these models, and are explicitly described in EMT, PACTE and Scarpa and Orlando's approach (cf. Biel 2017). Thus, the consultation or the creation of corpora in translator training can contribute to the active development of these competences.

References

Baker, M. (2000), 'Towards a Methodology for Investigating the Style of a Literary Translator', *Target*, 12: 241–66.
Bazerman, C. (1994), 'Systems of Genres and the Enactment of Social Intentions', in A. Freedman and P. Medway (eds), *Genre and the New Rhetoric*, 79–101, London: Taylor and Francis.
Bhatia, V. K. (2004), *Worlds of Written Discourse*, London: Continuum.

Biel, Ł. (2010), 'Corpus-based Studies of Legal Language for Translation Purposes: Methodological and Practical Potential', in C. Heine and J. Engberg (eds), *Reconceptualizing LSP. Online Proceedings of the XVII European LSP Symposium 2009*. Aarhus 2010. Available online: https://bcom.au.dk/fileadmin/www.asb.dk/isek/biel.pdf (accessed 6 June 2021).

Biel, Ł. (2014), *Lost in the Eurofog. The Textual Fit of Translated Law*, Frankfurt am Main: Peter Lang.

Biel, Ł. (2017), 'Enhancing the Communicative Dimension of Legal Translation: Comparable Corpora in the Research-informed Classroom', *The Interpreter and Translator Trainer*, 11 (4): 316–36.

Biel, Ł. (2018a), 'Corpora in Institutional Legal Translation: Small Steps and the Big Picture', in F. Prieto Ramos (ed.), *Institutional Translation for International Governance: Enhancing Quality in Multilingual Legal Communication*, 25–36, London: Bloomsbury.

Biel, Ł. (2018b), 'Genre Analysis and Translation', in K. Malmkjær (ed.), *The Routledge Handbook of Translation Studies and Linguistics*, 151–64, London and New York: Routledge.

Biel, Ł., J. Engberg, R. Martín Ruano and V. Sosoni, eds (2019), *Research Methods in Legal Translation and Interpreting: Crossing Methodological Boundaries*, Abingdon: Routledge.

Bowker, L. (2000), 'A Corpus-based Approach to Evaluating Student Translations', *The Translator*, 6 (2): 183–210.

Burdick, A., J. Drucker, P. Lunenfeld, T. Presner and J. Schnapp (2012), *Digital_Humanities*, Cambridge, MA: MIT Press.

Cao, D. (2014), 'Teaching and Learning Legal Translation', *Semiotica*, 201: 103–19.

Dobson, J. E. (2019), *Critical Digital Humanities: The Search for a Methodology*, Urbana, IL: University of Illinois Press.

Engberg, J. (2002), 'Legal Meaning Assumptions – What Are the Consequences for Legal Interpretation and Legal Translation?' *International Journal of the Semiotics of Law*, 15 (4): 375–88.

Fairclough, N. (2003), *Analysing Discourse. Textual Analysis for Social Research*, London: Routledge.

Fairclough, N. (2006), 'Genres in Political Discourse', in K. Brown (ed.), *Encyclopedia of Language and Linguistics*, 2nd edn, vol. 5, 32–8, Oxford: Elsevier.

Fantinuoli, C. and F. Zanettin (2015), 'Creating and Using Multilingual Corpora in Translation Studies', in Fantinuoli and F. Zanettin (eds), *New Directions in Corpus-based Translation Studies*, 1–10, Berlin: Language Science Press.

Favretti Rossini, R., F. Tamburini and E. Martelli (2007), 'Words from Bononia Legal Corpus', in W. Teubert (ed.), *Text Corpora and Multilingual Lexicography*, 11–30, Amsterdam: John Benjamins.

Göpferich, S. (1995), 'A Pragmatic Classification of LSP Texts in Science and Technology', *Target*, 7 (2): 305–26.

Goźdź-Roszkowski, S. (2011), *Patterns of Linguistic Variation in American Legal English. A Corpus-based Study*, Frankfurt am Main: Peter Lang.

Goźdź-Roszkowski, S. (2013), 'Exploring Near-Synonymous Terms in Legal Language. A Corpus-based, Phraseological Perspective', *Linguistica Antverpiensia*, 12: 94–109.

Goźdź-Roszkowski, S. and G. Pontrandolfo (2015), 'Legal Phraseology Today: Corpus-based Applications across Legal Languages and Genres', *Fachsprache*, 37: 130–8.

Hamann, H., F. Vogel and I. Gauer (2016), 'Computer Assisted Legal Linguistics (CAL[2])', in F. Bex (ed.), *Legal Knowledge and Information Systems. JURIX 2016: The Twenty-Ninth Annual Conference*, Amsterdam: IOS Press.

Hatim, B. and I. Mason (1990), *Discourse and the Translator*, Harlow: Longman.

Koehn, P. (2005), 'EuroParl: A Parallel Corpus for Statistical Machine Translation', *Conference Proceedings: The Tenth Machine Translation Summit*, 79–86, Phuket, Thailand: AAMT.

Laursen, A. L. and I. Arinas Pellón (2014), 'Exploring the Potential of Corpus Use in Translation Training: New Approaches for Incorporating Software in Danish Translation Course Design', in E. Bárcena, T. Read and J. Arús (eds), *Languages for Specific Purposes in the Digital Era*, 243–63, Wiesbaden: Springer.

Lombardi, A. (2004), *Collocazioni e linguaggio giuridico. Proposte per un'analisi semi-automatica delle unità complesse in testi del diritto penale italiano e tedesco*, Milano: EDUCatt Università Cattolica.

Marín Pérez, M. J. (2014), 'A Proposal to Exploit Legal Term Repertoires Extracted Automatically from a Legal English Corpus', *Miscelánea: A Journal of English and American Studies*, 49: 53–72.

Marín Pérez, M. J. and C. Rea Rizzo (2012), 'Structure and Design of the British Law Report Corpus (BLRC): A Legal Corpus of Judicial Decisions from the UK', *Journal of English Studies*, 10: 131–45.

Martìn Ruano, R. (2019), 'Beyond Descriptive Legal Translation Studies: Towards Engaged Research, towards Critical Practices', in I. Simonnæs and M. Kristiansen (eds), *Legal Translation: Current Issues and Challenges in Research, Methods and Applications*, 129–53, Berlin: Fran & Timme.

Monzó Nebot, E. (2008), 'Corpus-based Activities in Legal Translator Training', *The Interpreter and Translator Trainer*, 2 (2): 221–52.

Mouritsen, S. (2011), 'Hard Cases and Hard Data: Assessing Corpus Linguistics as an Empirical Path to Plain Meaning', *Columbia Science and Technology Law Review*, 13: 156–205.

Mouritsen, S. (2017), 'Corpus Linguistics in Legal Interpretation. An Evolving Interpretative Framework', *International Journal of Language & Law*, 6: 67–89.

Olohan, M. (2004), *Introducing Corpora in Translation Studies*, London: Routledge.

PACTE (2003), 'Building a Translation Competence Model', in F. Alves (ed.), *Triangulating Translation: Perspectives in Process Oriented Research*, 43–66, Amsterdam: John Benjamins.

Pearson, J. (1998), *Terms in Context*, Amsterdam/Philadelphia: John Benjamins.

Pontrandolfo, G. (2012), 'Legal Corpora: An Overview', *Rivista Internazionale di Tecnica della Traduzione*, 14: 121–36.

Pontrandolfo, G. (2015), 'Investigating Judicial Phraseology with COSPE: A Contrastive Corpus-based Study', in C. Fantinuoli and F. Zanettin (eds), *New Directions in Corpus-based Translation Studies*, 137–60, Berlin: Language Science Press.

Prieto Ramos, F. (2011), 'Developing Legal Translation Competence: An Integrative Process-Oriented Approach', *Comparative Legilinguistics. International Journal for Legal Communication*, 5: 7–21.

Prieto Ramos, F. (2014), 'Legal Translation Studies as Interdiscipline: Scope and Evolution', *Meta: Translators' Journal*, 59 (2): 260–77.

Prieto Ramos, F. and D. Guzmán (2018), 'Legal Terminology Consistency and Adequacy as Quality Indicators in Institutional Translation: A Mixed-Method Comparative Study', in F. Prieto Ramos (ed.), *Institutional Translation for International Governance: Enhancing Quality in Multilingual Legal Communication*, 81–101, London, New York: Bloomsbury.

Šarčević, S. (1997), *New Approach to Legal Translation*, The Hague: Kluwer Law International.

Scarpa, F. and D. Orlando (2017), 'What It Takes to Do It Right: An Integrative EMT-based Model for Legal Translation Competence', *The Journal of Specialised Translation*, 27: 21–42.

Schäffner, C. (1998), 'Parallel Texts in Translation', in L. Bowker, M. Cronin, D. Kenny and J. Pearson (eds), *Unity in Diversity? Current Trends in Translation Studies*, 83–90, Manchester: St. Jerome.

Scott, J. (2012), 'Can Genre-Specific DIY Corpora, Compiled by Legal Translators Themselves, Assist Them in "Learning the Lingo" of Legal Subgenres?', *Comparative Legilinguistics*, 12: 87–101.

Steinberger, R., B. Pouliquen, A. Widiger, C. Ignat, T. Erjavec, D. Tufiş and D. Varga (2006), 'The JRC-Acquis: A Multilingual Aligned Parallel Corpus with 20+ Languages', *Proceedings of the 5th International Conference on Language Resources and Evaluation (LREC'2006), Genoa, Italy, 24–26 May 2006*, 2142–7, Paris: European Language Resources Association (ELRA).

Steinberger, R., M. Ebrahim and M. Turchi (2012), 'JRC EuroVoc Indexer JEX. A Freely Available Multi-label Categorisation Tool', *Proceedings of the 8th International Conference on Language Resources and Evaluation (LREC'2012), Istanbul, 21–27 May 2021*, 798–805, Paris: European Language Resources Agency (ELRA).

Steinberger, R., A. Eisele, S. Klocek, S. Pilos and P. Schlüter (2012), 'DGT-TM: A Freely Available Translation Memory in 22 Languages', *Proceedings of the 8th International Conference on Language Resources and Evaluation (LREC'2012) Istanbul, 21–27 May 2012*, 454–9, Paris: European Language Resources Agency (ELRA).

Steinberger, R., M. Ebrahim, A. Poulis, M. Carrasco-Benitez, P. Schlüter, M. K. Przybyszewski and S. Gilbro (2014), 'An Overview of the European Union's Highly Multilingual Parallel Corpora', *Language Resources & Evaluation*, 48: 679–707.

Stetting, K. (1989), 'Transediting: A New Term for Coping with the Grey Area between Editing and Translating', in G. Caie, K. Haastrup and A. L. Jakobsen (eds), *Proceedings from the Fourth Nordic Conference for English Studies*, 371–82, Copenhagen: University of Copenhagen.

Swales, J. M. (2004), *Research Genres: Explorations and Applications*, Cambridge: Cambridge University Press.

Teubert, W. and A. Cermakova (2004), 'Directions in Corpus Linguistics', in M. A. K. Halliday (ed.), *Lexicology and Corpus Linguistics, An Introduction*, 113–67, London: MPG Book Ltd.

Tiedemann, J. (2009), 'News from OPUS. A Collection of Multilingual Parallel Corpora with Tools and Interfaces', in N. Nicolov, G. Angelova and R. Mitkov (eds), *Recent Advances in Natural Language Processing*, vol. 5, 237–48, Amsterdam: John Benjamins.

Tiedemann, J. and L. Nygaard (2004), 'The OPUS Corpus. Parallel and Free', *Proceedings of the 4th International Conference on Language Resources and Evaluation (LREC)*, 1183–6, Lisbon, Portugal: European Language Resources Association (ELRA).

Tognini-Bonelli, E. (2001), *Corpus Linguistics at Work*, Amsterdam: John Benjamin.

Varantola, K. (2002), 'Disposable Corpora as Intelligent Tools in Translation', *Cadernos de Tradução IX – Tradução e Corpora*, 1 (9): 171–89.

Vogel, F., H. Hamann and I. Gauer (2018), 'Computer-Assisted Legal Linguistics: Corpus Analysis as a New Tool for Legal Studies', *Law & Social Inquiry*, 43 (4): 1340–63.

Zanettin, F. (2002), 'Corpora in Translation Practice', in E. Yuste-Rodrigo (ed.), *Language Resources for Translation Work and Research, LREC 2002 Workshop Proceedings*, 10–14, Las Palmas de Gran Canaria.

Zanettin, F. (2012), *Translation-driven Corpora. Corpus Resources for Descriptive and Applied Translation Studies*, Manchester: St. Jerome.

Zanettin, F. (2014), 'Corpora in Translation', in J. House (ed.), *Translation: A Multidisciplinary Approach*, 178–99, Basingstoke: Palgrave.

7

A comparative study of emotive language in English and Italian migrant narratives in digital museums

Cinzia Spinzi and Anouska Zummo

1. Introduction

The United Nations High Commissioner for Refugees' statistics estimated 79.5 million forcibly displaced people worldwide 'as a result of persecution, conflict, violence, human rights violations or events seriously disturbing public order' (UNHCR 2020), of which 85 per cent are hosted by developing countries. Yet in more economically developed countries, 'xenophobic and racist discourse has been normalized [...], with certain media outlets and politicians blaming refugees and migrants for economic and social problems' (Tsitsanoudis-Mallidis/Derveni 2018: 3). Social media platforms and news reporting play a significant role in the formulation of public opinion towards migrants. Linguistic strategies enable the depiction of the so-called 'migrant crisis' or 'refugee crisis' to either fortify or contradict political and societal stances. Regardless of whether the public upholds anti-migration or sympathetic viewpoints, it is inevitable that the views in question are, in part, molded by the opinions of outside perspectives (journalists, activists, reporters, politicians). The polarized stances have historically been the anti-migrant propaganda of the far right that creates a collective, nameless, dehumanized mass versus a more humanitarian, left-wing reference to people, children and named individuals, with the intention of summoning sympathy, solidarity and compassion. The

---

Even though the two authors conceived the article together, Anouska Zummo is primarily responsible for Sections 1, 2, 4.2. and 5.1 and Cinzia Spinzi is responsible for Sections 2.1, 3, 4.1 and 5.

two polarized approaches weaponize emotive language,[1] appealing either to a populist fear of the 'Other', an 'Invader', a growing 'threat'[2] or to an empathetic sense of humane responsibility based on a more non-nationalistic sentiment. Both strategies present migrants in a way that objectifies them, even in instances where the intention may be to summon support and understanding. Indeed, the unrelenting usage of 'the word "crisis" automatically leads to present people as "media objects", instead of media subjects. Overall, media paid little and scattered attention to the context of refugee and migrant plight about migrants' and refugees' individual stories, their lives and culture' (CNMC–MNRA[3] Report 2018: 6). Likewise, Browning addresses the use of the word 'illegal' in the description of migrants as a word choice that 'functions within the fearful imagination' and, framing her appeal in postcolonial ethics, she calls for 'just speech', arguing that it is an 'essential component in the creation of just policy towards migrants' (2009: 242).

One hope of this study is that it might contribute to efforts (principally in language mediation and museum platforms) of reducing the binaries present in migrant narratives by placing the focus on the linguistic choices of migrants within their own writing. It is for this reason that digital museum platforms were chosen for gathering data, given the relatively recent role of museums as interactive, multimodal and accessibility-orientated institutions which contribute to the re-construction and re-narration of migrants' social identities, foregrounding migrant voices and humanizing an otherwise predominantly objective discourse. As a matter of fact, museums are seen as enablers for the shift of perspective from objectified victims to epistemic and poietic agents (Rizzo/Spinzi/Greco forthcoming 2022) and, fundamentally, create individual narratives which can function as being more relatable.

While numerous studies have highlighted the role of linguistic choices within journalistic or politicized discourse about migrants and refugees (see Hayat Taha 2019; for effects of media coverage in Europe, see Eberl *et al.* 2018), the role of such choices within narratives written *by* migrants is relatively unexplored. As a matter of fact, 'the role of emotion in people's mobile lives has long been marginal in migration studies' (Alinejad/Ponzanesi 2020: 621), and within the sociological[4] tradition of migration research 'the explicit consideration of emotions has largely been ignored' (Albrecht 2016: 26, see also Alencar/Camargo, forthcoming). From a linguistic perspective, to the best of our knowledge, relatively little attention has been paid to the emotive language used in migrant discourse where displaced persons are themselves the narrators.

Framing itself within the 'emotional turn'[5] (see Gonzalez 2017: 27 and Lemmings/Brooks 2014), this work intends to fill this gap by starting a preliminary investigation of the frequency and mode of usage of words that evoke emotion within migrant narratives in English and Italian, in order to assess the intention and effect of these linguistic choices. Drawing upon a combination of methods (e.g. corpus techniques and the Appraisal Theory, Martin/White 2005), more particularly, this work sets out to analyse manifestation of emotion, based on data obtained from digital museum contributions, seeking to understand whether subjective narratives authored by migrants apply emotive language as a means of integrating or as a means of formulating a distinct identity. Finally, this study is also of interest from the translation perspective in that 'the way people interpret their own emotions depends, to some extent at least, on the lexical grid provided by their native language' (Wierzbicka 1999: 26).

Such angles critically connect corpus linguistics with translation studies; migrants often write in a second or subsequent language (L2) and the usage and nature of their L2, when examined as part of a collective corpora of data, become indicative of behaviour, emotional norms and intercultural communication. Applying corpus linguistic methods for the analysis of digital data positions the research within the realm of the Digital Humanities, defined by Smith Rumsey (2013: 158) as 'the use of digital evidence and method, digital authoring, digital publishing, digital curation and preservation, and digital use and reuse of scholarship'.

After an overview of the background to this research in the following section, data and methodology are explained in Section 3, followed by the combination of quantitative and qualitative exploration in Section 4 where findings led us to conclude that first-hand narratives seek to avoid the tendency of victimizing the migrant figure.

2. Background and theoretical framework

Before exploring the literature on emotive language, a definition befits the interests of this research. Macagno and Walton (2014: 5) maintain that emotive words 'affect our decisions concerning their referents' and consider them as 'effective instruments to direct and encourage certain attitudes and choices'. Furthermore, the two scholars distinguish them from ethical words which are strictly bound to moral values leading to value judgments.

A less manipulative but more articulate definition adopted in this study is provided by Tsitsanoudis-Mallidis and Derveni (2018: 5):

> Emotive language is word choice that is used to evoke emotion and is intended to cause an effect (emotional response) on the audience. Different words can be used to cause different reactions in the audience. Loaded words are these highly emotional words, which elicit an emotional response (positive or negative) beyond their literal meaning and can significantly contribute to persuading the audience to adopt a specific point of view.

Research on the types and role of emotions has been extensively carried out across such a variety of disciplines (i.e. philosophy, psychology, sociology, anthropology and linguistics) that summarizing it here would not do justice to all of them. That is why in this section only those studies that are more relevant to the connection of emotive language and social migration will be explored. As a matter of fact, given its inherent intersections between sociological, anthropological, geographical and psychological accounts, Boccagni and Baldassar (2015) describe work in the field of emotions and migration as an emerging field and underline the necessity of examining migration via a multidisciplinary perspective. They additionally foreground the reciprocal significance of migration studies for the social study of emotion and critically observe that

> transnational migration, and mobile lives more generally, offer a privileged lens through which to observe emotions. The migration process is a powerful catalyst of change in emotional life – one that may make it physically and symbolically 'out of place'. As people move away from home–or indeed, *between* 'homes' – emotions themselves are on the move.
>
> (Boccagni and Baldassar 2015: 74)

Other studies have pointed out the importance of exploring subjective narratives since they provide stories as opposed to statistics and personalize public engagement with the often diversified 'Other' (Albrecht 2016). Alencar and Camargo (forthcoming 2021) go further by underlining the relevance of investigating the dynamics of refugees' emotional experiences 'for a better understanding of their agency, subjectivities and interactions with old and new reference groups, as well as across time and space'.

It is beyond the scope of this paper to demonstrate the ways in which binaries are created but rather to highlight the necessity for platforms through which migrant narratives occupy their own space, unhinged by ulterior motives in other forms of public discourse. Through analysis of certain linguistic expressions, we may begin to ascertain trends and norms within migrant narratives – possibly as indicative or representative of their own genre, although this for now remains a promising avenue for future research.

From an intercultural perspective, no consensus has been achieved in terms of universality of human emotions; on the contrary, the humanities perhaps lean towards what Lindqvist, K. (2013) calls the 'constructionist model', meaning that emotions are 'quintessentially, by all measure, a matter of culture' (Boccagni and Baldassar 2015: 75). Regardless of these conflictual stances, what is relevant to this study is that aspects of emotional experience are determined by socialization and cultural construal (Bednarek 2008: 5; see also Harkins/Wierzbicka 2001).

Apart from the cross-cultural approach, a plethora of studies have also shown an interest in emotive language from other standpoints such as cognitive (Kövecses 2000), diachronic (Halliday *et al.* 2004) and pragmatic (Stubbs 1996) to mention just a few. This study is closer to Bednarek's (2008) linguistic analysis of emotion talk in different registers where she adopts the functional framework of the Appraisal Theory (Martin/White 2005), which focuses on interpersonal meanings in language, namely those concerned with the ways in which solidarity is negotiated, with speaker/writer commitment and evaluation.

The claim of the two functionalist scholars that they complement their taxonomy with quantitative methods was addressed by Bednarek (2008) who takes up the challenge and elaborates the model relying on empirical data by the means of corpus linguistics techniques with the aim of setting up a Local Grammar of Affect, that is one of the three semantic resources which constitute Attitude. In other words, she attempts to uncover all the patterns in language that express Affect in a more implicit way.

2.1. System of attitude

Appraisal Theory, which distinguishes emotion (i.e. affect) from opinion (i.e. evaluation), organizes both in three main semantic domains: ENGAGEMENT, ATTITUDE and GRADUATION. The subdomains of Attitude are Affect, involving emotional reaction, Judgement, referring to assessments of ethical behaviour and Appreciation, which looks at aesthetics, that is, all resources for constructing assessments of artefacts, texts and natural objects in terms of how they are assigned value socially. The second dimension, Engagement, covers the resources which position the textual voice inter-subjectively and, finally, Graduation concerns all those resources for 'up- or down-grading' the intensity of the speaker's meanings. For the purpose of this research only Affect will be considered, seen as the 'core system with Judgement and Appreciation as its institutionalized versions' (Miller 2007: 163). Drawing upon further revisions of the Appraisal Theory (Bednarek 2008, Fuoli/Hommerberg 2015), the Affect system comprises five semantic domains for emotions: un/happiness, in/security, dis/satisfaction, surprise, dis/inclination, each realized in a direct way ('inscribed') or indirectly ('invoked') which is known as 'attitudinal token' and, in this case, evaluation is construed through mechanisms of 'association' and 'implication'. Further variables for the categorization of these groups are given by polarity (positive and negative), intensity (e.g. adore, love and like), grammatical metaphor (e.g. use of nominalizations instead of verbal processes) and stimulus (e.g. realis or irrealis). Bednarek's contribution to this model lies in the distinction between 'overt' and 'covert Affect'. In her words: 'Resources of overt Affect directly name an emotional response of Emoters (*fear, love, hate*), whereas resources of covert Affect only indirectly denote such an emotional response' (2009: 166).

3. Data and methodology

The data consulted for the analysis come from an *ad-hoc* comparable corpus of migrants' narratives from digital museums in the United States, the UK, Australia and Italy. The stories were downloaded from museums which have set forth discursive practices of social equality and inclusion through stories of immigration and cultural identity, past and present. The digitization of museum collections and the fact that migrant discourse in the public domain is predominantly found on digital platforms result in the increasingly intercepted spheres of Humanities research and technology. The capacity of computer software for reading vast amounts of online data enables researchers to access crucial data on a mass scale, facilitating our understanding of representation of different sectors of society in online archives. As both disciplines (i.e. museum studies and corpus linguistics) use computer-aided linguistic analysis, both inevitably incorporate the rising global relevance of the Digital Humanities. The Alliance of Digital Humanities Organizations (ADHO, founded in Toronto in 1997) refers to the phenomenon as 'humanists engaged in digital and computer-assisted research' (Forest *et al.* 2019: i1), and the mission of the ADHO focuses on 'knowledge mobilization, public-facing scholarship, collaboration among scholars and communities, open access to code, software, research and results, and aspects of digital humanities research and publication involving accessibility technologies' (Forest *et al.* 2019: i2). The non-hierarchical and accessibility-orientated drive behind the development of the digital humanities is particularly relevant to the subject of the language of migration, which transcends the boundaries of various academic disciplines and humanist interests. Sandrini and Garcia Gonzales (2015: 177) reiterate this sentiment in his plea that 'there is a more profound rationale behind the concept of openness, touching the question of social equality when referring to knowledge and education, as well as to the ownership of knowledge in general'. Digital museums have thus provided a voice for migrants to communicate their counter-narratives[6] as opposed to mainstream narratives, and have tended to acknowledge – and even celebrate – the cultural heritage of migrants in their adoptive territories through audiovisual translation modes. In this way – as noticed by De Fina and Tseng (2017: 382) – underrepresented communities are given voice to build 'knowledge about processes of displacement and relocation' and to express emotions negotiated through multiethnic interaction.

The museums considered for the English corpus are the *Tenement Museum* in New York, the *Battersea Arts Centre*, the *Migration Project Museum* in London and, finally, the *Immigration Museum, Victoria Culture* in Melbourne. The Italian corpus assembles stories from three Italian museums: *Memoria e Migrazione* (MEM) in Genova, where stories recount a cross-section of the Italian society, from the mid-nineteenth century to the present day, tracing a picture of the migration processes, past and present; the *Migrador Museum*, conceived only as a virtual museum, and from the *Museo Italiano delle Migrazioni* (MIM),[7] housed in Belluno. The corpus provisionally stands at 55,569 words for the English sub-corpus and at 38,090 words for the Italian counterpart.

In order to ascertain the ways emotive language is deployed in terms of polarity and strategy the corpus was interrogated by means of the software *AntConc* (Anthony 2020). From the methodological point of view, in the wake of Hunston (2004), our analysis starts with the reading of random narratives which serve as the basis for further corpus-assisted investigation with the corpus working as an 'echo-chamber' (see for example Miller 2006). The first utility used for quantitative observation was the wordlist from both sub-corpora which was functional for a preliminary identification of all the adjectives as expressions of overt Affect of the speaker (authorial Affect). In the interests of thoroughness, this step was also supported by the list of adjectives considered by Bednarek as potential seed list of overt Affect (2009: 189). Then verbs which were considered as potential candidates for expressing emotions were taken into account. Adjectives and nouns (happy vs happiness) and verbs (based on previous research Rizzo/Spinzi/Greco forthcoming 2022) were classified according to polarity (positive and negative) and strategy (overt vs covert). The cluster list was also retrieved to detect patterns of Affect as manifestation of covert Affect, following those identified by Bednarek (2009). Concordances were relied upon for the investigation of context to identify the cause of emotion (trigger).

4. Analysis

4.1. Results from the English subcorpus

The canonical form in which emotions are manifested in language is the adjectival form, hence Affect is expressed as a quality which can be either attributed to participants or used to describe them. Further manifestations of Affect in language are through processes, usually of the Mental and Behavioural type, and through comment adverbs (Modal Adjuncts). In this analysis adverbs are left out because they are not frequently used, thus the main focus is on adjectives and processes. Following Martin/White (2005) and Bednarek (2009), the classification of attitudinal lexis – only emotions and not opinions – can be visualized in the following tables.

Table 7.1 Overt instantiations of Affect

Overt Affect type	Positive	Negative	Examples from the corpus
Un/happiness -a) quality -b) process	happy (11); excited (3); cheerful (1); fond of (1); enjoyable (1); glad (1); love (44); like (14); laugh (2); enjoy (8)	sad (5); hurt (1); hate (2) don't enjoy (1)	(1) I am very **happy** that I find myself in this land, this land that has embraced all the migrants. (2) I **loved** all the dishes she made, and being at home surrounded by it all made me feel **comfort** and warmth.
In/security -a) quality -b) process	sure (5); safe (3); calm (3); confident (1); fear (1); peaceful (1); protect (13)	not sure (2); scared (2); not safe (2); afraid (1); anxious (1); unsure (1); worried (2); –––	(3) I turned to my friend and said, we are **safe** and finally going back home. (4) My husband was over the moon. We were in Melbourne within 24 hours. I was very **anxious**. 'What was going to happen in the future'.

Overt Affect type	Positive	Negative	Examples from the corpus
Dis/satisfaction -a) quality -b) process	proud (17); pleased (4); grateful (3); thankful (3); delightful (1) ——-	homesick (4); angry (2); never warm (1); stressed (1) ——-	*(5) With such a great tie to our heritage our family can be **proud** of where we came from, and show it.* *(6) And there I was very **homesick** and I think that mostly happens to a lot of people.* *(7) It was so nice because I **remember eating** the cocoa beans before the coffee.*
Dis/inclination -a) quality -b) process	interested (8); desire (2); hope (11) want (13); remember + ing (10); miss (5); long (2); crave (1); willing (1)	don't want (5)	*(8) It was one of the many dishes I **miss** about my country, but also reminds me of my grandma who took care of me for four years while my mom was in the United States.* *(9) I **longed for** some stability.*
Surprise	amazing (10)	shocked (1); crazy (1)	*(10) So if your ever in the area definitely stop by and try the sesame bread it is **amazing** and definitely feels a little bit like home.*

Table 7.2 Covert instantiations of Affect

Covert Affect type	Positive	Negative	Examples
Un/happiness -a) quality -b) process	happiness (8) love (8); joy (1)	sadness (6); grief (1)	*(11) Migration is a very mixed experience. You can certainly find freedom, peace and a new life but there is **pain** and **sadness** <u>leaving so much behind.</u>*
In/security -a) quality -b) process	protection (5); safety (1); together (39); peace (5); guardian angel (2) warmth (1)	screaming (2); loneliness (2) don't belong (5)	*(12) The cookies to me mean family in a way and it's <u>what brings us all together.</u>* *(13) I'm forty. I **feel** like I **don't belong** anywhere.*

Covert Affect type	Positive	Negative	Examples
Dis/satisfaction -a) quality -b) process	pride (2) ———	aching (1) ———	(14) *When I was eating it was remember back home. It connects to me because by pieces of grilled meat or typically chicken.*
Dis/inclination -a) quality -b) process	prefer (2); hope (1); intention (2) —————	rejection (1) ————-	(15) *I **hope** that this recipe reaches others so they may make them for people they **love** as well.*
Surprise	—————	————-	

The narratives were expected to reveal heightened degrees of emotional content, in accordance with media entities that sympathize with the migrant plight; instead, they seem to evade such victimization, appealing to notions of originally culturally relevant aspects or episodes which contribute to the reconstruction of their identity intrinsically projected towards the past. Findings displayed in the two tables and quantified in the Figures 7.1 and 7.2), show that the narrator is happily disposed to the subject of communication. Indeed, the affective narrator's disposition of happiness (65 per cent of the instantiations of Affect are related to happiness) is mostly construed through the canonical mental processes of median intensity (i.e. in 51 per cent of the overt Affect instances, the verb *love* is used) where the trigger is related (in order of frequency) to food, to a member of the family, quite often grandparent and to the country of origin. Triggers do not change when love is realized as a noun that is covert.

The category of insecurity, which is more covertly constructed (65 per cent of examples of covert Affect vs 16 per cent occurrences of overt Affect), reveals feelings of anxiety in relation to the new life in a new place and manifests the willing of staying together to overcome worries. In a stereotypically gendered community, these feelings are connected to 'mothering in the home' (Martin/White 2005: 49), as shown by the following example:

> My grandmother's recipes <u>are very important to</u> our family, and we **love** to cook with them. Some of these recipes were passed down to her from her mother-in-law (my great-grandmother, Martha Randolph). My grandma's mother-in-law taught my grandmother how to cook and wrote some of these recipes! […] We use the chocolate roll recipe for dessert on Christmas, and sometimes we also use them when we have friends over, or have parties. These <u>are very important to</u> me because my grandmother **loved** to cook, and although I never met her I **feel** that I have a **strong connection with** her when I use the recipes that she wrote.

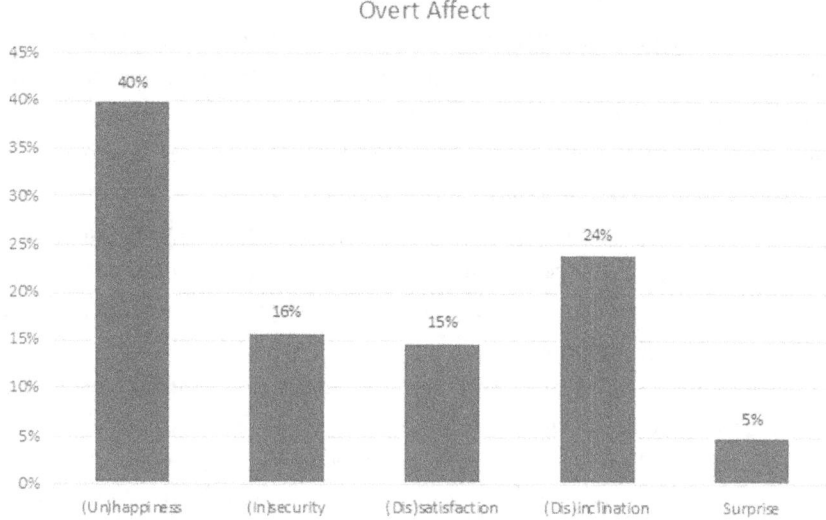

Figure 7.1 Quantitative distribution of overt Affect in English subcorpus

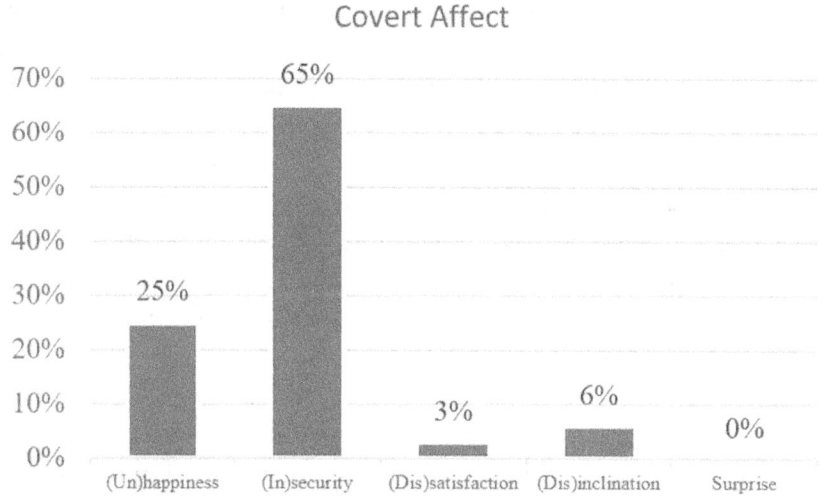

Figure 7.2 Quantitative distribution of covert Affect in English subcorpus

The memory of the grandmother is crucial to the process of identity reconstruction and, metaphorically described as the *guardian angel*, this motherly figure becomes the symbol of past time spent cooking traditional recipes. People may move to new places but their identity is strongly connected with their place of origin. It is through reminiscence that home becomes not only a physical place but also a mental place of identity, in short, it is a feeling. The different degree of transience is construed through the fracture between the new home where migrants are happy and the feeling, or better the desire, of belonging to a place (e.g. inclination). In the extract above, where the narrator's family comes from the UK to settle in the United States, not only does food represent an expedient to retain cultural memory and heritage but it also represents a means of achieving community unity, and thus reassurance. The pervasive use of the attitudinal token *together* and the cluster *together as a family* contributes to construing an implicit feeling of comfort by staying united, by connection, by religious gatherings for praying.

Defensiveness is present in certain verb choices (e.g. *protect*), and in the yearning for the cultures they have left behind, in the feeling of nostalgia (e.g. *miss, homesick*). Nostalgia is instrumental here in that it stirs up established habits from the past to lead narrators to new moods and often to new discoveries: it brings them close to the vital sources that flow within themselves. Nostalgia is not a discomfort to be eliminated, but a useful reminder to make those in question what they already are deep down, an invitation to leave home to rediscover the life force within themselves that calls out to them and assists them on their existential journey. Migrants' feeling of pride (e.g. satisfaction) of their culture and of their land is thus simultaneously constructed with the feelings of gratitude for being in a new place even though *to migrate is like to be born again*.

Emotion is summoned through structural argument, through factual/mental recounting (e.g. remember+ing), intentionally unelaborate, which is possibly owing to the perceived formality of the museum as a forum, as the subjects do not know their audience. In specific reference to migrants who fall into the category of 'refugee' or 'asylum seeker', the public may be more familiar with portrayals that are re-narrated by charitable agencies looking to obtain public support or donations for their causes. Such agents inevitably seek to heighten the sense of emotion in their secondhand presentation of migrant narratives through increasing the portrayal of subjects as victims, in contrast to the portrayal of those who donate and sympathize as 'saviours'. It is, in effect, harder to stimulate human compassion without highlighting the dependent nature of a victim and the, subsequently, noble nature of those who sympathize and help; this results in a natural tendency for (vulnerable) migrants and non-migrants to assume roles. In the museum setting, with first-hand accounts authored by migrants, a tendency towards victimization might exist to evoke empathy but, interestingly, as the intention of their narratives is communication and preservation of identity, many instances of emotive language relate to pride, self-sufficiency, cultural expression and determination.

During a Creative Writing project (*Write Here, Sanctuary*) for refugees and people seeking asylum in the UK, Stickley et al. (2018: 11) observed:

> The theme of place, home and identity was explicitly addressed through group activities. This was a complex subject for individuals who may have experienced instability and danger in terms of location. The potential existed for difficult and traumatic experiences to be articulated. However, the main expression was pride and fond memories of their homes.

As results show, pride and a desire to communicate memories of tradition and culture from societies of origin are recurring emotional triggers within the data. 'This way, it is possible to recognize the actors and narrators as individuals who shape transitions themselves instead of constructing them as executors of cultural logic or victims of their presumed conflicts' (Breckner 2005: 56, cited in Albrecht 2016: 28).

4.2. Results from the Italian subcorpus

In the Italian language, covert expressions of emotions (64 per cent) were found to be more frequently interspersed in the corpus. This first finding induced a manual checking of the narratives through reading in order to identify

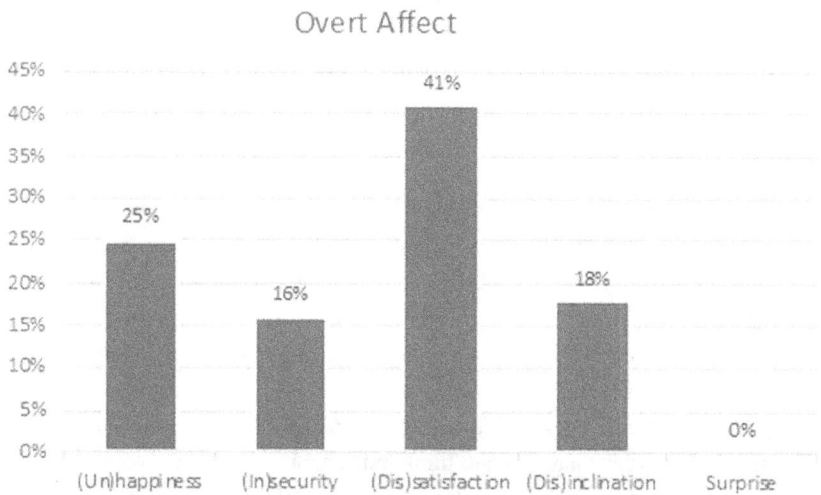

Figure 7.3 Quantitative distribution of overt Affect in Italian subcorpus

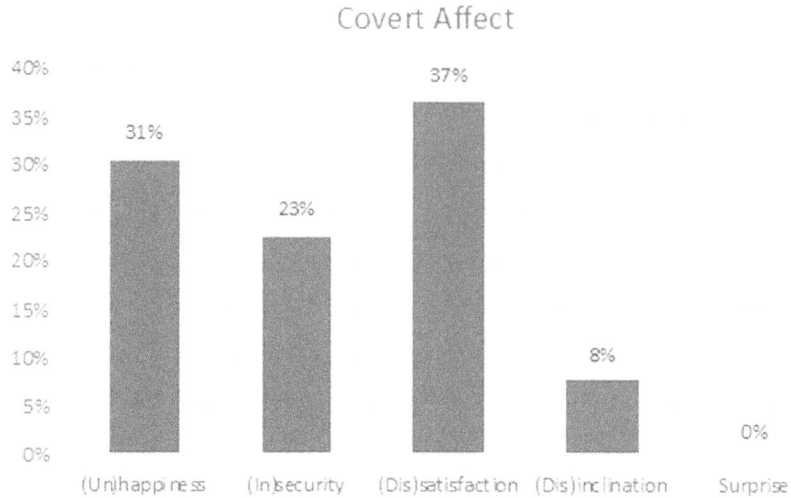

Figure 7.4 Quantitative distribution of covert Affect in Italian subcorpus

occurrences of implicit manifestations of emotion and prosodic realizations. The presence of indirect expressions of appraisal is not due to the narrator's predilections for a covert manifestation of emotions, but since it is a common feature in the Italian narratives regardless of the original provenance of the speaker, it is justifiable by the Italian implicit style of communication and higher preference for nominal formulations (see Katan 2004).

The following citation is one of the many examples of how appraisal is realized through a cumulative effect built upon invoked emotions. Affect constructed as inclination (e.g. so busy) is followed by expressions of disappointment and frustration triggered by the negative experience of the refusal and the shock of feeling for the first time the extra-community sentiment.

(1) *All'inizio ero **così impegnato** a cercare un alloggio e un lavoro per mantenermi che non avevo tempo di riflettere tanto su quello che stavo vivendo. Però, ho provato per la prima volta sulla mia pelle il **sentimento** anti-immigrato o anti-extracomunitario. <u>Nessuno voleva affittare casa a un ragazzo albanese,</u> nemmeno in una città grande come Torino, che mi sembrava già abbastanza multietnica.*

[In the beginning I was so busy looking for accommodation and a job to support myself that I didn't have time to think much about what I was experiencing. However, for the first time I felt the anti-immigrant or anti-extra-community sentiment. No one wanted to rent a house to an Albanian boy, not even in a city as big as Turin, which seemed to me to be already quite multi-ethnic.]

As shown by Figures 7.3 and 7.4, the major positive Affect is satisfaction which stems from the feelings of gratitude and being lucky either to live in Italy or for having achieved objectives in Italy mainly through work (example 2). Achievements coming after efforts and sacrifices trigger feelings of pride. Satisfaction mingles with narration of happiness for the country, its culture, its people and their hospitality (example 3):

(2) *Mi sento **fortunato** a vivere in Italia. <u>Sono riuscito a trovare lavoro</u>* (Positive Satisfaction).
[I feel lucky to live in Italy. I was able to find a job]

(3) *Sono dell'avviso che alla bellezza e all'ospitalità italiana, politiche come quella di Mare nostrum non facciano del bene […] **Felice** di essere arrivato in Italia e di viverci da più di metà della mia vita, sono **contento** e **fiero** di contribuire nel mio piccolo nel renderla un paese pienamente integrato, dove un giorno i miei nipoti si potranno dire **fieramente** italiani.*
[I believe that policies such as Mare Nostrum do not do Italian beauty and hospitality any favours […] Happy to have arrived in Italy and to have lived there for more than half my life, I am happy and proud to contribute in my own small way to making it a fully integrated country, where one day my grandchildren will be able to proudly call themselves Italian.]

(4) *Di quella <u>giornata infinita</u>, mi è rimasto il ricordo di mio fratello **affamato** e **piangente** e lo sguardo pieno di **dolore** di mio padre <u>perché non era in grado di soddisfare quella necessità primaria del suo piccolo</u>.*
[Of that endless day, I am left with the memory of my brother, hungry and crying, and my father's look of sorrow because he was unable to meet his little one's basic needs.]

(5) *Col passare del tempo, mi sono sentita italiana ed albanese a fasi alterne … perché con entrambe i paesi ho avuto **amore** e **odio** a fasi alterne. I primi anni vissuti qui li '**odiavo**' entrambe: <u>l'Albania che ci aveva costretti ad andare via, e l'Italia che mi costringeva a nascondermi come una ladra insieme alla mia famiglia</u>. Per tanti anni sono stata, e mi sono considerata, però principalmente 'albanese'.*
[As time went by, I felt Italian and Albanian in alternating phases … because I had love and hate for both countries in alternating phases. The first years I lived here I 'hated' them both: Albania which forced us to leave, and Italy

which forced me to hide like a thief together with my family. For many years I was, and considered myself, mainly 'Albanian'.]

(6) *Sono **orgogliosamente** marocchino **e ci tengo a dimostrare agli italiani** che marocchino non è sinonimo di povertà e di maleducazione.*
[I am proudly Moroccan and I want to show the Italians that Moroccan is not synonymous with poverty and rudeness.]

(7) *Comunque non venivo accettata, ero sempre l'albanese, forestiera e 'chi si crede di essere'. I primi tre anni sono stati di 'combattimento', il **desiderio** di integrazione si scontrava con una barriera forte.*
[However, I was not accepted, I was always the Albanian, a foreigner and 'whoever she thinks she is'. The first three years were of 'combat', the desire for integration clashed with a strong barrier.]

Listening to the voices of migrants encourages us to engage with ethics, with people as similar to our 'selves' (6), within a moral order and conscience based on feelings of invoked compassion (4). Compassion activates victimization in order to appeal for sympathy, since the intention in these stories is understanding and acceptance, rather than monetary aid negotiated by organizations as in the case of mainstream narratives.

Example (5) blends manifestations of un/happiness, even in conflictual terms with covert sentiment of dissatisfaction (5), frustration, again to stimulate solidarity that develops from processes of inclusion and belonging. The fragility that emerges from this struggle between the two identities and the resistance to integration coming from societal barriers (8). And what they have to offer is their aptitude to work, their desire for a better life and their willingness to make it happen.

It is possible that the narratives position themselves accordingly within the societies of reception. Italy has a history of emigration (and migration, from South to North) for economic reasons and there is a tendency within the accounts to foreground acquisition of employment and hard work whilst separated from family or through hardship. Some accounts are written by Italians who have migrated out of necessity and, therefore, empathy and comprehension are likely to be forthcoming. Traditionally, the importance of family and a sense of welcome go hand in hand with Italy's macro-narrative, and the migrant accounts predominantly reinforce this sense of integrative society. The narratives in English appeal to societies where mass emigration has not historically been an economic necessity, and indeed the narratives tend not to focus on assimilation into the host society, at least not hand in hand with ease of preservation of their original identities. The accounts have been published in recent years, amidst increasingly insular and nationalistic policies in the Anglophone territories selected and this undoubtedly affects the sense of national welcome and personal integration, perceived or real.

5. Concluding remarks

This research has used digital humanities tools in order to disseminate human migration creatively. The digitization of archival databases as well as storytelling applications have opened new ways of acquiring knowledge about people, places and politics that are crucial to the long histories of human movement across the world.

By examining the language of migrant narratives, in addition to offering an inside perspective, the paper also sought to highlight the role of emotive language as an inclusion-targeted tool diversely applied by the subjects, in comparison to Western media trends of reporting on immigration. The purpose of migrant narratives is to share experiences with the host country, or 'society of arrival' (Pries 2001, cited in Albrecht 2016), possibly in order to justify their place in that society, but also to share information about the 'society of origin' (Pries 2001, cited in Albrecht 2016), which is also often subject to misrepresentation or biased portrayal in the media.

In digital museums migrants are given a name, are individuals with their own stories and are thus empowered in that they can choose what to share to evoke sympathy. Emotive language is crucial to this purpose; in both languages positive affect is foregrounded even though negative appraisal is critical to the construction of compassionate stories, above all in the Italian narratives. Hence, the level of humanitarian compassion is heightened in the Italian data where these people are perceived as having been enforced to start a new life in a new country. As such, they are not criminalized for disrespecting the rule of law for, as Browning (2009: 241) argues, when the term '"illegal immigrant" is used in public speech or policy, a barrier is created that impedes compassion', resulting in a tendency to dehumanize.

The tendency to prefer manifestations of positive emotions in both languages may be explained by the intention to achieve integration by claiming identity recognition in English stories and by aspiring to full integration in Italian narration.

By contrast, in the English narratives original identity is an obstacle to integration shown by the migrants' inclination to keep memories from the past. Identity is more mentally constructed through a constant remembrance of objects, prayers, human connections. While emotive language highlights effects of translocation in English, assimilation is the target objective in Italian where the place of birth is not an obstacle anymore to such an extent that most storytellers forget their original nationality to start 'feeling' Italian.

By uncovering real facts through the use of displaced emotions from history, museums' digital platforms may perform an incredibly socially integrative function in that they help to mitigate the fear of home-grown terrorism and the incapacity of societies to amalgamate multiethnic and multi-faith denominations.

We may also conclude from the nature of the emotive language and the way in which it is used to reference pride, hard work and deservedness, that it is fundamental to counterbalance the negative press in the media with accounts that re-humanize and which 'produce positive representations that speak of the rich cultural contributions refugees and asylum seekers bring to cities and communities' (O'Neill 2004: 4).

The corpora pave the way for future research to address the role of digital technologies in communicating and representing migrant narratives, to explore the very 'condition of migrancy'[8] (Alinejad/Ponzanesi 2020: 621) and to look at the ways in which such online platforms are 'reshaping migrant subjectivities' (Alinejad/Ponzanesi 2020). Furthermore, in terms of Appraisal, further research may also highlight patterns of evaluation in terms of opinions, values and beliefs that were found to be quite pervasive in the data but not focused on. Despite the effort to measure emotive language, limitations are inevitable in this research and are mainly due to the subjectivity existing in classifying emotions in one category rather than in another.

5.1. Implications in/for translation

The implications of this research into emotion and language for Translation Studies are manifold. It is fundamental that translation, as a practice of linguistic mediation, be intently concerned with cultural sensitivity. Particularly at a time when English dominates as a lingua franca, agents working as interpreters and mediators need to be sensitive to the fact that emotion, as one of the most volatile components of language exchange, may be lost or misconstrued in its interlingual transfer. As observed (Raga/Sales/Sánchez 2020: 104), 'The cultural formulation of basic emotions can intensify, minimise, modify or mask their expression'. Translation negotiates and liaises between intricate cultural differences that manifest themselves (and indeed reveal themselves) in language; yet in our increasingly globalized world, language barriers[9] can seem resolvable without critical engagement of such difference. The art of translation lies in its *protection* of that nuance of difference. Intercultural comprehension therefore relies on proactive and in-depth analysis of the ways in which language is used, and emotion – particularly in terms of its relevance in multi- and interlingual communication settings[10] – is fast emerging as a core focus.

As most migrant accounts involve nostalgia, departure, transition and adaptation, they are of an emotional nature and, viewed thus, 'migration narratives go hand in hand with translation and interpreting narratives' (Ruiz-Cortés 2020: 218). If we consider that different languages construct emotion differently, and migrant narratives are often written in a second (or subsequent) language, we can assume from the outset that emotive word usage might indicate diverse cultural norms, in terms of expression of emotion. If, as mentioned, we veer away from the notion that there is a single universal measure for human emotions (see Pavlenko 2008), we can therefore surmise that migrant narratives which incorporate emotive words in a language other than their mother tongue do so either as successful translations into the nearest cultural equivalent, or that the words are borrowings from the cultural models of emotions in their first language and/or culture. Dewaele (2014: 359, referring to a study by Schrauf/Durazo-Arvizu 2006) writes that 'How well emotional experiences are remembered is not just a matter of congruence but also whether the recall happens in the language in which the event happened. Immigrants recalling L1 memories from childhood in an L2 typically lose some emotional intensity'. Bilingual, or second and subsequent language acquisition, does not inherently equate to native conceptualization of emotion in a new language and/or cultural environment, though Albrecht draws attention to Mona Lindqvist's assumption that 'emotion work is an intrinsic element of the cognitive process of integration, which is often primarily regarded as a rational process of learning the language, norms and rules of the society of arrival' (2013: 231 cited in Albrecht 2016: 27). Mesquita (2010: 83, cited in Dewaele 2014: 357) claims that 'emotions are first and foremost a type of connection with our social worlds'; the strong cultural attitude towards the verbalization of emotions is a notably Western norm. In order to accurately analyse these possible factors, Pavlenko (2008: 147) writes that:

> models need to address crosslinguistic differences in emotion concepts and ways in which bilinguals' representations may differ from those of monolingual speakers. On the processing level, models need to incorporate the affective

processing dimension, recognizing affective priming effects and differences in emotionality across bilinguals' languages and word types.

Linguistic study, coupled with ethical translation practices, enables scholars and mediators to address not only the ways in which emotions are expressed, but the ways in which such expression of emotion might indicate cultural differences in the perception and subsequent communication of emotion. Analysis of emotive language is one means of understanding the manipulation of language to evoke certain sentiments; whether or not this is intentional might depend on significant cultural differences in perception of emotional words.

Through further collaboration between studies in translation, migration and corresponding public platforms, such as museums, efforts can be made to reduce stigmatization, providing alternative, non-ethnocentric dialogue and interchange, 'thus offering a counterbalance to the often-negative views about marginalized social groups circulated through political discourse and the mainstream media' (De Fina/Tseng 2017: 382).

Notes

1. Emotive language is regarded by Macagno and Walton (2010: 2) as 'a particular dialectical and rhetorical strategy whose distinctive feature is the persuasion through emotions'; Browning (2009: 235) suggests that with regards to immigration policies, 'emotive language runs high on all sides of the issue'.
2. 'Media also differed widely in terms of the predominant themes to their coverage. For instance, humanitarian themes were more common in Italian coverage than in British, German or Spanish press. Threat themes (such as to the welfare system, or cultural threats) were the most prevalent in Italy, Spain and Britain' (Berry/Garcia-Blanca/Moore, 2015 Online *UNHRC Report*). The Italian example illustrates the contradictory stance of the media.
3. CNMC is Spain's National Authority for Markets and Competition, while MNRA is: The Mediterranean Regulatory Authorities Network, which 'was created in 1997 to strengthen the historical and cultural links between Mediterranean countries. The Network counts 26 member authorities representing 22 countries from both shores of the Mediterranean Sea' (*Report on Media coverage of Migrants and Refugees in Audiovisual Media*, 2018).
4. Emotion, although previously subsumed under 'attitude' within the Humanities, may be 'understood as a social construct [that has] a strong relationship with language' (Belli *et al.* 2010: 249).

5   Following other such 'turns' in the social sciences and humanities, the 'emotional turn' bridges many academic disciplines and is gathering momentum in terms of its perceived significance and effect. Prior and van Hoef (2018: 48) address its increasing relevance within political science, which in 'traditionally emphasising the "rational" public sphere rather than the "emotional" private sphere, has increasingly questioned this dichotomisation'; for an in-depth exploration of the 'emotional turn' and its impact on international relations, see Clément/Sangar (2018).
6   Rizzo (2019: 95) writes of such museums as 'spaces of re-narration of marginalised narratives which "speak out" and offer oppositional stories'.
7   https://www.tenement.org/ (accessed September 2020); https://bac.org.uk/ (accessed 30 September 2020); https://www.migrationmuseum.org/ (accessed 30 September 2020); https://museumsvictoria.com.au/immigrationmuseum/ (accessed 30 September 2020); http://www.memoriaemigrazioni.it/ (accessed 30 September 2020); https://www.migradormuseum.it (accessed 30 September 2020); https://www.mimbelluno.it/ (accessed 30 September 2020).
8   Boccagni and Baldassar (2015: 74) also refer to this notion of 'the migrant condition' [as] a reference to the characteristic ambiguities and tensions around emotional connections to 'here' and 'there'.
9   On the notion of 'language barrier' and its evolving connotations in the UK, see Federici (2020).
10 For a discussion of cognitive empathy in a translation setting, see Rudvin/Carfagnini (2020).

References

Albrecht, Y. (2016), 'Emotions in Motion. How Feelings Are Considered in the Scope of Migration Sociological Studies', *Digithum: A Relational Perspective on Culture in Late Modernity*, 18: 25–33.

Alencar, A. and J. Camargo (forthcoming, 2022), 'Stories of Migration: Exploring the Links between Emotions and Technologies in the Narratives of Venezuelan Refugees in Brazil', in T. Panayiota (ed.), *Digital Inclusion: Enhancing Vulnerable People's Social Inclusion and Welfare*, London: Palgrave Macmillan.

Alinejad, D. and S. Ponzanesi (2020), 'Migrancy and Digital Mediations of Emotions', *International Journal of Cultural Studies*. Special Issue: *Migration, Digital Media and Emotion*, 23 (5): 621–38.

Anthony, L. (2020), *AntConc* (Version 3.5.9) [Computer Software], Tokyo, Japan: Waseda University.

Bakamo Public Project for the Friedrich Ebert Stiftung (A) (2018), 'Migration Narratives in Europe through Conversations on Public Social Media'. Available online: http://library.fes.de/pdf-files/bueros/budapest/15374-20190510.pdf (accessed 6 June 2021).

Baynham, M. and A. De Fina (2016), 'Narrative Analysis in Migrant and Transnational Contexts', in M. Martin-Jones and D. Martin (eds), *Researching Multilingualism*, 31–45, London: Routledge.

Bednarek, M. (2008), *Emotion Talk across Corpora*, Houndmills/New York: Palgrave Macmillan.

Bednarek, M. (2009), 'Language Patterns and Attitude', *Functions of Language*, 16 (2): 165–92.

Belli, S., R. Harré and L. Íñiguez-Rueda (2010), 'What Is Love? Discourse about Emotions in Social Sciences', *Human Affairs*, 20 (3): 249–70. DOI: http://dx.doi.org/10.2478/v10023-010-0026-8.

Berry, M., I. Garcia-Blanca and K. Moore (2016), *Press Coverage of the Refugee and Migrant Crisis in the EU: A Content Analysis of Five European Countries*. Report prepared for the United Nations High Commission for Refugees. Cardiff School of Media, Journalism and Cultural Studies.

Boccagni, P. and L. Baldassar (2015), 'Emotions on the Move: Mapping the Emergent Field of Emotion and Migration', *Emotion, Space and Society*, 16: 73–80.

Breckner, R. (2005), *Migrationserfahrung – Fremdheit – Biografie: Zum Umgang mit polarisierten Welten in Ost-West- Europa*, Wiesbaden: VS Verlag.

Browning, M. D. (2009), 'Reexamining Our Words, Reimagining Our Policies: Undocumented Migration, Families, and the Moral Imagination', *Journal of Poverty*, 13 (3): 234–53. DOI: http://dx.doi.org/10.1080/10875540903163844.

Clément, M. and E. Sangar, eds (2018), *Researching Emotions in International Relations. Methodological Perspectives on the Emotional Turn*, New York: Palgrave Macmillan.

CNMC-MNRA Report (2018), 'Media Coverage of Migrants and Refugees in Audiovisual Media'. Available online: https://www.rirm.org/wp-content/uploads/2018/12/Report-CNMC-_Workshop-Migrants-Refugees_2018-November.pdf (accessed 6 June 2021).

De Fina, A. and A. Tseng (2017), 'Narrative in the Study of Migrants', in S. Canagarajah (ed.), *The Routledge Handbook of Migration and Language*, 381–96, London: Routledge.

Dewaele, J. M. (2014), 'Culture and Emotional Language', in F. Sharifian (ed.), *The Routledge Handbook of Language and Culture*, 357–70, Oxford: Routledge.

Eberl, J. M., C. E. Meltzer, T. Heidenreich, B. Herrero, N. Theorin, F. Lind, R. Berganza, H. G. Boomgaarden, C. Schemer and J. Strömbäck (2018), 'The European Media Discourse on Immigration and Its Effects: A Literature Review', *Annals of the International Communication Association*, 42 (3): 207–23. DOI: http://dx.doi.org/10.1080/23808985.2018.1497452.

Federici, F. (2020), '"Language Barrier" in UK Newspapers 2010–2020: Figurative Meaning, Migration, and Language Needs', *Cultus: Mediating Narratives of Migration*, 13: 191–216.

Forest, D., D. Jakacki, C. Raynor, M. E. Sinatra and S. Sinclair (2019), 'Introduction', *Digital Scholarship in the Humanities*, 34 (Supplement_1): i1–i2, https://doi.org/10.1093/llc/fqz077.

Fuoli, M. and C. Hommerberg (2015), 'Optimising Transparency, Reliability and Replicability: Annotation Principles and Inter-coder Agreement in the Quanti-Cation of Evaluative Expressions', *Corpora*, 10 (3): 315–49.

González, A. M. (2017), 'In Search of a Sociological Explanation for the Emotional Turn', *Sociologia, Problemas e Práticas*, 85: 27–45.

Halliday, M. A. K., W. Teubert, C. Yallop and A. Cermáková (2004), *Lexicology and Corpus Linguistics: An Introduction*, London: Continuum.

Harkins, J. and A. Wierzbicka, eds (2001), *Emotions in Crosslinguistic Perspective Series: Cognitive Linguistics Research* [CLR], 17, Paris: Mouton De Gruyter.

Hayat Taha, S. (2019), 'Refugees, Migrants and Citizens in U.K. Socio-political Discourse: A Postcolonial and Discourse Analytical Critique', *Journal of Global Faultlines*, 6 (1): 17–38.

Hunston, S. (2004), 'Counting the Uncountable: Problems of Identifying Evaluation in a Text and in a Corpus', in A. Partington, J. Morley, and L. Haarman (eds), *Corpora and Discourse*, 157–88, Bern: Peter Lang.

Katan, D. (2004), *Translating Cultures*, London: St Jerome.

Kövecses, Z. (2000), *Metaphor and Emotion: Language, Culture, and Body in Human Feeling*, Cambridge: Cambridge University Press.

Lemmings, D. and A. Brooks (2014), *Emotions and Social Change. Historical and Sociological Perspectives*, New York: Routledge.

Lindqvist, K. (2013), 'Emotions Emerge from More Basic Psychological Ingredients: A Modern Psychological Constructionist Model', *Emotion Review*, 5 (4): 356–68.

Lindqvist, M. (2013), '"Like a White Crow": Migrant Women and Their Emotion Work in Sweden', *International Journal Work Organisation and Emotion*, 5 (3): 229–42. Available online: http://dx.doi.org/10.1504/IJWOE.2013.055903 (accessed 6 June 2021).

Macagno, F. (2010), 'The Argumentative Uses of Emotive Language', *Sistemi Intelligenti*, 24 (3): 1–33. DOI: http://dx.doi.org/10.1422/38984.

Macagno, F. and D. Walton (2010), 'The Argumentative Uses of Emotive Language', *Revista Iberoamericana de Argumentacion*, 1: 1–33.

Macagno, F. and D. Walton (2014), *Emotive Language Argumentation*, Cambridge: Cambridge University Press.

Martin, J. R. and P. R. White (2005), *The Language of Evaluation: Appraisal in English*, London: Palgrave Macmillan.

Mesquita, B. (2010), 'Emoting. A Contextualized Process', in B. Mesquita, L. F. Barrett and E. R. Smith (eds), *The Mind in Context*, 83–104, New York: Guilford.

Miller, D. (2006), 'From Concordance to Text: Appraising "Giving" in Alma Mater Donation Request', in G. Thompson and S. Hunston (eds), *System and Corpus. Exploring Connections*, 248–68, London: Equinox.

Miller, D. (2007), 'Towards a Typology of Evaluation in Parliamentary Debate: From Theory to Practice – and back again', *(R)evolution in Evaluation, Textus*, 20 (1): 159–80.

O'Neill, M. (2004), 'Global Refugees: Forced Migration, Diaspora and Belonging', in D. Robinson, C. Horrocks, N. Kelly, and B. Roberts (eds), *Narrative, Memory & Identity: Theoretical and Methodological Issues*, 1–21, Huddersfield: University of Huddersfield.

Pavlenko, A. (2008), 'Emotion and Emotion-Laden Words in the Bilingual Lexicon', *Bilingualism: Language and Cognition*, 11 (2): 147–64.

Pries, L. (2001), *Internationale Migration*, Bielfeld: Bielefeld Verlag.

Prior, A. and Y. van Hoef (2018), 'Interdisciplinary Approaches to Emotions in Politics and International Relations', *Politics and Governance*, 6 (4): 48–52.

Raga, F., D. Sale and M. Sánchez (2020), 'Interlinguistic and Intercultural Mediation in Psychological Care Interviews with Asylum Seekers and Refugees: Handling Emotions in the Narration of Traumatic Experience', *Cultus. The Journal of Intercultural Mediation and Communication: Mediating Narratives of Migration*, 13: 94–121.

Rizzo, A. (2019), 'Museums as Disseminators of Niche Knowledge: Universality in Accessibility for All', *Journal of Audiovisual Translation*, 2 (2): 92–136.

Rizzo, A., C. Spinzi and G. Greco (forthcoming, 2022), 'Accessible Stories Within Mediascapes: Voicing Otherness in Digital Museums', *Journal of Audiovisual Translation*, 4(1).

Rudvin, M. and A. Carfagnini (2020), 'Interpreting Distress Narratives in Italian Reception Centres: The Need for Caution when Negotiating Empathy', *Cultus. The Journal of Intercultural Mediation and Communication: Mediating Narratives of Migration*, 3: 123–44.

Ruiz-Cortés, E. (2020), 'To Translate or Not to Translate: Narratives and Translation in the UK Home Office', *Cultus. The Journal of Intercultural Mediation and Communication: Mediating Narratives of Migration*, 13: 218–35.

Sandrini, P. and M. Garcia Gonzalez, eds (2015), 'Digital Scholarship in Translation Studies: A Plea for Openness', in P. Sandrini and M. Garcia Gonzalez (eds), *Translation and Openness*, 177–94, Innsbruck: Innsbruck University Press.

Schrauf, R. and R. Durazo-Arvizu (2006), 'Bilingual Autobiographical Memory and Emotion: Theory and Methods', in A. Pavlenko (ed.), *Bilingual Minds: Emotional Experience, Expression, and Representation*, 284–311, Clevedon: Multilingual Matters.

Sevinc, Y. (2020), 'Embodying Emotion in Migration and in Language Contact Settings', in G. L. Schiewer, J. Altarriba and B. Chin Ng (eds), *Handbook on Language and Emotion*, 2048–60, Berlin: Mouton De Gruyter.

Smith Rumsey, A. (2013), 'New-Model Scholarly Communication: Road Map for Change', *Scholarly Communication Institute Reports 9, 2004–2011*, 157–88, Charlottesville, VA: University of Virginia Library. Available online: https://libraopen.lib.virginia.edu/downloads/x633f104mpdf (accessed 6 June 2021).

Stickley, T., A. Hui, M. Stubley, F. Baker Michelle and M. Watson (2018), '"Write Here, Sanctuary" Creative Writing for Refugees and People Seeking Asylum', *Arts and Health: An International Journal for Research, Policy and Practice*, 11 (3): 246–63.

Stubbs, M. (1996), 'Collocations and Semantic Profiles: On the Cause of the Trouble with Quantitative Studies', *Functions of Language*, 2 (1): 23–55.

Tsitsanoudis-Mallidis, N. and E. Derveni (2018), 'Emotive Language: Linguistic Depictions of the Three Year-old Drowned Refugee Boy in the Greek Journalistic Discourse', *Interface. Journal of European Languages and Literatures*, 6: 1–38.

UNHCR 2020. Available online: https://www.unhcr.org/figures-at-a-glance.html (accessed 6 June 2021).

Wierzbicka, A. (1999), *Emotions across Languages and Cultures: Diversity and Universals*, Cambridge: Cambridge University Press. DOI: http://dx.doi.org/10.1017/CBO9780511521256.

8

Learning analytics at the service of interpreter training in academic curricula

Francesca Bianchi, Davide Taibi,
Philipp Kemkes and Ivana Marenzi

1. Introduction

The Web is a fundamental resource for interpreters, as it offers free access to an immense array of content-based databases (i.e. Wikipedia, encyclopaedias, institutional websites, scientific publications, thematic blogs), and language-based databases (monolingual and bilingual dictionaries, glossaries, Linguee or Reverso); but profitably using such material for professional preparation requires some experience and practice. Teachers of interpreting are in a position to offer advice on how to prepare for an interpreting event and to assess the results of their student's preparation, but have few means to monitor the learning process, especially when it involves the use of online resources.

The current chapter illustrates an online learning and competence development environment, called LearnWeb (Marenzi 2014a), which has recently integrated a set of affordances aimed at supporting students of dialogue interpreting in autonomous terminology management-and-acquisition work, and at assisting teachers in overseeing the students' work from a distance. In particular, LearnWeb has been expanded with a tool for the creation of glossaries, a tracking system for logging students' searches on the Web, and a learning analytics system to support teachers in monitoring their students' progresses in the creation of personal glossaries and in their use of Web resources. The system will soon also support self-monitoring by the students. By integrating Web resources with data tracking and data analysis systems, LearnWeb favours investigations into the way students use the Internet as source for relevant material in the creation of glossaries, and can provide insight into the learning, cognitive and/or material processes that students of interpreting apply during the preparation phase and in glossary compilation, and into their preferences.

These affordances were developed having in mind specific learning scenarios: the interpreting modules offered at the University of Salento (Lecce, Italy). This university has a three-year undergraduate degree in cultural mediation with one module in sight translation and dialogue interpreting (focusing on tourism), and a two-year MA degree in translation and interpreting with two modules of interpreting: sight translation and dialogue interpreting in the first year, and consecutive in the second year, both focusing on medical topics. It is not infrequent in the academic panorama that translation and interpreting are taught to the same students within the same curriculum (Gile 2009) and that dialogue interpreting is introduced in the final year of modern language curricula to boost communicative competence (Sandrelli 2001). For this reason, we believe that this system could be of interest to the wider community of teachers of interpreting.

This chapter presents the newly developed tools to support teachers and students of interpreting, with particular emphasis on the theoretical and pedagogical aspects that informed the development of these affordances. Furthermore, it offers some ideas of how the system could be used for teaching and research purposes in the field of interpreting.

To these aims, the rest of the chapter is organized as follows. Section 2 discusses the needs of trainee interpreters and academic institutions offering interpreting modules, with exclusive reference to content and vocabulary acquisition, as these are the only needs targeted in the LearnWeb system. Section 3 discusses existing systems for terminology management. Section 4 illustrates the LearnWeb environment and its newly created affordances. Section 5 offers an example of how these tools could be integrated into class activities. Section 6 suggests possible uses of the system and its affordances for both teaching and research in the field of interpreting.

2. Needs analysis

2.1. Professional needs and habits

Interpreting is a highly complex task involving several cognitive, linguistic and practical skills (see Gile 2009, Pöchhacker 2003). Some professional skills and habits vary according to the type of interpreting technique adopted (e.g. simultaneous vs consecutive interpreting) or the professional context in which the given technique is applied (e.g. conference vs non-conference settings), but others cut across techniques and contexts and apply in greater or smaller extent to all of them. The current chapter targets dialogue interpreting (a form of consecutive interpreting; for compact descriptions see: Andres 2015, Dam 2010, Merlini 2015, Viezzi 2013), as well as sight translation (for a compact description of this form of interpreting, see Cenková 2010, 2015). It also focuses on the preparation phase to interpreting tasks, a common aspect in the life of all interpreters which is related to the need to acquire and/or develop domain knowledge and terminology.

All interpreters need to acquire and/or develop domain knowledge and terminology connected to the assignment they have accepted (Moser 1978, Seleskovitch 1978, Gile 2002, Fantinuoli 2017). Domain knowledge facilitates the processing and understanding of informative texts, inferencing and memorization (for a review of empirical studies see Díaz-Galaz 2015: 42–6), all of these being core skills in consecutive interpreting (Jones 1998, Kalina 1998, Pöchhacker 2003), and is fundamental to correctly situate terminology (Will 2007). At the same time, terminology should be an active, readily available resource, especially for dialogue interpreting and sight translation. In fact, while glossary consultation is a viable solution in case of terminological doubts during simultaneous interpreting (Fantinuoli 2016), this is not possible in dialogue interpreting, where the interpreter is clearly visible to all participants in the communicative event, needs to maintain eye contact with the participants in order to understand and manage translation turns, and may be engaged in some form of note-taking. In dialogue interpreting, requests for clarifications by the interpreter are possible, but they slow down the interaction and disrupt the expected flow of the discourse, and should thus be limited or possibly avoided. Glossary consultation is equally not viable in sight translation, as the interpreter is expected to translate the contents of the source text into the target language *impromptu*, delivering at natural speed and without unnecessary hesitations or reformulations (Cenková 2010, 2015). Domain and terminological knowledge are primarily acquired prior to the event itself, that is, during the preparation phase.

Preparation is a fundamental practice characterizing professional interpreting (AIIC 2004, Gile 2002, 2009, Díaz-Galaz 2015). The preparation phase, which generally culminates in the creation of a glossary (Díaz-Galaz *et al.* 2015, Fantinuoli 2016), includes searching for, reading and critically using textual resources, and in particular – when preparing for non-conference settings – comparable texts (Gile 2009, Fantinuoli 2017). The linguistic aspects to focus on include semi-technical terms (i.e. general terms that recur frequently in the given domain), high-frequency and low-frequency technical terms, but also phraseological patterns (Fantinuoli 2017). In the preparation phase, the tasks of reading to acquire content knowledge, identifying useful and technical vocabulary and preparing the glossary are interrelated; thus, interpreters discover vocabulary and phraseology while reading to acquire domain knowledge, and learn something about the topic itself while creating a glossary (Gile 2002, Fantinuoli 2017).

A typical interpreter's glossary would generally include a list of terms and their translations in one or more languages, both terms and translations being chosen for a wide range of possible reasons (Setton 2003). This is to say that the glossary records only part of the knowledge system that interpreters constitute in the preparatory phase, since 'the terminological part is included [in the glossary] while the domain knowledge – definitions, conceptual systems, example of usage, etc. – is generally omitted' (Fantinuoli 2016: 43). Such decontextualized lists – however used by professional interpreters – have been recognized to have some limits, including the fact that they 'do not allow a clear term disambiguation' (Fantinuoli 2018: 159). One possible way to re-contextualize the terms in a glossary is structuring the glossary into themes and sub-themes (e.g. Gile 2009). Furthermore, some interpreters and researchers of interpreting have suggested that glossaries should include other types of information. In particular, banking on the needs of conference interpreting, Rodríguez and Schnell (2009) recommend recording the following types of information in the glossary: theme and sub-theme, the term in the source language and its target language equivalent, a definition, an illustration, hypernyms, synonyms, abbreviated forms, proper names, names of products and items that come up frequently in the discourse, information on register, preferences of the client and the organization, pronunciation, phraseology and verb-noun collocations.

It is undeniable that these types of information would be highly useful also in dialogic contexts and consecutive interpreting scenarios. Some of them are functional to memorization and glossary organization: theme and sub-theme help to organize the glossary and anchor terms in the given domain, while source and target terms are of course the core elements in any glossary. Other pieces of information are functional to source text comprehension and/or the delivery phase. Recording a definition or a picture of the term would guarantee that the interpreter knows exactly what the term refers to when s/he hears or uses it. At the same time, if in want of a technical term, during the delivery phase the interpreter may resort to defining or describing the concept or to substituting the term with a hypernym – and having a definition or a hypernym at hand is certainly useful. Knowing the correct pronunciation of terms is fundamental in both the reception and production phases, while being familiar with the specific phraseology (including verb-noun collocations) used when talking about the given concept will help the interpreter in the production phase in many ways: it supports anticipation processes in the comprehension phase (Stoll 2009), it facilitates paraphrasing in the target text (Rodríguez/Schnell 2009) and it makes the target text more idiomatic, thus increasing its acceptance by a specialized audience and giving the interpreter a more professional profile (Fantinuoli 2017). Synonyms and information on register (tenor, in Systemic Functional Linguistics terms) will prove useful in the production phase, especially in cases of unbalanced knowledge relations between the participants. Abbreviated forms, acronyms and product names play a fundamental role in some specialized types of language, such as medical jargon (Loiacono 2013). Proper names are tricky to decode if their connection to the given topic is not known. Finally, preferences of the client and the organization are strictly connected to specific professional assignments.

2.2. Pedagogical needs

In academic curricula like the ones outlined in the Introduction, interpreting modules are generally taught by (former) interpreters and aim at providing students with basic professional skills, as well as a view of professional practice. However, in our experience, the students attending these types of curricula are not comparable to attendees of professionalizing courses in interpreting. Due to their young age and lack of any type of professional experience, they often have below-C1 command of their foreign languages, still-imperfect command of their native language, limited world knowledge and very limited domain knowledge of specialized fields. Thus, their need for domain and terminological knowledge is much greater than that of a professional interpreter. Furthermore, these students are generally not aware of the importance that domain knowledge plays in interpreting, and of the linguistic and terminological aspects they should pay attention to in order to achieve good results in an interpreting task. Finally, they still need to develop good practices to apply in the preparation phase.

In this respect, glossary making is certainly a suitable and interesting activity to engage the students in, as part of class and/or exam work. However, suggesting or asking students to compile glossaries containing only terms and their translations – that is, restricting the product of the preparation phase to context-free lists of words, albeit organized into multi-layered structures – is likely to lead them to believe that words are the ultimate concern of an interpreter. Conversely, a glossary tool aimed at guiding interpreting students during the preparation phase should draw the students' attention to many, if not all, of the elements listed by Rodríguez and Schnell (2009; see Section 2.1, above).

Curiously, although teachers of interpreting have long recognized the importance of domain knowledge (Sawyer 2004) and technical vocabulary (Sawyer 2004, Corsellis 2008), vocabulary development (and acquisition of domain knowledge) is a task which is often underestimated by interpreting students (e.g. Crezee 2013, Bancroft/Allen 2015), who then enter the profession unprepared. Indeed, according to a 2010 survey among professional interpreters, young interpreters lack good terminology knowledge and would benefit from specific training in the use of resources, possibly through the use of technology (Setton 2010).

Working on content and vocabulary knowledge is time-consuming, and doing this in class subtracts class time to the teaching and training of other cognitive and procedural skills, many of which require much time and effort to master and cannot be acquired without the teacher's help. This is particularly true in learning scenarios like the ones described in the Introduction, where students take one or two modules on interpreting in their whole academic career and each module includes a few dozen hours of contact time.

Hence our idea of finding a way to allow teachers to delegate content and terminology work to the students themselves, as autonomous work done outside class hours, to spur the students to expand their vocabulary and to help teachers to oversee whether and how the students are attending to this task. We felt we needed a glossary tool linked to monitoring and self-monitoring tools (for teachers and students respectively) and possibly supported by learning analytics technologies.

3. Software tools supporting terminology management

Although many professional interpreters still use general tools such as MS Word or MS Excel for creating their glossaries (Jiang 2015), more than one software program specifically developed for terminology management in interpreting is available on the market. Some of these computer-aided interpreting (CAI) tools – the so-called 'first generation tools', which include Interplex,[1] Terminus[2] and Interpreters' Help,[3] – provide graphic interfaces for managing multilingual glossaries similar to MS Word or Excel lists, support the categorization of entries into two- or multi-level ontologies and may provide features to store additional information; finally they offer functionalities to look up glossaries in the booth (Fantinuoli 2018: 164–5). Other tools – such as InterpretBank,[4] classified as 'second generation' tools – 'present a holistic approach to terminology and knowledge management for interpreting tasks and offer advanced functionalities [...], such as features to organize textual material, retrieve information from corpora or other sources (both online and offline), learn conceptualised domains, etc'. (Fantinuoli 2018: 165).[5]

All these tools seem to have been created to target the needs of simultaneous interpreting in conference settings; the literature that discusses them certainly has this particular focus. Furthermore, excluding Interpreters' Help, which is browser-based and works regardless of the operating system, they are all platform-dependent (e.g. Terminus is for Windows only). Even more importantly for the current learning scenarios, none of them has been thought for class use and/or training purposes, and none of them would easily allow teachers to monitor the students' activities *in absentia*.

To find a glossary tool that is integrated with a tracking system allowing teachers to monitor students' activities we need to look at learning management systems (LMSs). The most widely spread LMS at academic level is Moodle. Moodle's glossary tool has been used in academic curricula of translation for the creation of bilingual glossaries by students (e.g. Seghiri 2013), and has been tested with good results in the context of specialized language teaching and learning (e.g. Bocanegra Valle/Perera Barberá 2011, Pospíšilová *et al.* 2011, Breeze 2014). Although Moodle's glossary offers some interesting features for students of interpreting, such as the possibility to link a picture or a document file to a glossary entry, to categorize entries, and to search the glossary using a simple search box, its structure is based on two fields only: 'concept' (where the term is to be entered) and 'definition'. The definition field is a text box in which any type of information can be entered, including a translation in one or more target languages. The result is thus a list of terms ordered alphabetically, each one accompanied by long textual information, and the display format is rather different from that of professional CAI tools. Furthermore, this glossary tool was thought for collaborative learning and cannot be easily used for the creation of personal glossaries by the students in a large class. Finally, although Moodle allows teachers to monitor what the students do, it does not integrate a learning analytics technology.

None of the systems available on the marked seemed to meet the needs of the interpreting teachers at the University of Salento, so we decided to expand an existing learning environment with specifically created tools.

4. The LearnWeb platform and its affordances for students and teachers of interpreting

LearnWeb is an online learning and competence development environment. It is characterized by an iterative, evaluation-driven, design-based research approach (Marenzi 2014a), that is, an approach in which the system is cyclically assessed in real-world settings by practitioners and improved by researchers on the basis of the practitioners' needs and suggestions (Wang/Hannafin 2005: 6). Through the years, LearnWeb has been continuously expanded in order to provide teachers with a range of customized environments (Marenzi/Zerr 2012, Marenzi 2014b, Bianchi/Marenzi 2016).

When we decided to use it with students of interpreting, LearnWeb already included the following key features: an integrated Web search engine, personal learning spaces for individual users, website archiving and, most importantly, automatic logging of the students' actions. To meet the needs described in the previous sections, the following features were added: a tool for the creation of glossaries, a tracking system for logging students' searches on the Web and a learning analytics system aimed at monitoring the students' interactions with the glossary and the Web during the creation of personal glossaries.[6]

4.1. The Glossary tool

The Glossary tool could be classified as 'first generation'. It was designed considering all the types of information on which interpreters should focus during the preparation phase (Section 2), and balancing this with the functional need of having a manageable, easily readable interface. In particular, what fields to include in the interface was decided on pedagogical considerations and needs. Flexibility and professional habits were also considered. The result is an interface that includes only a minimum amount of compulsory fields, accompanied by several optional fields, and text boxes whose contents can be freely decided by the user (Figures 8.1a and 8.1b). These elements are described in detail in the following paragraphs.

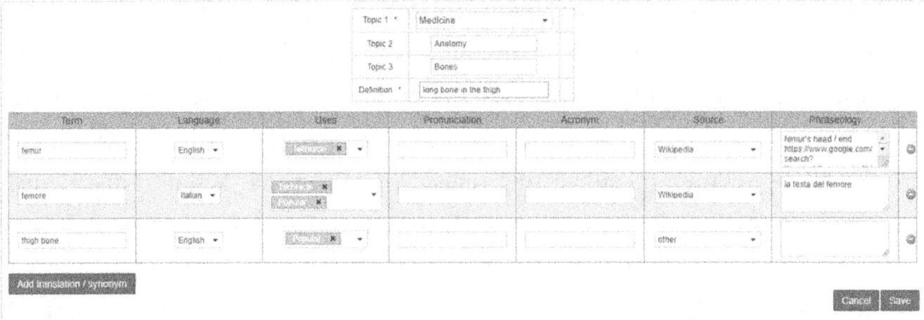

Figure 8.1a Glossary interface with sample entries: 'creation mode'

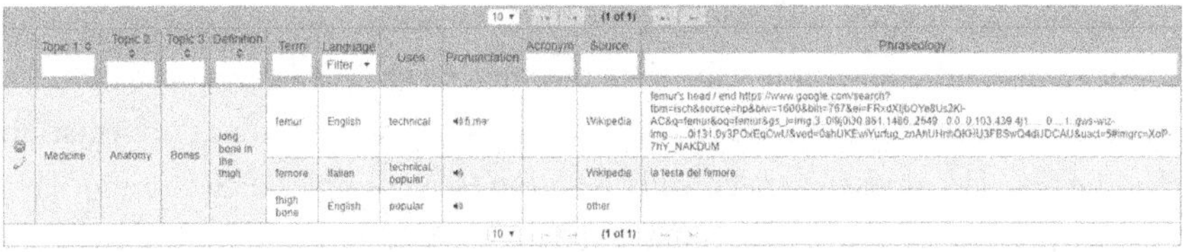

Figure 8.1b Glossary interface with sample entries: 'consultation mode'

Our glossary offers a three-tier categorization system (Fields *Topic 1*, *Topic 2*, *Topic 3*, to be intended as domain, subdomain and sub-sub-domain). Users are free to decide how many layers they want to use, since only the first level is compulsory. For their module, some teachers wanted domain (*Topic 1*) and subdomain options (*Topic 2*) to be provided in the form of a drop-down menu, in order to guide the students in creating meaningful classifications. However, even when a drop-down list is present, the user can add a new value by writing in the box itself.

The interface also includes a compulsory *Definition* field, which serves more than one purpose. In the context of interpreting, definitions have all the advantages described in Section 2. From a pedagogical perspective, obliging the students to create (or even select and paste a definition from an existing document) is fundamental to draw their attention to content knowledge, and to anchor the term in its context. Finally, from a technical perspective, this field allows storing a term, its synonyms and translations in a single entry (or 'concept', in LearnWeb's terminology). Though unusual in CAI tools and more typical of terminological databases such as SDL Multiterm, storing several terms and translations in a single entry could prove useful for interpreters, too (Costa *et al.* 2014a), and we considered it particularly important for students.

The only other compulsory fields are the *Term* boxes, in the source and target languages. Each term is accompanied by a set of descriptive fields. None of these fields is compulsory, to cater for different levels of lexical knowledge and needs. These fields, however, are intended to draw the student's attention to *Uses* (a drop-down menu suggesting register/tenor, fundamental to distinguish between synonyms), *Pronunciation* (a text box that accepts characters of any type, including IPA symbols, and in 'consultation mode' displays a loudspeaker icon through which the student can listen to native speaker's pronunciation), and *Acronym*(s) (a text-box that could be used also to store short forms). The *Phraseology* box is a text box that accepts any type and number of characters. It was named in this way to lead students to focus on and record useful collocations and colligations (for the relevance of phraseology see Section 2), but, if necessary, it can be used to add to the glossary other kinds of information that the interface does not specifically mention (see examples in Section 5). This is something that the teacher should explain when presenting the glossary tool to the students.

Finally, the *Source* field was added for two reasons. On the one hand, it was considered important to make the students think about the reference material they use in compiling the glossary. On the other hand, it is needed by the teacher to understand what kind of sources of information the students resort to. This field is automatically analysed by the learning analytics system and the teacher is given a summary view of the sources specified by each student (Section 4.3.1). To achieve automatic analysis of this field it was necessary to provide a drop-down menu with a list of possible sources; the list includes content-based items (Wikipedia, encyclopaedia, institutional website, scientific publication, non-institutional website or blog), but also language-based items (monolingual dictionary, bilingual dictionary, glossary, Linguee or Reverso). Language-based resources are not intended as suggestions – and the students should be made well aware of this by the teacher when she introduces the Glossary tool – but were included because experiments on strategies of L2 vocabulary acquisition and language learning have shown that students tend to consider dictionaries as their primary resource (Gu/Johnson 1996), a trend that had been observed in interpreting classes at the University of Salento, too.

The green button *Add translation/Synonym* allows users to add one or more Terms (and the corresponding list of optional fields) to the given entry, in any of the glossary languages. This was done, for example, in Figures 8.1a and 8.1b. Our glossary can be bilingual or multilingual; the teacher specifies the languages needed for the specific module when s/he defines the type of LearnWeb environment needed; the student defines the glossary languages when s/he creates the object 'glossary'.

Finally, like all CAI software, various search features are available, allowing users to filter the glossary by field, as well as to search the entire glossary (i.e. all fields) for a particular word or part of. Although in CAI literature search features are generally, if not exclusively, discussed with reference to the booth, they are important regardless of it. In fact, as the glossary expands, the user should be able to check what terms the glossary contains, to avoid repetitions and quickly add synonyms if necessary. Search features will also be useful when revising technical vocabulary prior to the interpreting task (e.g. the exam).

The Glossary tool is connected to data tracking, data analysis and data display features to create a seamless environment that, in our view, can support students, teachers and also researchers of interpreting in some of their activities. A more detailed description of these affordances is offered in the next section.

4.2. Tracking and logging students' searches on the Web

As we have seen, terminology work is not limited to filling in glossary entries, but also involves searching the Web for comparable texts or other resources. We thought that tracking the web pages that the students consult while compiling their glossaries would provide teachers and researchers with important information about how the students face the preparation phase.

From a technical point of view, however, tracking Web searches outside the given environment is not an easy task, and the attempts described in the literature so far required a controlled environment, such as a classroom, where the course manager can fully control Internet access or has the privilege to install logging or screen recording software, the latter option requiring manual analysis of the recordings.[7] Differently from previous experiments, the LearnWeb system takes advantage of a specifically developed novel tracking framework – which we call Web Analytics Proxy Service (WAPS) – that allows researchers to unobtrusively track all the pages a student views during a learning session, including external websites such as Wikipedia.org or Google.com, without requiring changes on the student's computer and regardless of the student's location (from home or in a classroom).[8]

Our system tracks fine-grained information, such as the user's mouse movements and keyboard inputs (scrolling, clicking and typing) on a web page, as well as the time and position of these events on the page; it also detects when the user actively interacted with a web page, and saves the sequence of actions performed by the student. Tracking is activated when the student accesses a specific URL and continues as long as the student works within that window.

The web pages visited by each student are presented to the teacher through a learning analytics dashboard, in the form of a chronologically ordered list of websites (see Figure 8.7, in Section 4.3.1). This way the teacher can see what types of resources each student browsed. Similar data will be displayed also in the student dashboard. For a student, a list of web addresses can act as electronic notes of the searches s/he did, a sort of personal memo.

Finally, for each log entry the system can show statistics, including how much time the user spent on the specific site and how long he was active (moved the mouse, scrolled, clicked or typed). Our system also offers the possibility to 'playback' the user's actions. This set of data is accessible at the WAPS domain, and we believe it may constitute a relevant source of information for researchers.

4.3. The learning analytics system

Learning Analytics is defined as 'the measurement, collection, analysis and reporting of data about learners and their contexts, for purposes of understanding and optimizing learning and the environments in which it occurs.'[9] In Learning Analytics, data are collected and elaborated not to support automated assessment processes, but to increase teachers' awareness of the students' learning process (Baker/Siemens 2014). Thus, teachers acquire insights that enable them to provide prompt, personalized interventions with their students, mainly while the learning activities are taking place. For this reason, Learning Analytics approaches have also been successfully adopted to support formative assessment (Taibi *et al.* 2014).

In the field of Learning Analytics, log data are used to register students' interactions with educational online tools, while dashboard tools are increasingly used to visualize students' activities.

Learning dashboards provide graphic interfaces based on the data collected (or a selection of these), which enables and supports the analysis of students' learning processes (Dietz-Uhler/Hurn 2013). They have been used to support teachers in monitoring students' involvement in a given task, in providing prompt intervention in case of low engagement and in detecting patterns of students' interaction with the system (Romero-Zaldívar *et al.* 2012, Blikstein 2014 *et al.*, Agudo-Peregrina *et al.* 2014). Dashboards are also useful to support students in self-monitoring their learning progress, by displaying individual learning patterns compared to the class average (Dyckhoff *et al.* 2012, Verbert *et al.* 2013). However, to achieve these aims, it is fundamental that learning analytics be informed by 'research knowledge about learning and teaching' (Gašević *et al.* 2015: 65).

Our system logs all the student's interactions with the LearnWeb system, and in particular their interactions with the Glossary tool. Some of the data thus collected are analysed and displayed in dashboards. Our system offers a teacher dashboard, described in the next section, and will soon include also a student dashboard. Through the latter, each student will be able to see his/her progress in the glossary task, compared to the class average.

4.3.1 *The teacher dashboard*

The teacher dashboard implemented in the LearnWeb environment was specifically designed to support teachers in monitoring students' involvement in a given task, in providing prompt intervention in case of low engagement, and in detecting patterns of students' interaction with the system. It was developed in close collaboration with an interpreting teacher at the University of Salento and bearing in mind the needs described in Section 2. Data are aggregated into graphs and tables in order to provide insight on the following:

(1) General activity on the glossary task (Figures 8.2 and 8.3). This part of the dashboard shows general information on students' activity (e.g. periods of activity/inactivity), the number of concepts and terms entered into the glossary and the number and types of sources the students declared to use most frequently. These data are provided both for individual students and for the whole class.

(2) Glossary organization (Figures 8.4 and 8.5). This part of the dashboard provides information about whether, and to what extent each student filled in the compulsory and optional fields; this includes a list of the definitions entered and their length.

(3) Sources and reference materials (Figures 8.6 and 8.7). This part of the dashboard shows the preferred sources of reference as declared by the student (glossary field *Source*), as well as a list of all the Web addresses that were visited by the students and tracked by the WAPS tool.

The student dashboard will include the same types of data as the teacher dashboard. Through the dashboard, each student will be able to see his/her own positioning with respect to the whole class. We believe that this may spur students to devote more time and energy in the preparation phase, by way of competition with his/her colleagues.

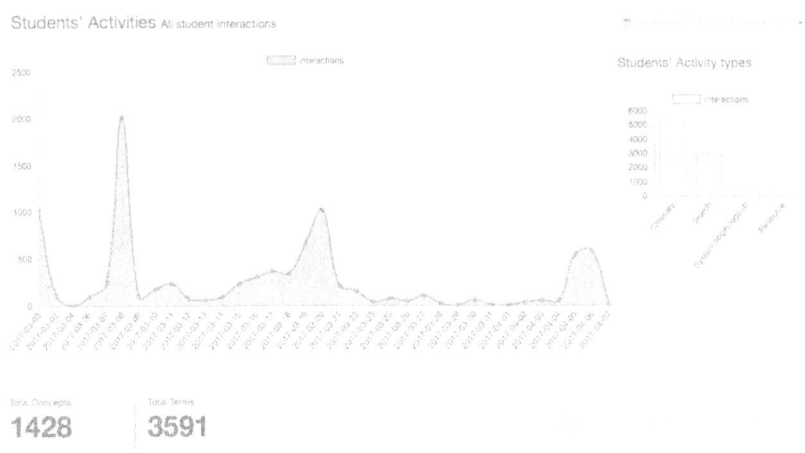

Figure 8.2 General information on students' activity (class view)

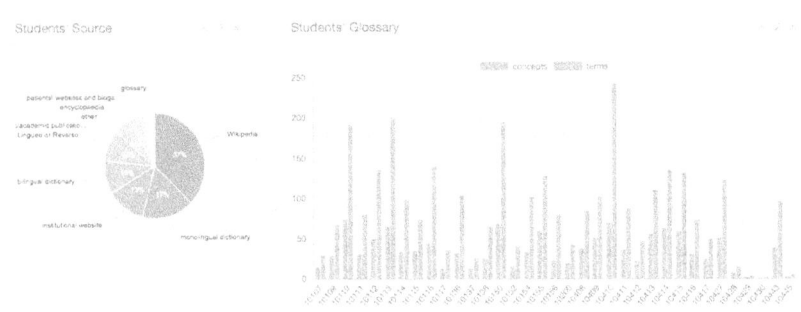

Figure 8.3 Number of concepts and terms entered into the glossary, and number and types of sources the students declared to use most frequently (class view)

Fields

	terms	pronunciation	acronym	phraseology	uses	source	AVG %
10110	211	27.49%	9.95%	30.81%	86.73%	59.24%	42.84%
10112	162	46.91%	4.32%	70.99%	96.91%	91.98%	62.22%
10113	228	35.09%	18.86%	69.30%	96.49%	97.37%	63.42%
10150	214	17.76%	12.15%	36.92%	86.45%	56.07%	41.87%
10410	243	4.12%	3.70%	1.23%	22.22%	41.15%	14.49%
10430	34	100.00%	0.00%	100.00%	100.00%	100.00%	80.00%

Figure 8.4 Whether and to what extent each student completed the compulsory and optional fields (class view)

Learning Analytics

Username ⇕	Definition ⇕	Word count ⇕
Student 1	any substance that plants or animals need in order to live and grow	13
Student 1	a substance in food that plants, animals, and people need to live and grow	14
Student 2	a serious illness caused by a group of cells in the body increasing in an uncontrolled way. Cancer is often treated by chemotherapy (=special drugs) or by radiotherapy	28
Student 3	It's a long-term medical condition in which the blood pressure in the arteries is persistently elevated.	16
Student 4	The back posterior end of the foot	7
Student 4	The small animal with a spiral-shaped shell. Especially well-known in the French traditional food, it can be eaten.	18
Student 5	A nutrient is a substance used by an organism to survive, grow and reproduce.	14
Student 5	a unit for measuring how much energy you get from food.	11

Figure 8.5 A list of the definitions entered and their lengths (class view). In the picture, the student's names have been replaced with placeholders for privacy reasons

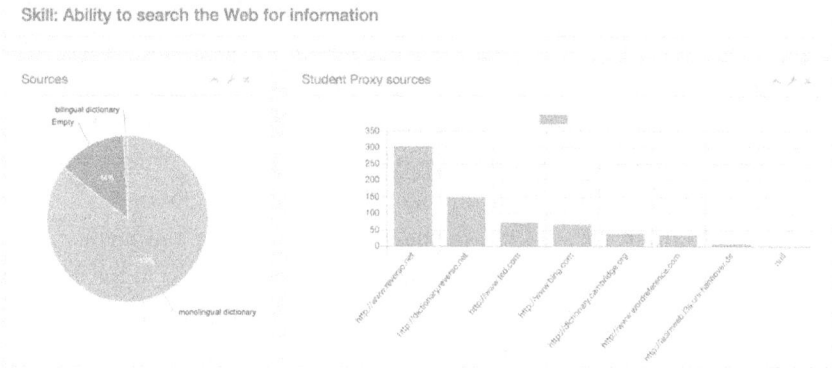

Figure 8.6 Preferred sources and reference pages (referring to a single student)

Url	Title	Total events	Created at
http://it.wikipedia.org/secure.waps.io/wiki/Intestino_tenue	Intestino tenue - Wikipedia	203	2017-03-16 19:09:36.0
http://learnweb.l3s.uni-hannover.de/lw/showGlossary.jsf?resource_id=...	Glossario - Learnweb	3012	2017-03-16 19:08:17.0
http://www.linguee.com.waps.io/english-italian/search?query=small%2...	small intestine - Italian translation – Linguee	186	2017-03-16 19:06:26.0
http://www.linguee.com.waps.io/english-spanish/translation/small%20in...	small intestine - Spanish translation ? Linguee	38	2017-03-16 19:06:18.0
http://learnweb.l3s.uni-hannover.de/lw/search.jsf?query=small+intestin...	Cerca - Learnweb	84	2017-03-16 19:06:13.0

Figure 8.7 List of Web addresses visited, tracked by the WAPS tool (referring to a single student)

5. Integrating the LearnWeb tools into class activities: an example

The LearnWeb Glossary affordances described in this paper are not intended as e-learning tools, but rather as tools to integrate and support traditional class work. They can be incorporated into modules of interpreting in many ways. This section describes how they are used at the University of Salento, as way of example. For a clearer picture, an overview of the entire module(s) is provided.

Since February 2017, the LearnWeb tools have been used at the University of Salento in five modules: two fifty-four-hour Bachelor modules on interpreting in tourism settings, each comprising over 100 students; and two thirty-six-hour MA modules focusing on medical interpreting, each attended by about thirty-five students. All these modules train students in dialogue interpreting and sight translation; the module structure is similar in all cases, and all explanations and activities are carried out in class. At the end of each module, the students sit an oral exam in which they are tested in sight translation from English (their main foreign language) into Italian (their native language) and dialogue interpreting; at the exam the students are expected to perform at near-professional level, banking on content and terminology knowledge, as well as on the interpreting strategies they were taught and practiced during the course (see following paragraphs). At the exam, the students are also supposed to bring a personal glossary of about 300 words on the module's topic. The glossary can be in printed or electronic format. The thematic areas of tourism and medicine are rich in technical terminology, thus lending themselves perfectly to the creation of glossaries. Obliging the students to compile and hand in a glossary was felt necessary to avoid students sitting the exam without any content-language preparation (a bad habit that had been observed in previous years, at both undergraduate and MA level).

In all the modules, a few initial classes are devoted to introducing the students to the existence of a range of interpreting techniques and their possible uses in different types of settings, monologic vs dialogic interaction, and general professional ethics. Next, the cognitive, linguistic and practical skills involved in dialogue interpreting and sight translation are explained. Emphasis is placed on the preparation phase, including how to perform content and language searches, but also on the delivery phase. Thus, a range of interpreting strategies applicable in one or both tasks are illustrated and exemplified, including deduction, inference, use of hypernyms, explanations, generalizations, visualization, reformulation, explicitation, text reorganization. Throughout the module, the students practice sight translation and interpreting under the constant supervision of and feedback from the teacher. Practice entails daily class simulations of interpreting assignments.

With reference to the preparation phase, the students are introduced to the need for both content and language knowledge, and how the two are interconnected. In this teaching phase, the teacher familiarizes the students with the Web as a repository of precious information. Different types of resources are suggested for doubts about general language (e.g. monolingual dictionaries, corpus-based resources, thesauruses) and for content and technical vocabulary searches (e.g. online encyclopaedias, institutional websites and academic publications on the given topic). They are also provided with criteria for evaluating web pages (taken from Montalt Resurreció/Gonzales Davies 2014). Next, they are shown how to use comparable texts written by native speakers to acquire content and vocabulary knowledge. Explanations are followed by class exercise where the students are provided with comparable texts on the given topic (one in English and one in Italian, selected by the teacher), asked to read them, highlight technical terms, multiword units and interesting phrases in each text, and to identify how the concepts they underlined in one text are expressed in the other. This approach to terminological searches generally allows students to find a suitable translation for many of the terms/phrases they highlighted, but not all of them. To find a correct target language equivalent to the unsolved expressions, the students are instructed to autonomously search the Web for more comparable texts.

At this point, the students are explained that professionals fix their searches in glossaries, and are then introduced to glossary creation in LearnWeb. They are presented the LearnWeb Glossary tool, and instructed to use it and create a personal glossary to support their preparation on the exam topics. The teacher discusses the glossary interface in class with the students, and illustrates the role and logic of each field and menu option. The students are invited to enter technical terms that are new to them or which they consider particularly important in the given domain, to fill in as many fields as necessary for each term and to use the phraseology box to enter collocations and colligations, but also other things that they consider useful, such as links to images, links to useful reference material, examples or grammatical information. Finally, they are told that they are expected to work on their personal glossaries at home as part of their individual preparation for each class simulation of interpreting assignments and for the final exam.

Thanks to the LearnWeb tracking features, its learning analytics system and the dashboard, the teacher is able to unobtrusively check each student's work on the glossary throughout the module, and provide remedial feedback when necessary. By way of example, the following paragraphs illustrate how the dashboard helped the teacher to identify some students who were disregarding content knowledge. The data refer to an MA module on medical discourse attended by thirty-five students.

Two weeks after the MA students were introduced to glossary creation and the LearnWeb tool, the section of the dashboard relating to the Internet resources specified by the students themselves (*Source* field; Figure 8.8) showed that this group of students had primarily been consulting content-based resources (62.9 per cent), and in fewer cases language-based resources (37.1 per cent). Among the content-based resources, Wikipedia was by far the preferred one. This type of profile suggested that most students in the group had understood the aims of the preparation phase and the importance of extended reading on the given topic.

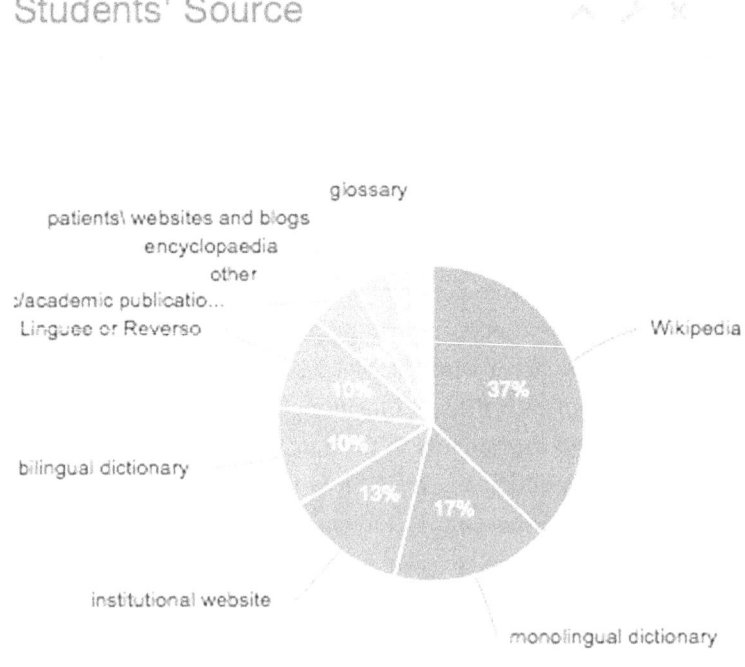

Figure 8.8 Group view of the data entered by the students in the source field

However, observation of the number of sources declared by each student highlighted that some students, such as Students 10413, 10443 and 10111, seemed to resort to a very limited number of sources for a high number of entries. A closer examination showed that student 10413, for example, resorted exclusively to a monolingual dictionary. Similarly, student 10111 made ample use of dictionaries (bilingual as well as monolingual) and very limited use of content-based sources. Individual conversations with the two students confirmed that they had not understood that the preparation phase includes learning something about a given topic and, more generally, that they had not understood the importance of content and context in interpreting. In the weeks after personalized feedback was given, the dashboard registered change in the behaviours of those particular students.

6. Possible uses of these affordances for teaching and research in interpreting

In the modules where the system has been used, the glossary tool has proven useful to and has been appreciated by students and teachers of interpreting (Taibi *et al.* 2019). However, the most innovative and interesting aspect of our tool is its integration with data tracking and data analysis systems.

As shown, the dashboard offers teachers a view of what the students are doing, and guides them in identifying students who need extra help or advice and in providing personalized remedial feedback. This makes it possible to delegate terminology work to the students themselves, as autonomous work done outside class hours.

However, the tracking and logging systems also present teachers and researchers of interpreting with a wide range of data that may provide insight into the learning, cognitive and/or material processes that students of interpreting apply during the preparation phase and in glossary compilation, and into their preferences. An analysis of the data in the dashboard, at individual, group or across-groups level, may provide, for example, an answer to questions such as: Do students fill in their glossaries on a regular basis or at specific points in time (e.g. when spurred to do so; immediately before an assignment)? Which fields do students compile and which do they disregard? What kind of information do students enter into the Phraseology box? What kind of resources do the students consult? What kind of resources do they find more useful? Insight into these issues may support teachers in planning their classes, and lead them to improve or change the way they introduce the preparatory phase and the needs of interpreters to their students.

If similar data were collected from professional interpreters, students' and professionals' habits could be compared, with potentially interesting implications at both practical and theoretical level. Furthermore, an analysis of the ways students (or professional interpreters) interact with online pages during the preparation phase – a possibility which is offered by the WAPS tool – could open unexpected views on the cognitive processes involved in such an activity. Finally, correlating glossary data to students' exam results may offer an insight into the relationship between specific patterns in content and vocabulary work and acceptability/quality of an interpreter's performance.

Notes

1. http://www.fourwillows.com/interplex.html.
2. http://www.wintringham.ch/cgi/ayawp.pl?T=terminus.
3. https://www.interpretershelp.com/.
4. http://www.interpretbank.com/.
5. Technical details of the software programs listed above can be found in Costa *et al.* (2014a, 2014b) and Rütten (2014a, 2014b).
6. In compliance with European privacy rules and regulations, all students using a LearnWeb environment are informed that their data will be tracked and stored for a given period of time (agreed with the module's teacher), and are invited to sign a consent form. The data of those who deny permission are not tracked.
7. For a more detailed discussion of behavioural log data and ways to collect and analyse them, see Taibi *et al.* (2018).
8. For a technical description of this tool, see Taibi *et al.* (2018).
9. Introduction to 1st International Conference on Learning Analytics and Knowledge (LAK2011) https://tekri.athabascau.ca/analytics/.

References

Agudo-Peregrina, Á. F., S. Iglesias-Pradas, M. A. Conde-González and A. Hernández-García (2014), 'Can We Predict Success from Log Data in VLEs? Classification of Interactions for Learning Analytics and Their Relation with Performance in VLE-Supported F2F and Online Learning', *Computers in Human Behavior*, 31: 542–50.

AIIC (2004), *A Practical Guide for Professional Conference Interpreters*. Available online: http://aiic.net/page/628 (accessed 6 June 2021).

Andres, D. (2015), 'Consecutive Interpreting', in F. Pöchhacker (ed.), *Routledge Encyclopedia of Interpreting Studies*, 84–7, London: Routledge.

Baker, R. and G. Siemens (2014), 'Educational Data Mining and Learning Analytics', in K. R. Sawyer (ed.), *The Cambridge Handbook of the Learning Sciences*, 2nd edn, 253–74, Cambridge: Cambridge University Press.

Bancroft, M. A. and K. Allen (2015), 'Not Your Mother's Latin: Honing Your Medical Terminology for Medical Interpreter Certification', *The ATA Chronicle*: 15–18. Available online: http://www.atanet.org/chronicle-online/wp-content/uploads/4405_15_bancroft_allen.pdf (accessed June 2021).

Bianchi, F. and I. Marenzi (2016), 'Investigating Student Choices in Performing Higher-Order Comprehension Tasks Using TED Talks in LearnWeb', *Lingue e Linguaggi*, 19, 23–40.

Blikstein, P., M. Worsley, C. Piech, M. Sahami, S. Cooper and D. Koller (2014), 'Programming Pluralism: Using Learning Analytics to Detect Patterns in the Learning of Computer Programming', *Journal of the Learning Sciences*, 23 (4): 561–99.

Bocanegra Valle, A. and M. D. Perera Barberá (2011), 'ICT-based Instruction for Specialised Vocabulary Development', in N. Talaván Zanón, E. Martín Monje and F. Palazón Romero (eds), *Technological Innovation in the Teaching and Processing of LSPs: Proceedings of TISLID'10*, 41–53, Madrid: Universidad Nacional de Educatión a Distancia.

Breeze, R. (2014), 'Moodle Glossary Tasks for Teaching Legal English', in E. Bárcena, T. Read and J. Arús (eds), *Languages for Specific Purposes in the Digital Era*, 111–28, New York: Springer.

Cenková, I. (2010), 'Sight Translation. Prima Vista', in Y. Gambier and L. van Doorslaer (eds), *Handbook of Translation Studies*, vol. 1, 320–3, Amsterdam: John Benjamins.

Cenková, I. (2015), 'Sight Translation', in F. Pöchhacker (ed.), *Routledge Encyclopedia of Interpreting Studies*, 374–5, London: Routledge.

Corsellis, A. (2008), *Public Service Interpreting. The First Steps*, Basingstoke, UK: Palgrave Macmillan.

Costa, H., G. Corpas Pastor and I. Durán-Muñoz (2014a), 'A Comparative User Evaluation of Terminology Management Tools for Interpreters', *Proceedings of the 4th International Workshop on Computational Terminology*: 68–76. Available online: https://www.aclweb.org/anthology/W14-4809 (accessed 6 June 2021).

Costa, H., G. Corpas Pastor and I. Durán-Muñoz (2014b), 'Technology-assisted Interpreting', *Multilingual* April/May 2014: 27–32.

Crezee, I. H. M. (2013), *Introduction to Healthcare for Interpreters and Translators*, Amsterdam: John Benjamins.

Dam, H. V. (2010), 'Consecutive Interpreting', in Y. Gambier and L. van Doorslaer (eds), *Handbook of Translation Studies*, vol. 1, 75–9, Amsterdam: John Benjamins.

Díaz-Galaz, S. (2015), *La influencia del conocimiento previo en la interpretación simultánea de discursos especializados: Un estudio empírico*. PhD dissertation,

Universidad de Granada. Available online: http://digibug.ugr.es/bitstream/handle/10481/23752/21167606.pdf?sequence=1&isAllowed=y (accessed 6 June 2021).

Díaz-Galaz, S., P. Padilla and M. T. Bajo (2015), 'The Role of Advance Preparation in Simultaneous Interpreting. A Comparison of Professional Interpreters and Interpreting Students', *Interpreting*, 17 (1): 1–25.

Dietz-Uhler, B. and J. E. Hurn (2013), 'Using Learning Analytics to Predict (and Improve) Student Success: A Faculty Perspective', *Journal of Interactive Online Learning*, 12 (1): 17–26. Available online: http://www.ncolr.org/jiol/issues/pdf/12.1.2.pdf (accessed 6 June 2021).

Dyckhoff, A. L., D. Zielke, M. Bültmann, M. A. Chatti and U. Schroeder (2012), 'Design and Implementation of a Learning Analytics Toolkit for Teachers', *Journal of Educational Technology & Society*, 15 (3): 58–76.

Fantinuoli, C. (20169, 'InterpretBank. Redefining Computer-assisted Interpreting Tools', *Proceedings of the 38th Conference Translating and the Computer*: 42–52. Available online: https://www.semanticscholar.org/paper/Redefining-computer-assisted-interpreting-tools-Fantinuoli/5617c59e3f2869d2e7d1b6da6b057ebff5944dfc (accessed 6 June 2021).

Fantinuoli, C. (2017), 'Computer-assisted Preparation in Conference Interpreting', *Translation & Interpreting*, 9 (2): 24–37.

Fantinuoli, C. (2018), 'Computer-assisted Interpreting. Challenges and Future Perspectives', in I. Durán-Muñoz and G. Corpas Pastor (eds), *Trends in e-tools and Resources for Translators and Interpreters*, 153–74, Leiden: Brill.

Gašević, D., S. Dawson and G. Siemens (2015), 'Let's Not Forget: Learning Analytics Are about Learning', *TechTrends*, 59 (1): 64–71.

Gile, D. (2002), 'The Interpreter's Preparation for Technical Conferences: Methodological Questions in Investigating the Topic', *Conference Interpretation and Translation*, 4 (2): 7–27.

Gile, D. (2009), *Basic Concepts and Models for Interpreter and Translator Training*, Amsterdam: John Benjamins.

Gu, Y. and R. K. Johnson (1996), 'Vocabulary Learning Strategies and Language Learning Outcomes', *Language Learning*, 46 (4): 643–79.

Jiang, H. (2015), 'A Survey of Glossary Practice of Conference Interpreters', *Aiic Webzine*, 66 (5). Available online: https://aiic.org/document/950/AIICWebzine_2015_Issue66_5_JIANG_A_survey_of_glossary_practice_of_conference_interpreters_EN.pdf (accessed 6 June 2021).

Jones, R. (1998), *Conference Interpreting Explained*, Manchester: St Jerome.

Kalina, S. (1998), *Strategische Prozesse beim Dolmetschen. Theoretische Grundlagen, empirische Fallstudien, didaktische Konsequenzen*, Tübingen: Gunter Narr.

Loiacono, A. (2013), *The Medical Alphabet. An English Textbook in Healthcare*, Andria: Matarrese.

Marenzi, I. (2014a), *Multiliteracies and e-learning2.0. Foreign Language Pedagogy Content- and Learner-Oriented*, vol. 28, Frankfurt am Main: Peter Lang.

Marenzi, I. (2014b), 'Interactive and Collaborative Supports for CLIL: Towards a Formal Model Based on Digital Literacy', in R. Kupetz and C. Becker (eds), *Content and Language Integrated Learning (CLIL) by Interaction*, 75–99, Frankfurt am Main: Peter Lang.

Marenzi, I. and S. Zerr (2012), 'Multiliteracies and Active Learning in CLIL: The Development of LearnWeb2.0', *IEEE Transactions on Learning Technologies (TLT)*, 5 (4): 336–48.

Merlini, R. (2015), 'Dialogue Interpreting', in F. Pöchhacker (ed.), *Routledge Encyclopedia of Interpreting Studies*, 102–7, London: Routledge.

Montalt Resurreció, V. and M. Gonzales Davies (2014), *Medical Translation Step by Step. Learning by Drafting*, London: Routledge.

Moser, B. (1978), 'Simultaneous Interpretation: A Hypothetical Model and Its Practical Application', in D. Gerver and H. Wallas Sinaiko (eds), *Language Interpretation and Communication*, 353–68, New York: Plenum Press.

Pöchhacker, F. (2003), *Introducing Interpreting Studies*, London: Routledge.

Pospíšilová, L., Z. Bezdíčková and D. Ciberová (2011), 'English for Science using LMS Moodle', *Interactive Collaborative Learning International Conference, 14th 2011 (ICL 2011)*: 169–71.

Rodríguez, N. and B. Schnell (2009), 'A Look at Terminology Adapted to the Requirements of Interpretation', *Language Update*, 6 (1): 21. Available online: https://www.btb.termiumplus.gc.ca/tpv2guides/guides/favart/indexfra.html?lang=fra&lettr=indx_titls&page=9oHAHvmFzkgE.html (accessed June 2021).

Romero-Zaldívar, V.-A., A. Pardo, D. Burgos and C. Delgado Kloos (2012), 'Monitoring Student Progress Using Virtual Appliances: A Case Study', *Computers & Education*, 58 (4): 1058–67.

Rütten, A. (2014a), 'Booth-friendly Terminology Management Programs for Interpreters: A Market snapshot', Available online: http://blog.sprachmanagement.net/booth-friendly-terminology-management-programs-for-interpreters-a-market-snapshot/ (accessed 6 June 2021).

Rütten, A. (2014b), 'Booth-friendly Terminology Management Revisited. 2 Newcomers'. Available online: http://blog.sprachmanagement.net/booth-friendly-terminology-management-revisited-2-newcomers/ (accessed 6 June 2021).

Sandrelli, A. (2001), 'Teaching Liaison Interpreting. Combining Tradition and Innovation', in I. Mason (ed.), *Triadic Exchanges. Studies in Dialogue Interpreting*, 173–95, London: Routledge.

Sawyer, D. B. (2004), *Fundamental Aspects of Interpreter Education*, Amsterdam: John Benjamins.

Seghiri Domínguez, M. (2013), 'Creating a Bilingual Glossary (English-Spanish) Based on Moodle for the Teaching and Learning of Scientific and Technical Translation', in M. Del Mar Rivas Carmona and M. Del Carmen Balbuena Torezano (eds), *Cultural Aspects of Translation*, 357–72, Tübingen: Gunter Narr.

Seleskovitch, D. (1978), *Interpreting for International Conferences: Problems of Language and Communication*, Washington: Pen and Booth.

Setton, R. (2003), 'Words and Sense: Revisiting Lexical Processes in Interpreting', *FORUM. Revue internationale d'interprétation et de traduction/International Journal of Interpretation and Translation*, 1 (1): 139–68.

Setton, R. (2010), 'From Practice to Theory and Back in Interpreting: The Pivotal Role of Training', *The Interpreters' Newsletter*, 15: 1–18. Available online: https://www.openstarts.units.it/dspace/handle/10077/4746 (accessed June 2021).

Stoll, C. (2009), *Jenseits simultanfähiger Terminologiesysteme*, Trier: Wvt Wissenschaftlicher Verlag.

Taibi, D., F. Bianchi, P. Kemkes and I. Marenzi (2018), 'Learning Analytics for Interpreting', *Proceedings of the 10th International Conference on Computer Supported Education*, vol. 1, *SCITEPRESS, Science and Technology Publications*: 145–54.

Taibi, D., F. Bianchi, P. Kemkes and I. Marenzi (2019), 'A Learning Analytics Dashboard to Analyse Learning Activities in Interpreter Training Courses', in B. M. McLaren, R. Reilly, S. Zvacek and J. Uhomoibhi (eds), *Computer Supported Education*, 268–86, Springer: Cham.

Taibi, D., D. Kantz and G. Fulantelli (2014), 'Supporting Formative Assessment in Content and Language Integrated Learning: The MWS-Web Platform', *International Journal of Technology Enhanced Learning*, 6 (4): 361–79.

Verbert, K., E. Duval, J. Klerkx, S. Govaerts and J. L. Santos (2013), 'Learning Analytics Dashboard Applications', *American Behavioral Scientist*, 57 (10): 1500–9.

Viezzi, M. (2013), 'Simultaneous and Consecutive Interpreting (Non-Conference Settings)', in C. Millán and F. Bartrina (eds), *The Routledge Handbook of Translation Studies*, 377–88, London: Routledge.

Wang, F. and M. J. Hannafin (2005), 'Design-Based Research and Technology-Enhanced Learning Environments', *Educational Technology Research and Development*, 53 (4): 5–23.

Will, M. (2007), 'Terminology Work for Simultaneous Interpreters in LSP Conferences: Model and Method', *MuTra 2007 – LSP Translation Scenarios: Conference Proceedings*. Available online. http://www.euroconferences.info/proceedings/2007_Proceedings/2007_Will_Martin.pdf (accessed 6 June 2021).

Exploring the construction and translation of film characters through a parallel corpus: The case of *Little Women* adaptations

Gianmarco Vignozzi

1. Introduction

This chapter presents some practical applications of corpus linguistics methods to the study of character building and translation in the dialogues of four films in their original and dubbed versions. The case study is centred on a self-compiled parallel corpus featuring the English original and the Italian dubbed transcribed dialogues of the big screen adaptations of *Little Women* (Cukor 1933, LeRoy 1949, Armstrong 1994, Gerwig 2019) and aims to unveil the key linguistic traits that contribute to constructing the personalities of the four protagonists. Using the *Sketch Engine* suite of tools (Kilgarriff *et al.* 2004) the parallel nature of the corpus is exploited to assess whether and how emerging key linguistic features depicting the main characters are preserved in the Italian dubbing, despite translational shifts. In order to do this, film speech is codified as written digital text so as to allow for automated triangulated analyses on original and translated dialogues.

The prolific interaction between translation studies and corpus methods was first highlighted by Sinclair (1991, 1992), who, after his pioneering works on the compilation of the first multi-million word corpora of written and spoken English (i.e. the *Longman-Lancaster English Language Corpus*) and on the potentialities of corpus linguistics as an empirical methodology, mentions translation studies as one of the fields that could benefit the most from the development and application of large language corpora. Building on Sinclair's approach, Baker (1993) implemented these new large-scale corpus methodologies to translation studies in an attempt to shed light on 'the nature of translated text as a mediated communicative event' and, most importantly, to establish some generalizable 'universals of translation' (1993: 243), that is, an array of 'linguistic features that typically occur in translation rather than original texts and are independent of the influence of the specific language pairs involved in the process of translation' (Laviosa 2002: 18).

Such a shift in attention from the theoretical intuition alone to the usage-informed findings drawn from large computerized corpora has favoured the study of the language of translated texts as a variety in its own right, with its distinctive features and 'shaped by its own goals, pressures and context of production' (Baker 1996: 175). As Baños Piñero *et al.* (2013: 1) explain, 'generalisations can thus be made on more solid ground not only because of the vast amount of data, but also because computer software makes it possible to detect patterns that would be difficult to identify through manual analysis'. In other words, the merger of corpus linguistics and descriptive translation studies (Toury 1995 [2012]) has made it feasible to deal with texts and translated texts based on numerical evidence and with a level of accuracy that would otherwise be impossible. Not only does this help to identify linguistic traits that could be overlooked through mere intuition, but also quantitatively helps validate claims about language features (Baker 1993, 1996, Kenny 2001, Johansson 2007, Oakes/Ji 2012).

The corpora, that is, the 'collection[s] of machine-readable authentic texts [...] sampled to be representative of a particular language or language variety' (McEnery *et al.* 2006: 5), which proved to be most frequently used in corpus-based translation studies are parallel, comparable and reference corpora. In parallel corpora the original source texts and the target translated texts are aligned one next to the other. Comparable corpora, instead, contain original texts in various languages within the same context of usage (e.g. text type, genre, topic, etc.). Their comparability lies in their similar sampling frame and balance (McEnery/Xiao 2008). An example of both a parallel and a comparable corpus is the *Pavia Corpus of Film Dialogue* (cf. Pavesi 2014), which consists in the transcriptions of the dialogues of a selection of British and American films aligned with the orthographic transcriptions of their Italian dubbed correspondents. Finally, reference corpora are collections of texts spanning over a wide range of sources and designed to represent a language as a whole, so that they can be used as benchmarks, for example, the BNC (*British National Corpus*) for British English and the COCA (*Corpus of Contemporary American English*) for American English.

Looking at audiovisual translation as an independent research avenue within translation studies (Dìaz-Cintas 2008), corpora and corpus linguistics as a methodology for assessing the translation of multimedia texts have been successfully applied to the analysis of original and translated verbal language

(Pavesi 2019), be it codified through the transcription of original and dubbed dialogues (cf. inter alia Pavesi *et al.* 2014), the original scripts (cf. *inter alia* Taylor 1999, 2004) or the intralingual or interlingual subtitles (cf. *inter alia* Dìaz-Cintas/ Ramael 2007). The corpus perspective has allowed researchers to systematically and empirically examine the distinguishing features and patterns of original and translated audiovisual texts, for instance for what concerns their written-to-be-spoken-as-if-not-written (Gregory/Carroll 1978: 42) or 'prefabricated' (Chaume 2012: 82) nature as compared to naturally occurring language. As a final remark, it is worth mentioning that besides combining quantitative and qualitative considerations, a specific peculiarity of corpus-based studies of audiovisual texts is that they often also consider the meaning-making contributions of the non-verbal codes and their potential influence on the translation strategies and the solutions adopted (cf. Taylor 2014).

Against this background, the present chapter is organized as follows: Section 2 briefly introduces the data used to compile the parallel corpus at the core of this case study, which is carefully described in Section 3, in which practical and theoretical reflections on the essential steps in parallel corpus building are outlined. Some of the potentialities of the corpus software *Sketch Engine* (Kilgarriff *et al.* 2004) are also presented as this is the tool used for the compilation and the subsequent analysis of the corpus. Section 4 features a corpus-driven analysis of the keywords in the dialogues of *Little Women* protagonists so as to observe how they provide narrative elements functional to their characterization. The analysis continues in Section 5, where the *Parallel Concordance* tool is used to evaluate some features that emerged from the inductive analysis carried out through the lens of interlinguistic translation. Finally, Section 6 recaps on the main points discussed throughout the paper.

2. *Little Women* and its big screen adaptations

Alcott's novel *Little Women* is centred around the daily life and the social interactions of the members of the March family. In particular, the protagonists are Meg, Jo, Amy and Beth, four sisters with very different temperaments who live in a modest house in Concord, Massachusetts, and experience the passage from childhood into womanhood during the challenges of the American Civil War. This coming-of age novel intertwines traits of romance and tragedy with the ordinary pains of growing up and 'hinges on some eternal truths, such as the search for one's identity and the desire to accomplish one's dream' (Bruti

2003: 62). These features have made it a canonical text capable of reaching any generation.

Given its enduring success, *Little Women* has periodically been adapted for the big and small screen (cf. Leitch 2017 on the telecinematic adaptation of literary classics). In fact, all its feature films have been very successful and well received by the public and the critics.

Cukor's version released in 1933 was the first adaptation of *Little Women* for the sound cinema and was a box-office hit. This film closely mirrors its historical context, that is, the difficulties of The Great Depression, by foregrounding key themes such as simplicity, frugality and resilience of the spirit to surmount difficulties, qualities that are especially embodied by the members of the March family.

In the wake of the acclaimed 1933 film, in 1949 LeRoy decided to revisit *Little Women* with a technicolor version and a new cast of Hollywood stars, but readapting the script and the music of the previous film. Therefore, the two versions are quite similar.

Fifty years later, in 1994 the Australian female director Gillian Armstrong readapted the classic tale of *Little Women* from a more feminist perspective. By foregrounding the intimate lives of strong female figures, such as the progressive matriarch March mother or the untamed and fiery daughter Jo, characters in this film are advocates of women as independent members of society.

The latest update of the story was in 2019, when another female filmmaker, Greta Gerwig, decided to refresh the literary classic and take it back to Hollywood. The peculiarity of this cinematic rendering is the orchestration of the tale's narrative in a non-linear fashion. The film, narrated by Jo's voice, proceeds on two different timelines. It starts *in medias res* when the four March sisters are already grown up and through flashbacks and memory fragments tells the story and the anecdotes of their younger years.

As normally happens with Hollywood productions, these films were concurrently dubbed and released in Italian, the only exception being the 1933 version that was dubbed into Italian only in 1990.

3. A parallel corpus of original and dubbed film speech: The *LittleWomenTalk* corpus

The dataset used to compile the corpus at the core of this study consists of the transcriptions of the English original and the Italian dubbed dialogues of the four cinematic renderings of *Little Women* described in Section 2. The original and translated dialogues were transcribed from scratch in Bruti and Vignozzi (2021) on the basis of the original soundtracks of the DVD film versions. Because of the nature of the research, transcription was essentially orthographic (cf. Bonsignori 2009 for an overview on media language transcription), even though spoken language phenomena (e.g. morpho-phonological reductions, hesitations, discourse markers, interjections) were carefully considered and transcribed. More in detail, the transcriptions were organized in Microsoft Word files (.doc), one per film, each of which containing a table with two columns: one for the speaker names and the other for the written codification of their speech. Hence, the turns of the characters, that is, the level taken as the minimal unit of transcription, were separated in rows.

In order to turn this eight-file dataset into a parallel corpus, I decided to use the corpus tool *Sketch Engine*. The reasons for choosing this web-based software among the many available are manifold. Firstly, for its versatility, as it allows users to upload, build, store and share corpora of different typologies. Indeed, corpora can be built with multiple documents in a variety of formats or with a single compressed file. Moreover, as explained in detail below, the software automatically recognizes manual mark-ups added before the compilation. Secondly, because the software offers a rich toolbox for analysing user-created corpora (e.g. *Concordance, Parallel Concordance, Keywords and terms*, just to mention a few) as well as a vast selection of ready-to-use corpora (e.g. the *British National Corpus* or the *Open American National Corpus*) that can be consulted, analysed or used as benchmarks when working with a do-it-yourself corpus.

Following the indications contained in the user guide[1] of the software for the compilation of parallel corpora, one spreadsheet Microsoft Excel file (.xls) per film was generated. In the first cell of the first column of each file was put the label *English* and in the second *Italian*. Correspondingly, in the English column were gathered the original dialogues and in the Italian column the corresponding dubbed ones. The original and the translated dialogues, copied and pasted from the.doc tables, were automatically sorted in rows, resulting in two columns of texts aligned turn by turn in the rows.

Character names were marked in each row through an xml-compatible attribute-value tagging system that permits to add metadata to the corpus in a way that the web interface of *Sketch Engine* can recognize and process. The following line is an explanatory example:

(1) <s speaker='Beth March'>You ought to publish it, Jo! Really! Not just in the Pickwick portfolio. </s>

A structure frame (i.e. <s </s>) must mark the beginning and ending of turns. The mark-up label, composed by an attribute and a corresponding value with the speaker name (i.e. speaker = 'name of the speaker'>), is then added to the beginning of the structure frame. Exactly the same rationale was applied to the dubbed dialogues pasted in the *Italian* column of the spreadsheet. Figure 9.1 features a random sample of the tagged pairs of texts as appearing in the aligned and tagged files.

Once the spreadsheets were prepared according to the format requirements described above, the actual compilation of the corpus was carried out by means of *Sketch Engine* corpus building interface. The guided procedure allows the user to upload the .xls files and automatically identifies the languages at stake. As a last step before finalizing the corpus building procedure, another level of attribute-value tagging was added, this time at document level. Thus, the built-in *Sketch Engine* metadata editor was used to label each of the uploaded documents (i.e. the spreadsheets with the tagged and aligned dialogues of the *Little Women* films) with the year of release of the film. Figure 9.2 illustrates this passage.

595	<s speaker="Jo March">Oh, no, Teddy. Teddy, don't. No, wait, Teddy We have to talk about this reasonably.</s>.	<s speaker="Jo March">Oh, no...Teddy...Teddy...no...no, aspetta Teddy...noi dobbiamo parlarne da persone ragionevoli.</s>.
596	<s speaker="Laurie">I have loved you... since the moment I clamped eyes on you. What could be more reasonable than to marry you?!</s>.	<s speaker="Laurie">Io ti ho amata, Jo, dal primo momento che ho posato i miei occhi su di te. Cosa può esserci di più ragionevole che sposarti?!</s>.
597	<s speaker="Jo March">We'd kill each other.</s>.	<s speaker="Jo March">Ma...sarebbe un inferno!</s>.
598	<s speaker="Laurie">Nonsense.</s>.	<s speaker="Laurie">Sciocchezze.</s>.
599	<s speaker="Jo March">Neither of us can keep our temper.</s>.	<s speaker="Jo March">Nessuno di noi due sa mantenere la calma.</s>.
600	<s speaker="Laurie">I can... unless provoked.</s>.	<s speaker="Laurie">Io sì. Se non sono provocato.</s>.
601	<s speaker="Jo March">We're both stupidly stubborn, especially you. We'd only quarrel.</s>.	<s speaker="Jo March">Siamo tutti e due stupidamente ostinati,sopratutto tu. Litigheremmo e basta.</s>.

Figure 9.1 Pairs of tagged texts taken from *Little Women* (Armstrong 1994)

Edit metadata

LW_2019_allineato_annotato.xls

Attribute   Value

Year   2019
_____   _____

Figure 9.2 *Sketch Engine* document metadata editor

At the end of the process, which culminates with an automatic part-of-speech tagging and the corpus compilation, the software issues two separate monolingual corpora aligned with each other: the first featuring the source texts and the second the target texts. They work as two aligned parallel subcorpora that can be questioned separately as well as comparatively through, for example, the *Parallel Concordance* tool.

The corpus under scrutiny was named *LittleWomenTalk* (hereafter LWT). Table 9.1 offers an overview of its size according to the numbers of tokens given by *Sketch Engine*.

Table 9.1 Total numbers in *LittleWomenTalk* corpus after the compilation

	LittleWomenTalk	
	Tokens in English subcorpus	Tokens in Italian subcorpus
Little Women (Cukor, 1933)	15,248	14,557
Little Women (LeRoy, 1949)	15,429	14,636
Little Women (Armstrong 1994)	12,062	11,960
Little Women (Gerwig, 2019)	15,434	14,995
	58,173	56,148
Total number of tokens of LWT	114,321	

LittleWomenTalk counts 114,321 tokens, which are distributed in a rather balanced way among the original and the dubbed films. Nevertheless, original dialogues appear to be slightly wordier than the dubbed ones, pointing to the tendency towards simplification that has amply been demonstrated to characterize translated texts (cf. Baker 1996, Pavesi *et al.* 2014).

To sum up, this annotated parallel corpus should allow for the systematic study of linguistic features defining the different characters and how they change across the four film versions, with the possibility of drawing comparisons between English original and Italian dubbed dialogues.

4. The construction of the March sisters' speech

4.1. Setting of the study: An overview of the research and the theoretical frameworks

This Section (4) and the next (5) present a case study aimed at showcase the potentialities of LWT by analysing the linguistic construction and some features of the dubbing into Italian of the four main characters in *Little Women*: Jo, Meg, Amy and Beth March. The choice of focusing in particular on the four March sisters is twofold. First, because they are the absolute protagonists of all the film adaptations: all the events taking place ultimately revolve around them or at least are filtered through them. Second, because they have very different personality types: Meg, the oldest March sister, is responsible, kind and compromising; Jo is fiery ambitious and untamed, but also very devoted to the family; Beth is virtuous, sensitive and shy; Amy is vain, social and sometimes overambitious. This makes it particularly interesting to see how these personalities are rendered in the dialogues.

According to Culpeper's (2001) model of characterization in fictional texts, characters are built in the mind of the audience through explicit and implicit 'textual cues that give rise to information about character' (Culpeper 2001: 163). Explicit cues are all information about characters that can be retrieved by their self-presentations:

(2) Jo March: Look at me, I'm homely and I'm awkward and I'm odd. (*Little Women*, Gerwig 2019)

or by their representations in the speech of other characters:

(3) Meg March: Oh Jo, please don't say 'awful'. It's slang. (*Little Women*, Armstrong 1994)

Conversely, implicit characterization cues are textual elements that indirectly contribute to sketching characters as they convey 'character information which has to be derived by inference' (Culpeper 2001: 172). A checklist of implicit characterization cues is provided by Culpeper (2001) and includes, for example, conversational structure, lexical and syntactic features in character speech, accent and dialect, paralinguistic features and visual features. This package of implicit information is to be searched only in the respective character's lines:

(4) Jo March: Christopher Columbus! What richness! (*Little Women*, LeRoy 1949)

These two exclamations point to the exuberant temperament of Jo, who is often outspoken and thus she is reproached by her more refined sisters.

The analysis presented in this paper exploits corpus linguistics tools to explore implicit characterization cues in particular and its potentials to build character identity in the dialogues of the March sisters. The different methodologies and theoretical frameworks that are used throughout the study to approach the analysis of the original and dubbed speech are presented in more detail where relevant. In a nutshell, the analysis mixes quantitative considerations, computed with the help of *Sketch Engine* toolbox, and qualitative analysis. In the quantitative computerized character-based analysis (cf. Bednarek 2012a, Lazzeretti 2019 for further examples) I extracted the keywords produced when comparing the dialogue of a character with that of the others. The results were then qualitatively evaluated by assessing the concordance lines. The subsequent analysis of dubbing choices is conducted resorting to *Sketch Engine* parallel concordancer, which is then integrated with an evaluation (Toury 1995 [2012]) of translation choices.

4.2. A character-based analysis through keywords extraction and evaluation

Thanks to the turn-by-turn tagging carried out on LWT, which distinguishes turns on the basis of the name of the character speaking, the lines of the March sisters in the original films were isolated into four subcorpora, one for each sister. This could be done automatically with the *Sketch Engine* subcorpora builder that allows for the creation of subcorpora from the corpus components marked with a tagging. The following Table 9.2 gives the numbers of the four subcorpora.[2]

As the size of subcorpora suggests, the character of Jo has a central role in all *Little Women* adaptations. In fact, she utters the highest number of words in all the film versions.

The character-based analysis was conducted by means of *Sketch Engine* keywords generator. Each of the March sister subcorpora was alternatively used as the focus corpus using the other subcorpora together as the reference corpus.[3] This methodology permitted to isolate the key textual cues profiling the four protagonists.

Keywords can be defined as 'linguistic features that are unusual in terms of frequency when a "node" text or corpus is compared to a reference corpus'

Table 9.2 Number of tokens in the four subcorpora

	Jo_subcorpus	Meg_subcorpus	Amy_subcorpus	Beth_subcorpus
1933	3,013	1,795	1,453	965
1949	2,945	1,679	1,421	867
1994	2,535	1,032	1,213	798
2019	2,820	1,342	1,532	919
	11,313	5,848	5,619	3,549

Table 9.3 List of top twenty-five keywords in the subcorpora

	Jo	Meg	Amy	Beth
Keywords	no; hate; truly; never; detest; not; we; Teddy; Beth; well; many; Aunt; n't; splendid; bilge; Beth; so; Auntie; writer; Christopher; Colombus; wonderful; love; sell; Friedrich	John; gloves; Brooke; thank; nice; sorry; please; sweet; hands; Jo; bonnet; lovely; dance; kind; such; thing; yes; they; quite; poor; darling; shall; boy; pair; embarrass	pencil; draw; Fred; pretty; elegant; wish; boyish; I, horrible; look; Jo; stop; unladylike; die; selfish; school; box; rude; terrible; picture; most; ashamed; Roderigo; foot; statirical	Marmee; Jo; Hummel; father; think; hungry; home; write; poor; good write; piano; thank; Santa; Claus; sick; house; Laurence; very; beautiful; God; wish; should; music; it; nest

(Bednarek 2012b: 4). In other words, they are not only frequent words, but also salient in terms of statistical significance.

The *Sketch Engine* keywords and terms tool identified hundreds of keywords in each subcorpus and it was beyond the scope of this case study to take all of them into account. Therefore, a selection of the most relevant among the top twenty-five keywords for each subcorpus (Table 9.3) was analysed in the following subsections.

4.2.1. Jo March

Starting with Jo's keywords, we can observe that the negation markers *no*, *not*, *n't* and *never* point to her tendency to be in contrast with what the other characters say. In fact, if we use *Sketch Engine* concordance tool to qualitatively evaluate the concordances, that is, the 'list of all instances of a search term in the corpus, including its co-text' (Bednarek 2012b: 206) produced for the negations above, which make up 30 per cent of the negative sentences in the whole corpus,[4] it appears that she often turns offers and requests down (5), she contradicts her interlocutors (6) or she affirms her strong opinions through disagreement (7).

(5) Laurie: May I engage you for this dance, Miss March?
Jo March: **No**, thank you, **I'm not** dancing. (*Little Women*, Cukor 1933)

(6) Marmee: Jo, you're crying.
Jo March: **No**, I'm **not**. (*Little Women*, Armstrong 1994)

(7) Marmee: I'm no different from many other mothers, but I'd rather see you as the happy wives of poor men or even respectable old maids, than queens on thrones, without peace or self-respect.
Jo March: Oh, I'm **never** going to get married, **never, never**! (*Little Women*, LeRoy 1949)

In a similar vein, the verbs *hate* and *detest*, which express strong negative attitudes, are salient in her dialogues. *Hate*, in particular, has twelve hits in the corpus, all of which are in Jo's turns.

(8) Jo March: How I **hate** to be elegant … (*Little Women*, LeRoy 1949)

Other traits which point to Jo's fiery temper are the words *truly* and *so* that often act as intensifiers.

The keyness of the pronoun *we* also tells us something about her personality. By looking at the seventy-four concordances, we may see that it often refers to her and her sisters (or the whole March family in general) (forty-three hits), or to her and Laurie (seventeen hits). This suggests that she has a strong sense of commitment to her family and to Laurie, the boy she does not end up marrying, but who she cares for.

Positive evaluative adjectives make up another group of keywords. It is interesting to notice that the adjectives *splendid* and *darling*, which are mostly targeted to her sisters or her mother only occur in the 1933 and 1949 versions, and *wonderful*, often used in exclamations showing joy, has one hit in the 2019 film, two in the one from 1994 and eight and seven respectively in the 1949 and 1933 versions. This could suggest that her character has slightly changed in the more recent versions or that the adjectives *splendid* and *darling* are perceived as dated.

The nouns *Teddy*, *Beth*, *Aunt* and *Auntie*, and *Friedrich* are commonly employed as terms of address. They indicate those with whom she has more interactions as compared to her sisters. Conversely, the nouns *Christopher*, *Columbus* and *bilge* always occur as exclamations, becoming a trademark of her rather colorful and expressive idiolect, for which she is sometimes frowned upon by her sisters.

(9) Jo March: Oh, **Christopher Columbus!** Look at that. (*Little Women*, Gerwig 2019)

A last remark could be made on *well*. Within its sixty-one concordances, forty-three correspond to uses as a discourse marker thus signaling the general informality that characterizes her interactions.

4.2.2. Meg March

One of the pivotal characteristics defining the dialogues, and thus also the personality, of Meg March is her adherence to conventions and her respectful behavior, which are especially conveyed by the words *thank*, *sorry* and *please*. The first two keywords are part of larger conventionalized routine formulae expressing gratitude (the first) or regret (the second) (10), the third one is also used in politeness rituals to indicate respect and courtesy in requests.

> (10) Amy March: I can pay for myself.
> Jo March: You will not come!
> Meg March: **I'm sorry**, my sweet, but Jo is right.
>
> (*Little Women*, Gerwig 2019)

This short exchange is emblematic of the difference between the personalities of Jo and Meg as far as politeness rituals are concerned. Jo uses a restrictive order to turn down her little sister's insistent requests to join her and Meg in their soiree. This constitutes what Brown and Levinson (1987) define as a face-threatening act menacing the negative face (i.e. a restriction of the hearer's personal freedom) of the hearer. Even though sharing the same position as Jo, Meg starts her turn with an apology that is accompanied by the endearment *sweet* (another keyword in her lines). Indeed, the evaluative words *sweet*, *nice*, *kind*, *lovely*, *poor*, *darling* as well as the expression of agreement *yes*, confirm her good, positive and compassionate disposition towards the others.

The nouns *John* and *Brooke* are most commonly terms of address that identify Meg's typical interactions. *John* is the man she marries. He is the tutor of her neighbour, Laurie, for whom she gives up her ambition to marry wealth. By looking at the concordances, it can be noticed that the first name *John* is used as an address only in scenes where the two characters are already acquainted. Conversely, his surname *Brooke*, preceded by the title *Mr*, is employed in first interactions before the two become intimate.

4.2.3. Amy March

The most distinguishing textual cues in Amy's dialogue appear to be evaluative adjectives. Differently from Jo and Meg, she frequently employs both positive evaluative adjectives (*pretty*; *elegant*) and, most typically, negative ones (*boyish*; *horrible*; *terrible*; *unladylike*; *rude, ashamed*). The concordances indicate that positive adjectives are generally targeted towards her sisters or Laurie and concern their appearance or their manners. This is very telling of her obsessions for aesthetics and good manners:

(11)   Laurie: Nice to meet you.
       Amy March: Oh, how **elegant**.

(*Little Women*, Cukor 1933)

Negative evaluations, instead, are either against things she hates, such as *school*, or they are addressed to her sister Jo, who refuses to submit to the conventions of ladyhood (12), which she takes as values to follow. In other words, Amy is Jo's foil.

(12)   Amy March: Jo! That's so **boyish**.
       Jo March: That's why I do it.

(*Little Women*, LeRoy 1949)

Also the keywords *wish* and *look* are quite revealing of the character's personality. *Wish* both occurs as a verb (thirteen hits) and as a noun (three hits) commonly expressing Amy's grandiose dreams (13). When it is a verb, it always colligates with the pronoun *I*, another keyword in her dialogue suggesting that she is rather self-centred as compared to her sisters.

(13)   Amy March: I have lots of **wishes**, but my favourite one is to be an artist in Paris and do fine pictures and be the best painter in the world. (*Little Women*, Gerwig 2019)

This line is also related to the passion for the arts that distinguishes Amy, confirmed by the keywords *pencil*, *draw* and *picture*.

The occurrences of *look* (twenty-four hits), of which nineteen as a verb, strengthen what emerged above concerning the character's passion for appearances:

(14)   Amy March: My nose will not simply **look** refined. (*Little Women*, Gerwig 2019)

Some last comments are in order on the word *statirical*. This rather peculiar word form, occurring in three out of the four film versions, is, in effect, a malapropism standing for 'satirical'. Especially in the first two adaptations, comic malapropisms are repeatedly used to characterize Amy's line and her wish to sound more grown up and refined, as testified by the following exchange between Amy and Jo, in which the younger sibling uses two malapropisms (*label* for 'libel' and *statirical* for 'satirical').

(15)   Amy March: Well, I don't think any of you suffer as I do, you don't have to go to that horrible school, with those impertinent girls who **label** your father, just because he's poor.

> Jo March: If you mean libel, then say so and stop saying label as if father was a pickle bottle.
> Amy March: I know what I mean and you needn't be '**statirical**' about that.
> Jo March: It's proper to use good words and improve one's vocabulary. (*Little Women*, LeRoy 1949)

4.2.4. Beth March

As the size of the subcorpus in Table 9.2 demonstrates, Beth is the least talkative among the four March sisters. Her most salient keywords clearly highlight the close relationship she has with her parents (*Marmee*; *father*), with her sisters (especially *Jo*) and her attachment to her *home* (16), which she also defines as a *nest*.

> (16) Beth March: I'd like the war to end so father can come **home**. (*Little Women*, Armstrong 1994)

The verbs *think*, *should* and *ought* are interesting keywords in terms of characterization, all pointing to the quiet and tentative attitude of Beth. For example, among the twenty-six occurrences of *think*, twelve have a hedging function lessening the impact of Beth's utterances and thus attenuating her position.

> (17) Meg March: We don't want any boys, this is a club for ladies!
> Beth March: I **think** we should leave him to do it. (*Little Women*, Gerwig 2019)

This contributes to building a discourse about humility and generosity around her character, which also surfaces from an attentive reading of the concordances of the keywords *Hummel, hungry, poor, sick, God*. These words revolve around the Hummel family, the poor German neighbuors of the March that Beth visits and from whom she catches the scarlet fever that will lead her to die like a heroine.

> (18) Meg March: You all haven't been to see the Hummel's. We should go.
> Jo March: Oh Bethy, we barely have enough food to feed ourselves. (*Little Women*, Gerwig 2019)

The sweet and gentle nature of Beth is also testified by the fourteen occurrences of *good*, which is used both as part of a leave taking formula (five hits) and as a positive evaluative adjective (nine hits). When it is used as a leave taking it is always targeted towards the mother, stressing their intimate relationship already emerged above.

(19) Beth March: **Good night**, Marmee. (*Little Women*, Cukor 1933)

Finally, as for Meg, *thank* is another important keyword expressing her polite, deferential and generous inclination.

5. The parallel concordance as a tool to compare the original and the dubbed dialogues

The parallel nature of LWT also allows for a systematic analysis of how key characterizing traits emerging from the character analysis are rendered in the Italian versions. In fact, the *Parallel Concordance* tool available on *Sketch Engine* represents an invaluable help to search translation correspondences. In short, it is a special type of concordancer for aligned parallel corpora that shows the occurrences of a search term or a phrase in its original context of use side by side the corresponding aligned segments in the target language corpus.

Figure 9.3 is a random sample of a parallel concordance taken from LWT. The search term taken as an example is *Marmee*, the famous idiolectal diminutive the March girls use both to refer to their mother in their interactions and as an affectionate vocative.

If we use the concordance interface to filter the 157 hits of *Marmee* according to the text types of the corpus, that is, the film versions, we can observe how the term was translated across the different adaptations of *Little Women*. Table 9.4 collects data referring to the distribution of *Marmee* in the corpus and its dubbing solutions.

doc#0	<s> No, Marmee . </s><s> I'm not tired. </s>	<s> No, mamma. </s><s> Non sono stanca </s>
doc#0	<s> Did you have a hard day, Marmee ? </s>	<s> Hai avuto una giornata faticosa, mamma? </s>
doc#0	<s> Let's... </s><s> Let's get something for Marmee with our dollar instead of for ourselves, shall we? </s>	<s> Ma, se coi nostri dollari comprassimo un regalo per mamma invece che per noi, che ne dite? </s>
doc#0	<s> Good night, Marmee </s>	<s> Buonanotte, mamma </s>

Figure 9.3 Sample of the parallel concordance of *Marmee* in LWT

Table 9.4 Distribution of *Marmee* in LWT and its dubbing solutions

	Marmee	**Dubbing solutions**
1933	50	mamma 42; Ø 8
1949	58	mamma 30; mami 23; mammina 5; Ø 1
1994	31	mami 25; mamma 6
2019	18	mami 18

As can be noticed, in the 1933 version the translation is always with the standard Italian noun *mamma* ('mum'), or, in some cases, the term is omitted. In the 1949 remake the translating solutions are more varied. Apart from *mamma* (thirty hits), which is still the most frequent option, *mami* (>'mummy') (twenty-three hits) is another recurrent translation. In fact, *mami* is a hypocoristic form of *mamma* that preserves the endearment connotation triggered by original term. In this film, both forms are used by the March sisters as a term of address or when talking about their mother. Interestingly, by filtering the concordances according to the speaker, we can observe that in Amy's turns *Marmee* is rendered as *mammina* (five hits) (>'little mummy'), a diminutive version of *mami* that expresses a rather higher degree of affection. The exchange in Table 9.5 is an illustrative example.

Table 9.5 Translation of *Marmee* in an exchange from *Little Women* (LeRoy 1949)

	Original	Italian dub
Jo March	Good bye, Marmee.	Buon viaggio, mami.
Beth March	Good bye, Marmee.	Arrivederci, mami.
Meg March	Good bye.	Arrivederci.
Amy March	Good bye, Marmee.	Ciao, mammina.
Mrs March	God bless us all.	Dio ci protegga tutti.

The translation of *Marmee* as 'mammina' also triggers a shift in the closing formula that it accompanies, which is not rendered with the formal/neutral leave taking *arrivederci* (>'good bye'), but with the more colloquial *ciao* (>'bye bye'). This dubbing choice could be meant to emphasize the extreme mannerism and affectation of the character of Amy, which, especially in LeRoy's adaptation, is particularly evident. In 1994 Armstrong's film, *mami* (twenty-five hits) outdoes the neutral *mamma* (six hits). By looking at the occurrences, it emerges that in this case the translation is constrained by the function of the term in the source text. The former option is used when *Marmee* corresponds to a vocative, the latter when the girls talk about their mother. Finally, in the latest 2019 adaptation *mami* is used as the only equivalent of *Marmee*, signaling a general tendency towards coherence in translation options.

5.1. An insight into apologies and their Italian dubbing

One of the most represented speech acts in the turns of the four March sisters, which contributes to characterizing their polite and respectful behaviour, is apologizing. Drawing on Searle (1969) and Goffman (1971), Holmes (1990: 164) defines apologies as 'a speech act addressed to B's face-needs and intended to remedy an offence for which A takes responsibility, and thus to restore equilibrium between A and B (where A is the apologizer, and B is the person offended)'. Hence, it is a remedial speech act through which the apologizer attempts to re-establish harmony with the other party thus balancing politeness relations between interlocutors. Contrary to other expressive speech acts (e.g. compliments), apologies are most of times explicit and ritualistic (Aijmer 1996, Coulmas 1981) meaning that English speakers tend to apologize by resorting to a rather routinized array of forms and constructions. This makes them particularly suitable for corpus-based analysis (Deutschmann 2003).

Hence, *Sketch Engine* parallel concordancer was used to query LWT starting from the eight words identified by Deutschmann (2003) as the core words for expressing an apology in English (i.e. *afraid, apologize, apology, excuse, forgive, pardon, regret* and *sorry*[5]) so as to get a full picture of the representation and the dubbing of explicit apologies in the corpus. Thanks to the tagging system of LWT, results could also be filtered according to the identity of the March sister and the film version. Moreover, concordances were qualitatively evaluated and filtered to leave out occurrences where the searched terms did not occur as apologies. Table 9.6 offers a breakdown of the results of this search.[6]

On a surface level, we can observe that not only in the 1933 and the 1949 originals apologies are less frequent than in the more recent adaptations, but they are also repeatedly omitted in the Italian dubbings. Generally speaking, in these older film versions, the translation of apologies seems to lean towards flattening. For example, emphatic expressions of regret in the turns of Jo and Meg, whose illocutionary intent is reinforced by degree adverbs such as *so* and *truly*, are rendered with the standard and non-emphatic *mi dispiace* (>'I'm sorry'), reducing the illocutionary force of the utterance and thus the emotional involvement.

On the contrary, in the 1994 and the 2019 films apologies are generally more frequent than in the previous ones and they are never omitted in the dubbed versions. Moreover, in different occasions the Italian dubbing also reinforces the illocutionary intent of the apology by adding the emphatic adjective *tanto* (>'very much'). This shift that concerns the degree and the intensity of the apology regularly happens in Jo's lines in the 1994 film and both in Jo's and Meg's lines in the 2019 film.

Table 9.6 Apologies in LWT

		1933		1949		1994		2019	
		Original	Dub	Original	Dub	Original	Dub	Original	Dub
apology	Jo					(1) My apologies	(1) mi dispiace molto		
excuse	Jo			(2) Excuse me	(2) Vogliate Scusarmi			(4) Excuse me	(1) chiedo scusa (2) scusatemi (1) scusa
	Meg								
Forgive	Meg			(2) forgive me	(1) scusatemi (1)	(1) forgive her	(1) Perdonala		
pardon	Jo	(2) I beg your pardon	(1) vi chiedo scusa (1) ti chiedo perdono						
	Meg	(1) I beg your pardon	(1) vi chiedo scusa						

Sorry	Jo	(3) I'm sorry	(2) scusatemi (1) Ø	(1) I'm sorry truly	(1) mi dispiace	(5) I'm sorry	(2) I'm sorry (1) mi dispiace (1) scusa
		(1) I'm so sorry	(1) mi dispiace	(2) I'm so sorry	(1) mi dispiace (1) Ø	(3) mi dispiace tanto (1) mi dispiace (1) scusate	(1) sorry (1) scusate
							(4) I'm so sorry (3) mi dispiace tanto (1) vi chiedo scusa
	Meg	(1) sorry	(1) Ø	(2) I'm sorry	(1) mi spiace (1) avete ragione	(3) I'm sorry (3) mi dispiace	(7) I'm sorry (4) mi dispiace (3) mi dispiace tanto
		(1) I'm so sorry	(1) mi dispiace	(1) I'm so sorry	(1) mi spiace	(2) I'm so sorry (1) mi dispiace tanto (1) chiedo scusa	(2) I'm so sorry (2) mi dispiace tanto
	Amy					(2) I'm sorry (2) mi dispiace	(3) I'm sorry (3) mi dispiace tanto
							(1) I feel sorry (1) mi dispiace tanto
							(1) I am the most sorry (1) sono dispiaciutissima
	Beth	(1) I'm sorry	(1) sono dispiaciuta				(1) I'm sorry (1) mi dispiace
		10	8	10	8	14	14	26	26

6. Wrap-up

This chapter attempted to illustrate how corpus linguistics methods could be applied to the study of characterization in English original and Italian dubbed film dialogues. The case study on the cinematic adaptations of *Little Women* in their original and translated versions was meant as a practical application of the methodology described throughout the paper.

The accurate description of the compilation of LWT presented some practical steps that can be followed and replicated to compile any type of parallel corpus of dialogic exchanges. The distinctive trait of this English-Italian parallel corpus is that it has a double level of mark-up so as to keep track both of the textual structure of each text and of the different corpus components. Such a mark-up adds value to the corpus in that it allows for the isolation of some parts of the corpus that can be queried alone, thus extending the range of research questions that the corpus can answer. This is particularly valuable for textual analysis, for which extra-linguistic information (e.g. the identity of the speaker) are crucial for the interpretation of the results.

The character-based analysis carried out through the extraction and the evaluation of the keywords in the dialogues of the four March sisters was aimed to identify the most distinguishing textual cues that contribute to their characterization. The results brought to light a series of salient lexical and pragmatic features that are used to profile the four characters and that contribute to their portrayal in front of the audience.

Given the parallel nature of the corpus, LWT could also be used to assess translation choices in the Italian dubbed dialogues. The analysis of the dubbing solutions of the noun *Marmee* and of apologies was taken as a sample to showcase how *Sketch Engine* parallel concordance can be exploited to compare and contrast originals with translated texts in a systematic way. Through the evaluation of the dubbing of apologies, for example, it could be noticed that their translation sometimes redefines the degree of intensity: in older films there is a tendency to downgrade the force of the speech act, whereas in the more recent ones it is often fostered to emphasize emotionality and commitment.

Notes

1 Available at: https://www.sketchengine.eu/guide/.

2   Corpora are sorted by size. From now on, the same order is followed throughout the study.
3   Keywords were calculated automatically by the *Keywords and terms* extractor tool of *Sketch Engine*, by leaving the settings as default. For overview of how keyness scores are calculated, see Kilgarriff *et al.* (2004).
4   Only sentences expressing a negative meaning were considered for this count. Jo's negative sentences are 478 out of the 1,588 present in the whole corpus.
5   All these words were searched as lemmas so as to include all relevant inflections (e.g. *apologies, excuses* and the like).
6   The words *afraid, apologize* and *regret* were excluded from Table 9.6 as they do not occur as apologies in LWT. The values between round brackets are the raw number of occurrences.

References

Aijmer, K. (1996), *Conversational Routines in English: Convention and Creativity*, London: Longman.

Baker, M. (1993), 'Corpus Linguistics and Translation Studies: Implications and Applications', in M. Baker, G. Francis and E. Tognini-Bonelli (eds), *Text and Technology: In Honour of John Sinclair*, 233–50, Amsterdam: John Benjamins.

Baker, M. (1996), 'Corpus-based Translation Studies: The Challenges That Lie ahead', in H. Somers (ed.), *Terminology, LSP and Translation*, 175–86, Amsterdam: John Benjamins.

Baños Piñero, R., S. Bruti and S. Zanotti (2013), 'Corpus Linguistics and Audiovisual Translation: In Search of an Integrated Approach', *Perspectives*, 21 (4): 1–7.

Bednarek, M. (2012a), 'Constructing "nerdiness": Characterisation in the Big Bang Theory', *Multilingua*, 31: 199–229.

Bednarek, M. (2012b), '"Get us the Hell out of here": Key Words and Trigrams in Fictional Television Series', *International Journal of Corpus Linguistics*, 17 (1): 35–63.

Bonsignori, V. (2009), 'Transcribing Film Dialogue: From Orthographic to Prosodic Transcription', in M. Freddi, Maria (ed.), *Analysing Audiovisual Dialogue: Linguistic and Translational Insights*, 185–200, Bologna: CLUEB.

Brown, P. and S. C. Levinson (1987), *Politeness: Some Universals in Language Usage*, Cambridge: Cambridge University Press.

Bruti, S. (2003), 'Reporting Signals in Fiction: *Little Women* and Its Italian Translations', *Rassegna Italiana di Linguistica Applicata*, 35 (3): 61–86.

Bruti, S. and G. Vignozzi (2021), 'The Representation of Spoken Discourse in *Little Women*: A Journey through Its Original and Dubbed Versions', *Textus*, 24 (1): 23–46.

Chaume, F. (2012), *Audiovisual Translation: Dubbing*, London/New York: Routledge.

Coulmas, F. (1981), 'Poison to Your Soul: Thanks and Apologies Contrastively Viewed', in F. Coulmas (ed.), *Conversational Routine: Exploration in Standardized Communication Situations and Prepatterned Speech*, 69–91, The Hague: Mouton.

Culpeper, J. (2001), *Language and Characterisation: People in Plays and Other Texts*, Harlow: Longman.

Deutschmann, M. (2003), *Apologising in British English*, Umeå: Umeå University.

Díaz-Cintas, J. (2008), 'Introduction: Audiovisual Translation Comes of Age', in D. Chiaro (ed.), *Between Text and Image*, 1–9, Amsterdam: John Benjamins.

Díaz Cintas, J. and A. Remael (2007), *Audiovisual Translation: Subtitling*, Manchester: St. Jerome.

Goffman, E. (1971), *Relations in Public*, New York: Basic Books.

Gregory, M. and S. Carroll (1978), *Language and Situation. Language Varieties and Their Social Contexts*, London: Routledge.

Holmes, J. (1990), 'Apologies in New Zealand English', *Language in Society*, 19: 155–99. Available online: /10.1017/S0047404500014366 (accessed 6 June 2021).

Johansson, S. (2007), *Seeing through Multilingual Corpora: On the Use of Corpora in Contrastive Studies*, Amsterdam: John Benjamins.

Kenny, D. (2001), *Lexis and Creativity in Translation*, Manchester: St. Jerome.

Kilgarriff, A., P. Rychlý, P. Smrz and D. Tugwell (2004), 'The Sketch Engine', in G. Williams and S. Vessier (eds), *Proceedings Eleventh EURALEX International Congress*, 105–15, Lorient: Université de Bretagne-Sud.

Laviosa, S. (2002), *Corpus-based Translation Studies: Theory, Findings, Applications*, Amsterdam: Rodopi.

Lazzeretti, C. (2019), 'The Characterization of Daisy Mason in the British Drama Downton Abbey', *Series-International Journal of TV Serial Narratives*, 5 (1): 33–44.

Leitch, T., ed. (2017), *The Oxford Handbook of Adaptation Studies*, Oxford: Oxford University Press.

McEnery, T., R. Xiao and Y. Tono (2006), *Corpus-based Language Studies: An Advance Resource Book*, London: Routledge.

McEnery, T. and R. Xiao (2008), 'Parallel and Comparable Corpora: What Is Happening?', in G. Anderman, (ed.), *Incorporating Corpora: The Linguist and the Translator*, 18–31, Frankfurt: Multilingual Matters.

Oakes, M. P. and M. Ji (2012), *Quantitative Methods in Corpus-based Translation Studies. A Practical Guide to Descriptive Translation Research*, Amsterdam: John Benjamins.

Pavesi, M. (2014), 'The Pavia Corpus of Film Dialogue: A Means to Several Ends', in M. Pavesi (ed.), *The Languages of Dubbing. Mainstream Audiovisual Translation in Italy*, 29–55, Bern: Peter Lang.

Pavesi, M. (2019), 'Corpus-based Audiovisual Translation Studies: Ample Room for Development', in L. Pérez-González (ed.), *The Routledge Handbook of Audiovisual Translation Studies*, 315–33, London: Routledge.

Pavesi, M., M. Formentelli and E. Ghia, eds (2014), *The Languages of Dubbing: Mainstream Audiovisual Translation in Italy*, Bern: Peter Lang.

Searle, J. (1969), *Speech Acts: An Essay in the Philosophy of Language*, Cambridge: Cambridge University Press.

Sinclair, J. (1991), *Corpus, Concordance, Collocation*, Oxford: Oxford University Press.

Sinclair, J. (1992), 'The Automatic Analysis of Corpora', in J. Svartvik (ed.), *Directions in Corpus Linguistics*, 379–400, Berlin: Mouton de Gruyter.

Taylor, C. (1999), 'The Translation of Film Dialogue', *Translation Studies Revisited*, Special Issue of *Textus*, 13 (2): 443–58.

Taylor, C. (2004), 'The Language of Film: Corpora and Statistics in the Search for Authenticity. Notting Hill (1998) - A Case Study', *Miscelanea*, 30, 71–86.

Taylor, C. (2014), 'Multimodality and Audiovisual Translation', in Y. Gambier (ed.), *Handbook of Translation Studies*, 98–104, Amsterdam: John Benjamins.

Toury, G. ([1995]2012), *Descriptive Translation Studies and beyond*, Amsterdam: John Benjamins.

Filmography

Little Women, Dir. George Cukor. RKO Radio Pictures, USA, 1933.

Little Women, Dir. Mervin LeRoy. A Mervyn LeRoy Production, produced by Loew's Incorporated, Metro-Goldwyn-Mayer, USA, 1949.

Little Women, Dir. Gillian Armstrong. Columbia Pictures, Sony Pictures Releasing, USA, 1994.

Little Women, Dir. Greta Gerwig. Columbia Pictures, Regency Pictures, Pascal Pictures, Sony Pictures Releasing, USA, 2019.

Subtitling in the digital era: TV crime drama series in domestic languages

Alessandra Rizzo

1. Introduction

As put in Chaume's terms, the new world of audiovisual media is marked by digital transformation, where '*[d]igitisation* refers to the technical conversion of analogue information into digital form', whereas '*[d]igitalisation* […] refers to the actual process of change in industries' (Chaume 2019: 103). Digital transformation is the '*effect* of digitization and digitalization on society' (ibidem), whose result is the increasing number of new generations of audiences who exploit and require the use of new digital devices. All this enables change and innovation when it comes to the consumption of all forms of audiovisual translation (henceforth AVT), and also of two or more AVT modes simultaneously. Digital transformations therefore involve

> the possibility to choose the (preferred) AVT mode (unlike the past, when audiences were obliged to consume dubbed products in dubbing countries, subtitled products in subtitling countries and voice-over products in voice-over countries).
>
> (Ibid.: 107)

This study is set within the context of extensive academic attention to and exploration of audio and visual data as resources, methods and practices in the Digital Humanities (henceforth DH) (Gallitelli 2016). DH are seen and understood 'as a large and heterogeneous container that accommodates different research areas and affects various media. It is a relatively young field of study, inextricably linked to the development of information technologies' (Gallitelli 2016: 53, my translation), within which the audiovisual dimension plays a central role. Audiovisual texts as forms of knowing, learning and entertaining have recently achieved a strategic position in the field of DH alongside current advances in computing. The digital access to audiovisual materials such as media communication and the visual arts has favoured the dissemination of digitalized audiovisual collections through for- and/or non-profit platforms, thereby enabling the circulation of audiovisual materials online.

It goes without saying that AVT and the digital spread of television programmes and series, films and documentaries as translated products have stimulated scholarly research on corpus-based studies combined with contrastive linguistic analyses of a variety of dubbed, subtitled and audio described products in different languages. Although audiovisual materials are often subject to degrees of copyright and access restrictions – often dictated by large multimedia producers – digital humanist research on certain digital collections and archives, such as television news programmes, feature films and TV series, has grown exponentially, and is contributing to the production of increasingly cutting-edge forms of experimentation in the field of AVT. In this context, the digital localization of audiovisual products – occurring now on a daily basis – has offered a wider choice to audiences, as well as 'a growing diversity in audiovisual content consumption and in the use of different translation practices' (Chaume 2019: 104). While accepting the need to view AVT in its wider scope, encompassing newer practices which are merging due to digitalization, we also have to look at patterns of internationally distributed formats that are systematically localized for other markets, thus encouraging the foreignization of digital genres, on the one hand, and their domestication within targeted contexts, on the other. In this pervasively digital world, humanities have the opportunity to broaden and rethink goals within the area of localized audiovisual forms of translation functioning on target levels.

In the context of digital TV crime drama series disseminated across streaming platforms, the scrutiny of original dialogues compared with their Italian translations (subtitles), and of interlingual subtitles produced in different languages, has the potential to shed light on the type of language which target publics are exposed to when they watch the audiovisual product itself in its subtitled version. First of all, this study describes and compares the linguistic features of original dialogues (in English) and their Netflix subtitles (in Italian), and of Netflix subtitles in English and Italian (where the English subtitles are used as templates (pivots) for the translation from Icelandic and Finnish originals into languages other than English). Then, the focus shifts to the strategies of interlingual translation that are employed for the creation of localized Italian subtitles which provide the accessibility of international TV crime drama series addressed to

Italian audiences as Internet consumers of digital products. Research is carried out by drawing on Halliday's concept of language as the expression of social reality within the context of Systemic Functional Linguistics (henceforth SFL) (1978, Halliday and Matthiessen 2004), together with the study of the sociocultural context of communication involved in the utterances chosen for the analysis within the selection of taxonomies of translation strategies (Gottlieb, 1992, Díaz Cintas and Remael, 2007, Ranzato, 2016).

Within the framework of a qualitative analysis of selected subtitles, the survey of translation strategies aims to pay attention to the linguistic features conveyed for the target audience. Attention is therefore given to the scrutiny of the most frequent translation strategies, recognizable in the Italian subtitled versions of the episodes in the TV crime drama series in question. The combination of two methods of investigation, that is, Functional Grammar (for the purpose of sociocultural analysis applied to recurrent language units used in communicative events) and taxonomical models of translation strategies (for the purpose of translation analysis with regard to the rendering of linguo-cultural features in Italian subtitling), has the purpose of showing to what extent the creation of Italian subtitles can contribute to the realization of unequivocal culture-specific frameworks within the setting of a local grammar (Hunston and Sinclair 2000), which appears to be functional to the identification of crime series as a digital genre in a (g)local dimension (i.e. Italian consumers of digital crime dramas).

For the purpose of this research, a Corpus of Police Procedurals has been compiled. It is an English–Italian parallel corpus including three episodes of contemporary police procedurals which contains, on the one hand, a transcript of source dialogues (English original) and its Italian subtitles and, on the other hand, the Netflix subtitles (English and Italian as language pairs). The three episodes belong to three different TV police crime dramas set in different geographical areas: the Icelandic *The Valhalla Murders* (henceforth *TVM*) (RÚV 2019, Netflix, BBC Four 2020), the Finnish *Deadwind* (originally *Karppi*, Yle TV2 2018, Netflix 2020) and the English *Luther* (BBC One 2010; Fox Crime, Netflix 2011). Against the backdrop of the phenomenon of digitalization of crime drama series in different languages through AVT, this chapter sheds light on the language employed in the interlingual translation of Netflix English, Icelandic and Finnish crime drama series into Italian. This multitude of digital subtitles as standardized and neutral written text types can become depositaries of culture-bound meanings belonging to source language (SL) genres (English, Icelandic and Finnish crime genres as the cases in point) and their relevant culture-specific features, and also containers of the linguistic and cultural elements relative to the domestic genres according to the conventions expected at the level of the target language (TL) and culture. In the process of interlingual transfer, forms of manipulation and adaptation are practised in order to recreate the genre within target-oriented contexts, that is, crime drama series are made more locally recognizable for the benefit of target audiences. In this way, subtitled languages are instrumental in the recreation of original digital genres by means of communicative and dynamic approaches to translation, thus strengthening the mobility of audiovisual genres.

After brief introductory sections focusing on the frameworks in which digital subtitling and crime genres are embedded, and on the translation settings by means of which these genres are internationally disseminated, the question of methodology is introduced, and the corpus is presented and observed from two perspectives, where linguistic analysis and translating strategies merge. On one level, the analysis is based on the investigation of the language choices in characters' dialogues in light of Halliday's interpersonal metafunction (i.e. the clause as exchange and the result of interaction based on speech functions) and also, partially, of the textual metafunction dimension (i.e. the text as message). On a second level, linguistic and translating differences and similarities in the context of English oral dialogues and Italian subtitles, and of subtitles in English and Italian, are taken into account in order to answer the following research questions: (a) to what extent is subtitling a fundamental translation resource for the spread of digital genres? (b) is it possible to talk about a local grammar (i.e. syntactic and lexical features as the most salient features in the context of arrival) as marking crime drama series in terms of genre-orientation in the target context (the Italian one)?

The final section illustrates the results and draws conclusive remarks.

2. Subtitling in digital settings

Today the vast tradition of English, Finnish and Icelandic crime genres appears digitally constructed and, to a very great extent, relies on processes of translation in a multitude of languages, since their accessibility depends on AVT modes, chiefly subtitling and dubbing, but also subtitling for the deaf and the hard of hearing and audio description for the blind and visually impaired, these last groups benefiting mostly from intralingual translation modes. The role of translation in the context of crime drama series is reinforced by the belief that since 'language [...] is precisely the only part of the audiovisual product that may be altered by translation professionals' (Arias-Badia 2020: 34), each final product is the result of translating strategies applied to subtitling for the benefit of target users.

Subtitling as the most common modality within AVT technologies is by definition one of the fundamental instruments by means of which human cultures are digitally spread. It is in particular the adoption of new digital applications and techniques that marks the relationship between the humanities and the digital world, where DH exploit technology (e.g. the technologization of subtitling) in the pursuit of humanities research, while interrogating technology in a line of humanistic questioning (Svensson 2010). Significant scholarly attention has been given to research on the implications of digital transformation in the processes of AVT – from the technological developments as key points in the description and application of AVT in international communication settings to localization processes fostering new audiences, and impacting reception at a target level (Di Giovanni and Gambier 2018, Chaume 2019, Díaz Cintas and Massidda 2020).

As a result of the enormous growth of subscription video-on-demand (SVoDs) platforms, among which are Netflix and Amazon Prime Video, digital series produced in different parts of the globe convey (foreign) contents (e.g. Icelandic and Finnish TV crime genres domesticated into Italian and many more languages) and are streamed both in their original languages and in numerous target languages. In the 1990s, developments in the subtitling industry evolved to the extent that sophisticated subtitling technologies took control of the spread of subtitles across channels, platforms and TV genres (Georgakopoulou 2018: 517).

In a nutshell, the widespread introduction of Information Technology in the field of media communication, while giving birth to 'the creation, production, distribution and potential manipulation of new audiovisual contents' (Chaume 2019: 104), has also raised digital technology to a pivotal role in the booming market of localization practices, where DH are involved. In line with Chaume's position, 'localization' is here used to refer to 'any kind of audiovisual translation – dubbing, subtitling, voiceover, subtitling for the deaf and the hard of hearing, audio description, surtitling, respeaking, etc. – and any kind of media adaptation – format licensing, adaptations, transcreations and remakes –' (ibidem), by means of which audiovisual products are digitally transmitted and reshaped within target contexts and the confines of language systems. The humanities – used as an umbrella term which includes the media and the arts – are today increasingly digitalized products, resulting from a process involving the 'multiplication of audiovisual distribution platforms and devices' (ibidem), and epitomizing 'the so-called age of convergence [...] where an audiovisual product can be broadcast across multiple platforms and formats through the use of current digital technologies' (ibidem). This has increased the coexistence of the global and local nature of localized products, and has facilitated comparative research on processes of adaptation of source culture (SC) into target culture (TC) ideologies and perspectives, within which translated audiovisual contents have encouraged the dissemination of fields and sub-fields within DH. In particular, the media and the visual arts, which have grown within the context of digital distribution channels, are reaching a wider audience thanks to the ever-increasing demand for AVT digital services.

Digitalized AVT has rendered DH inclusive by the removal of cultural and linguistic barriers, as well as the physical ones. The subtitling revolution can be considered 'a real catalyst which has accelerated all the changes recently witnessed' (Díaz Cintas 2010b: 109). From the distribution perspective, digital subtitles have stimulated 'greater dynamism in the traffic of audiovisual material, to the extent that exchanges are now instantaneous' (ibidem) and collaboration settings and amateur translation have grown exponentially. It is well accepted that an audiovisual text is the perfect combination of several elements belonging to the spheres of visual, verbal (verbal and non-verbal) and acoustic codes. In TV crime genres as part of DH, efforts are made in order to reproduce orality through the frequent use of short sentences and minimal responses, interjections and voiced hesitations, topicalisations, interruptions, informal colloquial speech, to list but a few, all of which give shape to social relationships and mark the interpersonal-interactional level which is fundamental to the creation of apparently spontaneous conversations. Therefore, translated communicative events play a crucial role in terms of genre recognition, since they indicate the peculiar traits of characters' identities and roles, as well as the context of situation in which actions occur. Therefore, the adaptation of a digital series is somehow part of the realm of localization, which implies that foreign products have to fit in the new target cultures and their translations are often influenced by existing domestic products belonging to the same genre (Cattrysse 2014).

Italian subtitling in the context of crime series is constructed through the use of linguistic items and structural devices that are supposed to satisfy the expectations of an audience which is accustomed to the conventionalized forms of the digital genre under examination and expects to find certain recurrent linguistic features. However, subtitles are, generally speaking, neutral, standardized and simple (Díaz-Cintas 2010a), which means that a certain number of the prototypical linguistic features of spoken language is lost. These features involve what is referred to as the 'prefabricated orality' (Baños Piñero and Chaume 2009, online) or 'fictive orality' (Arias-Badia 2020: 106–7) found in TV dialogues: screenwriters have linguistic resources at their disposal 'with which to elaborate believable dialogues that, despite having been carefully planned in advance, can be identified by viewers as true-to-life conversation' (Baños Piñero and Chaume 2009, online). When it comes to subtitling, what emerges is that 'some conversational features are eliminated from subtitles because this modality of audiovisual translation involves a transfer from oral to written discourse, which, in turn, entails the need for a significant amount of text reduction' (Bruti 2019: 193). This implies that Italian subtitles only partially imitate seemingly spontaneous conversations (more natural, dynamic and creative than written language).

3. The digital universe of TV genres: crime drama series

Crime dramatizations (Turnbull 2014, Piper 2015) are dominating our television and web screens, and the appetite for crime series (most of them, police procedurals) shows no signs of abating in 2021. BBC, ITV, SKY, Netflix, Rai Play, Discovery Channel, Amazon Prime, are airing dramas based on awful cases of murder and also feature acclaimed actors in the role of real-life serial killers.

The success of streaming services is rooted in the popularity of mobile devices around the world. In a binary perspective, Netflix is both a 'disruptor' and 'cultural institution' (Barker and Wiatrowski 2017), an art form able to adapt traditional television models to the Internet landscape. Research relating to the dissemination of crime drama genres and subgenres streamed on the Internet in different languages through subtitling and dubbing (Arias-Badia and Brumme 2014, Laudisio 2018, Sandrelli 2018, 2020, Arias-Badia 2020) continues to increase, especially from the perspective of localization intended as a 'hypernym for any kind of audiovisual translation' (Chaume 2019: 104), thus strengthening the increase of diversity in audiovisual content consumption.

Although some genres have never been part of TV programming grids (Mittell 2004), they are however recognized as such due to textual and content recurrences common to certain genres. As remarked in recent research, TV crime dramas (Turnbull 2014) are at 'the crossroads between fiction, specialized discourse and evocation of everyday conversation' (Arias-Badia and Brumme 2014: 110). There are a variety of crime genre types, such as detective, forensic/medical, procedural, etc. Some give more attention to action, while others, such as *Luther*, include conventions from different genres such as thriller genres. Subgenres may include broad categories of mystery, detective and crime, overlapping and open to subjective interpretation. Some of the widely recognized categories, which are rooted in the literary tradition, are mysteries, classic detective, police procedurals and thrillers, all of which have a basic set of structural components such as catching criminals or villains who threaten social order, and deduction and resolution.

The series under scrutiny have been chosen because they are comparable on both linguistic and thematic levels. They represent mystery, detective, thriller and crime dramas as a macro genre within which it is possible to identify police procedurals (also highly psychological and based on thriller effects) and Nordic Noir as subgenres. Key plot conventions of crime dramas involve: (a) committing and solving crimes; (b) medical, forensic and procedural investigations; (c) fictional accounts of real-life stories; (d) titles of the show as regularly eponymous (e.g. *Luther*, *Karppi* in the Finnish original); (e) the setting is usually the city and its suburbs; (f) the main character contrasts with the authority/the boss or the partner in crime; (g) typical character types include heroes and villains; (h) the story moves from patterns of chaos to the discovery of the crime that leads to a new equilibrium, then leading to the solving of the crime; (i) narrative connection among multiple episodes.

The background of Scandinavian (*Deadwind*) and Icelandic (*TVM*) crimes, which have attracted and entertained international audience with their dark, suspenseful and enthralling stories, their grey city streets, snowy landscapes, brutal crimes, tortured detectives and often strong female leads, share common features with the London-based crime episodes (*Luther*) which are embedded in the 1950s Noir conventions such as dark lighting, industrial gritty settings, female characters' pale faces with red lipstick as the symbol of the *femme fatale* (i.e. Alice Morgan in *Luther*) and reds and blacks as crime drama genre iconography.

4. The corpus and methodology

The series taken as case studies, *Luther*, *TVM*, *Deadwind*, are distributed in their original idioms by Netflix, as well as dubbed and subtitled in a myriad of languages. The data analysed in this research are part of the collection and transcription of all the episodes of the three series taken into account. However, for the purpose of this survey, the corpus of this analysis is based on a subcorpus that is composed of the first three pilot episodes of each series, as they are adequately representative of the linguistic and thematic traits of the conventions in TV crime dramas. As already anticipated in the introductory section, original language dialogues and translated (subtitled) versions (with regard to *Luther*), as well as the two sets of parallel subtitles (in *TVM* and *Deadwind*, the English subtitles function as both the template and target language, whereas the Italian subtitles function as a targeted version), have been manually transcribed and, therefore, are verbatim records of the authentic dialogue lines recited by the actors. Therefore, in the crime series in Finnish and Icelandic, English has been used as the language of departure. In fact, it has become common practice in digital settings to make use of English templates to provide translations into other languages. This signifies that in the context of DH, TV genres and subgenres are disseminated in their source languages as niche languages, but are mostly widely spread in their English versions or translated from English into other languages. This clearly puts emphasis on the role of English as the pivotal language that has gained the privileged position of de facto lingua franca worldwide.

The examples taken from the three episodes do not intend to be exhaustive, but are meant to offer an overview of translated crime genres, as they are linguistically and culturally represented through digital Italian subtitles (the final products as object of study), which are the expression of the genre itself in its written form, and also recognizable on the target level. Accordingly, manual annotations of the corpus have been undertaken and the results presented are those I have deemed as qualitatively most relevant.

The subcorpus (the sum of the three episodes) contains linguistic features taken from the fields of criminal investigation in legal, medical and police settings, and develops sequences based on recurrent themes, character and setting types, and prototypical narrative sequences accompanied by specific linguistic structures, which contribute to the phenomenon of genre recognition and pose challenges for Italian subtitling practices.

4.1 The corpus

The Valhalla Murders, *Brot* in Icelandic, literally meaning 'violation', is a police procedural or police crime drama, where attention is given to the investigative procedures conducted by a female police officer. Created and directed by Þórður Pálsson, and produced by Truenorth and Mystery Productions for RÚV, *TVM* is an eight-episode police procedural television series produced and originally aired in Island in 2019. The Icelandic crime series was then digitally released worldwide on Netflix in 2020, and also aired for free on BBC Four in the UK. The series explores serial murders which are set in Nordic Noir environments in Reykjavik, where Kata and Arnar collaborate to solve police cases and brutal murders.

Luther, a dark psychological crime drama, includes features belonging to the thriller (i.e. low key lighting, intense non-diegetic music, sirens, the *femme fatale* character) and to the horror genre, too. Created by BBC Drama Production and first distributed by BBC Studios in 2010, the British series ran for five seasons for a total number of twenty episodes on Netflix. It was written by Neil Cross with the purpose of reflecting current attitudes towards the role of women in society and attitudes towards racial equality. The narratives, often constructed as inverted detective stories, contain non-linear elements in the form of flashbacks, narrative strands and are articulated by Propp's character types (i.e. the hero, the villain, the helper, etc.).

The high-quality Nordic Noir, *Deadwind,* composed of twenty episodes distributed in two seasons, was created and directed by Rike Jokela, and premiered in Finland in March 2018 on Yle TV2 and in August 2018 on Netflix. The show introduces eponymous homicide detective Sofia Karppi, of the Finnish police, who is recently widowed in her 1930s with two children. Karppi buries herself in her work, almost to the point of neglecting her own two children. Clearly used to working her investigations alone, she is at first rather hostile towards her new partner, detective Sakari Nurmi, recently transferred from the financial crime unit to the homicide unit.

4.2. Methodology

The qualitative analysis concentrates on two sets of language data, which relate to the concept of clause as exchange in light of the sociocultural framework described in Halliday's SFL (i.e. interpersonal meanings and relations established between interlocutors involved in the language event according to social and discourse roles). The two linguistic sets involve: (a) morpho-syntactic realizations within the context of speech functions taking the form of interactional sequences of propositions and/or proposals: offers, commands, statements and questions; and (b) paralinguistic cues (vocal interferences, pauses both silent and filled, interruptions, overlaps). The typical traits of orality in crime drama series consist of a wide range of repeated linguistic features (within which lexical elements such as word repetitions, titles, specialized lexicon, etc. are also relevant) including above all interrogative clauses, pragmatic markers (marking speakers' personal meanings, organizational choices, attitudes and feelings), ellipsis, unfinished constructions. The recurrent kind of communicative events occurs within the context of interaction involving (a) police superiors and subordinates; (b) police officers and criminals; (c) friends and families.

To begin with, the first step is to identify the linguistic features in the original English dialogues and in the English templates within the framework of Halliday's SFL, since clauses are identified as interactive events involving two or more interlocutors (speaker-listener) engaged in social and discoursal relations based on their assuming social roles. In subtitling, 'manipulative behaviour' (Bruti 2019: 197) mostly impinges on the interpersonal dimension, thus resulting in 'the cleaning up of expressive markers' (ibidem). In Halliday's terms, the tenor (concerning the people involved in the language event) reveals the features of language and, specifically, the lexico-grammatical resources which have been chosen in order to construe the interaction. In particular, communicative functions are construed within the context of clauses by means of lexico-grammatical choices made within the mood system, which plays a special role in carrying out the interpersonal function of the clause. One particular component of the clause involved in grammatical variation is the mood block carrying 'the burden of the clause as an interactive event' (Halliday and Matthiessen 2004: 120).

In the second place, the second step is to evaluate how the range of repeated linguistic features (i.e. the use of situational ellipsis, pragmatic markers, specialized lexicon, interrogative clauses, etc.) which, as remarked by Arias-Badia and Brumme (2014), represent the stereotyped language in criminal drama series, are rendered in Italian subtitles. The translation strategies used for this purpose mostly draw on the strategies (text reduction implications) provided by Díaz Cintas and Remael (2007) as far as textual shifts are concerned, and on Ranzato's taxonomy adapted to fit the rendering of specific lexicon and cultural references (2016, 2010) in subtitling. In order to classify shifts on a textual level, Díaz Cintas and Remael's model (2007) has been used, since it provides a clear distinction between textual and cultural features in the translation dimension pertaining to subtitling. As to the rendering of culture-bound terms, Díaz Cintas and Remael's model, as well as Ranzato's classification, have been adopted. Ranzato (2010, 2016) adds strategies such as official translation, creative addition, generalization by hypernym and concretization by hyponym, elimination and also modifies the nuances of certain strategies that are present in Díaz Cintas and Remael's taxonomy.

5. Qualitative analysis

In order to put emphasis on the most significant features of orality (as a marker of the genre) in the STs and the TTs, and to evaluate whether Italian subtitles are genre-oriented and generally 'exhibiting neutral register' (Arias-Badia 2020: 362), the qualitative analysis takes into account three recurrent communicative events based on spoken interaction which functions within the framework of clause as exchange and conveys information about a character's personality. Dialogic sequences have been chiefly identified within three areas:

1. sequences of dialogue taking place between police officers having different ranks: Detective Chief Inspectors, Detective Sergeants, Superintendents (addressed as *boss* and *Gov*), usually occurring in the context of preliminary forensic analysis at initial stages of investigations, and of formulations of hypotheses and suspect profiling;
2. sequences of dialogue between police officers and criminals or suspects in the context of interrogations;
3. sequences of dialogue involving family members and friends, but also between police officers (Luther and Reed or Ripley; Karppi and Nurmi, Kata and Arnar) having discussions in more confidential tones.

Due to lack of space, the triple distinction mentioned above has only been applied to *Luther*, whereas, as for the other two series, *TVM* and *Deadwind*, a few examples and the relative translation choices are shown and commented. Some specific linguistic features, which have been identified as consistently present in the series, have been taken into account for translating purposes (Table 10.1).

Table 10.1 Linguistic features analysed in the corpus

Lexical and morpho-syntactical features
Idiomatic expressions
Colloquialisms
Pragmatic markers
Interrogative clauses
Ellipsis
Modality
Unfinished sentences
Specialized lexicon

These features mark the difference between recognized degrees of spokenness (simple and short sentences; contextualization, spontaneity given by hesitations and redundancy, fillers and pauses) and degrees of writtenness (lexical density, explicitness, complex clausal organization).

The tables below contain the most significant dialogues in the opening and most singular episode of the British series *Luther* (S1.E01). The uttered sequences involve dialogues between John Luther, Detective Chief Inspector, D.C.I., and (a) his boss, Rose Teller, Detective Superintendent (Table 10.2); (b) Justin Ripley, Detective Sergeant, D.S. (Table 10.3); and (c) Luther's colleague and friend, Ian Reed, D.C.I. (Table 10.4). Table 10.2 is used as a sample table for the purpose of a more in-depth analysis. Speech functions (i.e. in particular, meanings being exchanged through marked interrogative clauses) appear underlined, specific lexicon (i.e. medical or forensic jargon) is shown in bold, appellatives, interjections, colloquialism, idioms are displayed in capital letters, and special cases of morpho-syntax (e.g. modals as verbs and adverbs within the mood block) are put in italics. The linguistic analysis interacts with the survey of translation strategies and deleted terms are signalled as omissions/eliminations in further comments.

Table 10.2 also contains the Italian subtitles, which include words belonging to different parts of speech or interjection types, as well nominal groups that have

Table 10.2 Dialogic interaction between Luther and Rose and Italian subtitling

English oral dialogues	**Italian subtitles**
L.: BOSS?	CAPO?
R.: Rule number one, don't get yourself in this situation again, which means you observe **case-management protocol.** Any proactive strategies *are to be signed off* by me.	Regola numero uno, non metterti più in queste situazioni. Ciò significa che seguirai il **protocollo di ogni caso.** Qualsiasi iniziativa *va approvata* da me.
R.: You and Zoe, <u>You've spoken?</u> [...] <u>She feel the same?</u>	Tu e Zoe ... <u>Vi parlate</u>? [...] <u>Lei la pensa ugualmente?</u>
L.: Rose, I did everything she asked for - Got MYSELF TOGETHER, now we'll see.	Rose, ho fatto tutto quello che mi ha chiesto. Mi SONO RIPRESO. Vedremo.
R.: D.C.I. JOHN LUTHER. D.S. JUSTIN RIPLEY [...]	ISPETTORE CAPO JOHN LUTHER. IL SERGENTE JUSTIN RIPLEY.
R.: There is no **forensics**, no **witnesses**. Timeline alone gets it LAUGHED OUT of the CPS. Find me the gun. Put it in her hand.	Non ci sono **prove**, né **testimoni**. La cronologia non REGGEREBBE in TRIBUNALE. Trova l'arma, mettigliela in mano.

English oral dialogues	Italian subtitles
R.: Zoe did not see her face. No CCTV. No EYEWITNESSES, no nothing.	Zoe non l'ha vista in faccia. Non ci sono né REGISTRAZIONI né TESTIMONI.
L.: <u>You do know</u> this makes me Alice Morgan's next project?	<u>Lo sa</u> che questo mi rende il prossimo obiettivo di Alice Morgan?
R.: Section 8. Police and Criminal Evidence Act: 'A magistrate may issue a warrant […]'	Paragrafo 8. *Police and Criminal Evidence Act:* 'Un magistrato può emettere un mandato […]'
L.: It won't be traceable, she does not leave **evidence** Just an **evidence**-shaped absence. […] Come on! She kills her parents and **walks.**	——————- Non ha lasciato **prove**. Solo una **prova** sotto forma di assenza. Andiamo! Ha ucciso i suoi genitori e **resta impunita.**
R.: SO take the chilly bitch down. But slow down, calm down, find another angle.	Cattura quella stronza insensibile Ma rallenta, calmati, cerca un'altra prospettiva.
L.: There are no other angles, she left us nothing.	Non ce ne sono, non ha lasciato niente.

been deleted, partially omitted or condensed with respect to the original English audios. Among them are terms such as *proactive, now, so, sir* (translation strategy: elimination), *case-management protocol/protocollo di ogni caso* (translation strategy: hypernym). Generalizations by hypernyms have been found to be frequently used strategies for the translation of culture-specific jargon within the field of TV crime genres. It is also the case of *CSP*, standing for 'Crown Prosecution Service', which is relevant within the context of British criminal surveys. The acronym *CSP*, which is rendered through the generalized term, *tribunale*, is SL culturally and geographically oriented. In England and Wales, 'CSP' is an independent organization which decides whether cases brought by the police proceed to the criminal court. The same translation strategy has been adopted for the rendering of the acronym *CCTV*, standing for 'closed-circuit television', generalized with the Italian term *registrazioni*. Other terms have been generalized, among which the legal-specific term *prove* is used to translate both *forensics* and *evidence*. The abundant number of marked interrogative clauses signalling professional and private levels of spoken interaction are neutralized in Italian subtitles, since the Italian language does not require the addition of auxiliaries or inversions to formulate questions (i.e. *You've spoken?/Vi parlate?*; *She feel the same?/Lei la pensa ugualmente?*).

As to deontic modality, it is reduced in strength in Italian subtitles, although it appears to respond to the standards of Italian legal discourse as a specialized lexicon, where the indicative mood in the simple present of 'andare' (*va*, conjugated in the third person singular voice, and followed by the past particle *approvata*), translates the English deontic modality implying obligation. Besides, personal and object pronouns, formal forms such as *Lei*, or third personal voices such as [...] *lo sa che* [...], increase the level of formality in Italian subtitling but, on the other hand, contribute to marking Italian crime drama series in the context of translation (i.e. formal forms are used in the Italian subtitled versions in order to strengthen distance or closeness). Such level of formality in Italian is somehow compensated by the fact that idiomatic expressions (i.e. *got myself together/mi sono ripreso*) or colloquialisms (i.e. *babe, babe/ piccola*), also present in the Finnish series, *Deadwind*, when possible, are replaced with Italian idioms or equivalent expressions at the level of the context of situation reproducing the SL effect. There are also significant loans used as translation strategies such as the textual frame *Paragrafo 8. Police and Criminal Evidence Act* that is left untranslated and transferred to the Italian text as such. This process not only confers a sense of British identity to the crime genre localized in Italian, but also reinforces the concept of foreignization in translation practices with the scope of exalting authenticity, where this satisfies the target audience's expectations and does not compromise the level of comprehension. Expletives are kept in Italian, although formality in Italian subtitles reduces their use, or motivates subtitlers to use swearwords and cursing only when their degree of offensiveness is rather low: *chilly bitch* does not literally correspond to *stronza insensibile*, and *porca puttana* (in English, "chilly bitch"), further on, does not address anyone but is an exclamation of anger.

Tables 10.3 and 10.4 contain the dialogues between Luther and Justin, and Luther and Ian, in which the most common linguistic features imply the use of interjections, pragmatic markers, idioms and specialized lexicon. Whereas specialized lexicon is commonly translated through transfers, the spontaneous level of communication – commonly given by interjections which strengthen the speaker's emotions and feelings, redundant words and repetitions (i.e. *home invasion/intrusione; Mate, mate, mate, thank you!/Amico, grazie!*), and discourse markers (i.e. *so*) – is often lost. Some cases of ellipsis in Italian subtitling, which make clauses more implicit and what is common in Low-Context Cultures (i.e. *are* in *Victims are Douglas and Laura Morgan/Le vittime: Douglas e Laura Morgan*), the presence of idioms, although more formal in Italian (i.e. *Nice to meet you/Molto lieto*), the maintenance of unfinished and short sentences and, rarely, of interjections (i.e. *Sleeping pills/Pillole per dormire; Um/Ehm*) and the use of a specific lexicon (i.e. *Carbon steel spring and barrel/Canna*

Table 10.3 Dialogic interaction between Luther and Ripley and Italian subtitling

English oral dialogues	Italian subtitles
J.: Morning, sir.	Buongiorno.
L.: Nice to meet you. Do we need to have the chat?	Molto lieto. Dobbiamo parlarne?
J.: Um …, then, no, We don't need the chat.	No, non c'è bisogno di parlarne.
L.: So what we got?	Che cosa abbiamo?
J.: Um, home invasion. Murder. Victims are Douglas and Laura Morgan.	Ehm … intrusione, omicidio. Le vittime: Douglas e Laura Morgan.
L.: She live there?	Vive lì?
L.: Sleeping pills. Separate bedrooms. So no sign of burglary […]	Pillole per dormire … letti separati. Nessun segno di scasso […]
J.: Contract killing, maybe?	Un omicidio su commissione?
L.: Well, it is workable. I mean, the shooter has done his homework.	È possibile. L'assassino era preparato.
J.: Some kind of low-caliber handgun.	Una pistola di piccolo calibro.
L.: Yeah, see, someone that efficient, you'd expect them to ditch the gun at the scene. […] I'll meet upstairs, yeah?	Una persona così competente di solito lascia l'arma sulla scena. Ci vediamo su, ok?

Table 10.4 Dialogic interaction between Luther and Reed and Italian subtitling

English oral dialogues	Italian subtitles
L.: Ah, mate, mate, mate …. Thank you. […] So tell me what I need to know.	Ah, amico, grazie. Dimmi, che cosa devo sapere?
I.: All right, this is a Glock 26. Lightweight compact pistol. Carbon steel spring and barrel. Polymer frame and components.	Bene, qui abbiamo una Glock 26, una pistola compatta e leggera. Canna e molle in acciaio al carbonio, struttura e componenti in polimeri.
Polymer frame. […] Polymer. Plastic.	Struttura in polimeri. […] Polimeri, plastica.

e molle in acciaio al carbonio), guarantee a partial tone of orality to target texts and encourage crime genre recognition within the Italian setting.

Table 10.5 contains a selection of dialogues within the context of sequences between Luther and the suspected criminal, Alice Morgan, labelled by Luther himself as 'malignant narcissist', while Table 10.6 reports a few examples that include informal exchanges between Luther and his wife, Zoe. The interactional level between the police officer and the criminal is translated in a very formal way (i.e. they both address themselves by the use of the Italian third person singular voice, which sheds light on social roles). Distance is signalled by Luther when he addresses Alice as *Miss Morgan* at the beginning and the end of their chat at the crime police department in contrast with other neutral and more informal appellatives in English (i.e. *Alice, please/Alice, la prego; I'm coming for you/Not if I'm coming for you/La prenderò, Non se la prendo prima io*).

In the exchange with Zoe (Table 10.6), the woman with whom Luther is trying to re-establish a sentimental relationship, the omission of fillers and discourse markers (i.e. *well, I know, so, I mean, Yeah*) and of a massive number of interjections (i.e. *Um*) is very common. Nevertheless, the informal level in the

Table 10.5 Dialogue between Luther and Alice Morgan and Italian subtitling

English oral dialogues	Italian subtitles
L.: Miss Morgan?	Signorina Morgan.
A.: Alice, please.	Alice … la prego.
L.: Alice. Hello, I'm John Luther. Senior Investigating Officer.	Alice salve, sono John Luther, L'ispettore a capo dell'indagine.
L.: Do you have any idea who would wish harm on your parents? Hmm. […] I'm sorry […]	Ha idea di chi avrebbe voluto fare del male ai suoi genitori? […] Mi perdoni […]
L.: You saw nothing or anyone unusual?	Non ha visto niente e nessuno di strano.
L.: I'm coming for you.	La prenderò.
A.: Not if I'm coming for you.	Non se la prendo prima io.

Table 10.6 Dialogue between Luther and Zoe and Italian subtitling

English oral dialogues	Italian subtitles
L.: Hi, babe, it's me. […]	*Ciao, piccola, sono io.*
Z.: I mean I knew they would obviously, but –	Sapevo che sarebbe andata così, ma …
L.: Yeah, and I'm back at work. […] Well, they missed me.	Sì, e sono tornato al lavoro. […] Sentivano la mia mancanza.
L.: What's wrong, babe? […] 'Cause I think that we, well, we need to have that talk.	Che succede, piccola? Perché credo che dovremmo parlare.
L.: Um. So	—————

English oral dialogues	Italian subtitles
L.: I've got myself together, all right? I am back and I feel great. I'm good. I'm … I'm … You know?	Mi sono ripreso. Ok? Sono tornato e mi sento una meraviglia. Sto bene. Lo sai?
Luther and Zoe on the phone. Luther is at the office.	
L.: D.C.I. John Luther. Zoe? Wait. Babe, babe, what's wrong? Bloody hell!	Ispettore John Luther Ehi … cosa succede? Porca puttana!

original dialogues – given by the fact they are husband and wife and are arguing heatedly – is not lost but reinforced by the use of colloquialism such as *piccola* (in oral English *babe, babe*).

There are further examples of appellatives and original marked interrogatives used among the police officers in the London Serial Criminal Unit, among which *Gov*, often pronounced to address Martin Schenk and Rose Teller, the two Detective Superintendents (i.e. Rose: *Gov./Capo*; Martin: *You do know the man is nitroglycerin?/Sai che quest'uomo è nitroglicerina?*; Luther: *I mean, honestly, gov., you should have just let me hold her/Sul serio capo, dovevamo trattenerla*). Whereas the Italian subtitling translates both *gov* and *boss* as *capo* (translation strategy: generalization by hypernym), in the English originals, there is a wider variety of appellatives and titles: for instance, 'gov' is an informal term that describes the person in authority, one's employer. Lexical variation is often omitted, and interrogatives, as already specified and confirmed by the numerous cases in *Luther*, are often neutralized in Italian.

The Italian subtitling for *TVM* and *Deadwind* presents the same features highlighted in *Luther*'s analysis, and the sense of orality is partially lost.

In *TVM*, dubbed dialogues contain obvious cases of marked interrogatives in spoken English (i.e. *We have an ID?/L'abbiamo identificato?*; *Must be lots of old people there at this time of the day;/La piscina non è piena di vecchi a quest'ora del giorno?*), which implies that, in the English subtitles (where interrogatives are unmarked: *Do we have an ID?*), the level of spokenness is at risk. The Italian subtitles are neutral and add no unusual value to the numerous marked interrogative clauses (dubbed dialogues) in the series. Conversely, *Deadwind* offers cases of markedness in the English subtitles: (i.e. *You haven't been in touch with her since?/Non vi siete più sentiti da allora?*), a structural device which is naturally reflected in the Italian subtitles, although they cannot be defined as marked types. Italian subtitles, with respect to the English templates, are characterized by the choice of using third person singular voices (i.e. 'lei'), when people do not know each other, or when police officers address suspects or criminals, and colloquial personal pronouns when participants are closely acquainted (i.e. *What did you do Saturday night?/Mi racconti il suo fine settimana/I need a room and a couple of detectives/Dammi una stanza e due agenti*).

Interjections, interrogatives, discourse markers, etc. denoting orality in TV subtitled crime drama series are predominantly omitted in Italian subtitles both in *Deadwind* and *TVM*, although the Italian subtitling of *Deadwind* is more faithful to the reproduction of orality. In order to strengthen colloquialism and informality, and to adapt the language of crime to the target context of the situation, as well as to render social roles, not only in *Luther*, but also in the Icelandic and Finnish crime dramas, expletives are usually kept in Italian, if they do not directly offend anyone (i.e. *TVM: Yeah, fuck. Meet me at the burger joint/Sì, cazzo. Vediamoci al locale*; *Deadwind: That's bullshit*; *Quelle sono cazzate*). Among the linguistic features which help subtitled crime drama series increase levels of spokenness, and favour tones of informality (i.e. *Deadwind: Hey, bro;/Senti, amico*), are the use of idiomatic expressions and sayings such as the Italian adaptation of *But never mind that* with *Bando alle ciance* (meaning 'enough small talk'), as it appears in *TVM*, or the rendering of 'fare bisboccia nel bosco' to translate that a 'woman was partying somewhere in the hood'. Hedge markers and types of pragmatic markers are prevalently lost in Italian, since they literally follow the English subtitles produced for *TVM* and *Deadwind*.

To sum up, it is possible to say that the language of crime in Italian subtitled versions tends to maximize the reduction of interjections, fillers and discourse markers which, on the contrary, are central to the oral communicative events in crime drama series. Among the essential linguistic features which are maintained in the process of subtitling crime series in Italian are the unfinished constructions and short sentences which, like in *Luther*, are typically used in the context of criminal investigation for the depiction of criminals' profiles and the description of forensic surveys (i.e. *TVM: No wallet. No ID. Ten stab wounds at least/Niente portafogli. Niente documenti. Almeno dieci coltellate*). The specific lexicon, as also happens in the Italian subtitled version of *Luther*, is often rendered through translating mechanisms of generalization by hypernym (i.e. *TVM*: CCVT becomes *registrazioni* in Italian; *burger joint* become *locale*; *chief superintendent* becomes *sovrintendente*; *Deadwind*: *Helsinki Police Department* becomes *Polizia di Helsinki*). Loans are also used, as we can find in the Italian subtitling of *Luther*, when culture-bound terms are untranslatable because no cultural equivalent exists. For example, the acronym

'RLR', which in the Icelandic police context indicates 'Police Investigative Branch', referred to as 'RLR', is kept untranslated and gives a flavour of foreignization to the crime drama series localized in Italian. On other occasions, literal translations or transfers occur to replace culture-bound terms that are comprehensible on the level of the target culture such as in the renderings of […] *the SPA in Hämeenlinna* as […] *alla SPA, a Hämeenlinna*, or *Financial Crimes Unit as Unità Crimini Finanziari* in *Deadwind*.

6. Discussion and conclusive remarks

The Italian subtitles of the digital crime drama series under scrutiny are the result of a combination of spoken and written language, and occupy a space which stands in the continuum of spoken and written languages: on the one hand, subtitles seek neutral solutions that respect the conventions of written language, and, on the other, are fed through spoken language to render fictional characters real people.

The major translation strategies employed in the subcorpus, as shown in Table 10.7, are divided into subtitling strategies based on structural shifts and alterations pertaining to culture-bound terms.

As mentioned earlier in this chapter, the series have been selected as mutually comparable with the scope of detecting norms in SL dialogue construction and

Table 10.7 Translation strategies adapted from different taxonomies

TEXT REDUCTION	DESCRIPTION
Reformulation	The readaptation of what is relevant concisely.
Condensation	The elimination of what is not relevant for the comprehension of the message.
Omission	The deletion of redundant items.
CULTURE-BOUND TERMS	
Elimination	The act of making an element disappear from a text without any culture-specific reference replacement.
Generalization by hypernym	The use of one or more words having a broader meaning than the source element and/or the partial rendering of the ST.
Transfer	The adequate and accurate rendering of the SL text.
Loan	Words or phrases left untranslated in the TT.

for the translation of crime genres in Italian. The linguistic features used for satisfying genre norms are relevant in order to point out what happens in the context of Italian interlingual subtitling, which motivates the decision to pursue a linguistic characterization of dialogues and subtitled versions.

Broadly speaking, the whole corpus has shown that dialogues belonging to crime genres, regardless of their origins, hold elaborate features of 'fictive orality' (Arias-Badia 2020). All this affects the levels of syntax and lexicon within the context of communication, where dialogues occur in a way that is commonly informal, colloquial, repetitive, full of hesitations, apparently spontaneous and explicit. Conversely, in Italian subtitling, to certain degrees, dialogues are marked by a more formal stereotyped language, often standardized and neutral, since they are embedded within written forms where redundancies (repetitions of textual and interpersonal themes, interjections, specific hedges, emphatic use of conjunctions, etc.) are avoided. Discourse markers (e.g. *I mean, well, you kn*ow) voiced hesitations or filled pauses (e.g. *Um, Hmm, Ouch*), as well as culture-bound terms belonging to the SL specific lexicon and context of situation (e.g. *cps, case-management protocols, cctv*) are (a) usually reformulated or condensed in line with the context of arrival through standardization or underspecification procedures; (b) frequently eliminated due to the absence of cultural equivalents on a target level; (c) sometimes left untranslated (*Police and Criminal Evidence Act; RLR*) in the form of a loan. Titles and personal pronouns are all rendered according to the conventions and standards expected by the audience in the context of arrival (e.g. *ispettore capo, sergente, lei* and *tu*). In terms of morpho-syntax, verbal structures have been simplified, modals and modal adjuncts have often been weakened, whereas unfinished constructions, legal jargon used for criminal surveys and psychological investigation, idioms and colloquial phrases, have been kept and rendered in Italian.

In the pilot episodes selected, linguistic variation, while ranging from formal to informal conversations, is minimized in subtitles. It has been observed that the most frequent type of interaction in the procedural genre is informal conversation. Although dialogic interaction in Italian subtitles is weakened by linguistic absences already discussed, it is also possible to confirm nevertheless that the three series have guaranteed genre recognition by respecting the most significant norms in the context of arrival: subtitling in Italian has reproduced clauses as exchanges among participants who never appear to lose their expertise in the fields of law and order, and whose terminology shifts easily across different registers. Despite standardization and generalization procedures, on the one hand, and condensation and omission strategies, on the other, the transfer of syntagms from one language to another and the appropriate balance of spokenness and writtenness through linguistic inclusions and exclusions, have succeeded in giving a sense of orality to crime genres in Italian. Therefore, although the language of Italian subtitlers has often appeared conventionalized, it can be argued that when omissions and condensations in subtitling have taken place, these absences have been compensated by the presence of idiomatic renderings and a specific lexicon, colloquial expressions and interrogative clauses that have favoured the spread of crime genres subtitled in Italian through processes of localization.

In spite of the limitation of the subcorpus in quantitative terms, this study has shown that digital procedurals make use of genre conventions in terms of thematic sequences and repeated linguistic structures. This confirms that, generally speaking, the driving principle of Italian subtitling of foreign crime drama series tends to domesticate the products in order to facilitate the comprehension for the TL audience, ensure enjoyment and stimulate genre recognition. At the same time, forms of foreignization within the subtitling process reveal attention to authenticity and cultural difference, all of which, together with the digitalization of subtitles and their diffusion in a multitude of languages, enrich the value of the spread of DH in the multifarious emerging digital setting, where humanities have acquired a variety of modes of engagement, discursive and linguistic strategies. In this sense, subtitles become depositaries of both original and local target grammars and cultures.

Since the data analysed in this study refer only to the first episodes of the three series under scrutiny, our investigation cannot be regarded as exhaustive, insofar as the data are not corroborated by quantity and frequency effects. However, the analysis can be viewed as a satisfactory initial phase which has not only stimulated the identification of crime genre-specific products, but also encouraged further studies aimed at broader identification of local grammars in Italian interlingual subtitling produced for crime genres. Future research, therefore, may confirm statistically how far these results can be generalized.

References

Arias-Badia, B. (2020), *Subtitling Television Series: A Corpus-driven Study of Police Procedurals*, Oxford and New York: Peter Lang.

Arias-Badia, B. and J. Brumme (2014), 'Subtitling Stereotyped Discourse in the Crime TV Series Dexter (2006) and Castle (2009)', *Journal of Specialised Translation*, 22: 110–31.

Baños Piñero, R. and F. Chaume (2009), 'Prefabricated Orality: A Challenge in Audiovisual Translation', *InTRAlinea*, special issue. Available online: http://www.intralinea.org/specials/article/Prefabricated_Orality (accessed 2 June 2021).

Barker, C. and M. Wiatrowski, eds (2017), *The Age of Netflix. Streaming Media, Digital Delivery and Instant Access*, North Carolina: McFarland and Company.

Bruti S. (2019), 'Spoken Discourse and Conversational Interaction in Audiovisual Translation', in L. Pérez-González (ed.), *The Routledge Handbook of Audiovisual Translation*, 192–208, London and New York: Routledge.

Cattrysse, P. (2014), *Descriptive Adaptation Studies: Epistemological and Methodological Issues*, Antwerp: Garant.

Chaume, F. (2019), 'Audiovisual Translation in the Age of Transformations: Industrial and Social Implications', in I. Ranzato and S. Zanotti (eds), *Reassessing Dubbing: Historical Approaches and Current Trends*, 103–24, Amsterdam: John Bejamins.

Díaz-Cintas, J. (2010a), 'The Highs and Lows of Digital Subtitles', in L. Zybatow (ed.), *Translationswissenschaft: Stand und Perspektiven*, 105–30. Frankfurt and Main: Peter Lang.

Díaz-Cintas, J. (2010b), 'Subtitling', in Y. Gambier and L. van Doorslaer (eds), *Handbook of Translation Studies*, 344–9, Amsterdam: John Benjamins.

Díaz-Cintas, J. and A. Remael (2007), *Audiovisual Translation: Subtitling*, London and New York: Routledge.

Díaz-Cintas, J. and S. Massidda (2019), 'Technological Advances in Audiovisual Translation', in M. O'Hagan (ed.), *The Routledge Handbook of Translation and Technology*, 255–70, Oxford and New York: Routledge.

Di Giovanni, E. and Y. Gambier (2018), *Reception Studies and Audiovisual Translation*, Amsterdam: John Bejamins.

Gallitelli E. (2016), 'Digital Humanities come risorsa per i Translation Studies', *Status Quaestionis*, 10: 53–72. DOI: https://doi.org/10.13133/2239-1983/13781.

Georgakopoulou, P. (2018), 'Technologization of Audiovisual Translation', in L. Pérez-González (ed.), *The Routledge Handbook of Audiovisual Translation*, 516–39, New York: Routledge.

Gottlieb, H. (1992), 'Subtitling. A New University Discipline', in C. Dollerup and A. Loddegaard (eds), *Teaching Translation and Interpreting: Training, Talent and Experience*, 161–9, Amsterdam: John Benjamins.

Halliday, M. A. K. (1978), *Language as Social Semiotic: The Social Interpretation of Language and Meaning*, London: Arnold.

Halliday, M. A. K. (revised by) C. Matthiessen (2004), *An Introduction to Functional Grammar*, 3rd edn, London: Arnold.

Hunston, S. and J. Sinclair (2000), 'A Local Grammar of Evaluation', in S. Hunston and G. Thompson (eds), *Evaluation in Text*, 74–101, Oxford: Oxford University Press.

Laudisio, A. (2018), 'The Adaptation of Legal Culture-Specific References in Cross-Cultural Rewriting: The Case of Legal Drama', *ESP across Cultures*, 14: 131–58.

Mittell, J. (2004), *Genre and Television. From Cops Shows to Cartoons in American Culture*, New York and London: Routledge.
Piper, H. (2015), *The TV Detective. Voices of Dissent in Contemporary Television*, London and New York: I.B. Taurius.
Ranzato, I. (2010), *La traduzione audiovisiva. Analisi degli elementi culturospecifici*, Roma: Bulzoni editore.
Ranzato, I. (2016), *Translating Culture Specific References on Television. The Case of Dubbing*, London: Routledge.
Sandrelli, A. (2018), 'An Italian Crime Series in English. The Dubbing and Subtitling of *Suburra*', *Status Quaestionis*, 15: 161–89.
Sandrelli, A. (2020), 'The Translation of Legal References in the Italian Dubbing of a US TV Series. A Corpus-based Analysis', *Lingue e Linguaggi*, 40: 315–40.
Svensson, P. (2010), 'The Landscape of Digital Humanities', *Digital Humanities Quarterly*, 4 (1). Available online:http://digitalhumanities.org/dhq/vol/4/1/000080/000080.html (Accessed 6 June 2021).
Turnbull, S. (2014), *The TV Crime Drama*, Edinburgh: Edinburgh University Press.

Original Sources

Deadwind [*Karppi*] by Rike Jokela. Yle TV2, 2018, Finland; Netflix, 2020.
Luther, by Neil Cross. BBC ONE, 2010; Netflix 2011, UK.
The Valhalla Murders [*Brot*] by Þórður Pálsson. RÚV, 2019, Island; Netflix, BBC Four, 2020.

Index

affect 131-6, 141, 143
annotation 3-4, 45, 85
AntConc 4, 73, 133
AntGram 73
Appraisal Theory 129, 131-2, 140, 143-4
Association-defined approach 10, 73-4
attitude 95, 131, 145, 190

blogs 12, 28, 83, 153, 162

character analysis 12, 177, 191, 210
characterization 12, 177, 179, 184, 190, 196, 221
cluster(s) 10, 31, 69-70, 73, 85, 95, 134, 138
colligation 38, 53-5, 58, 69, 85, 162, 169
collocation 6-8, 10, 38, 53-5, 58, 68-71, 74, 85, 88, 118, 156-7, 162, 169
communication
　corporate 40
　intercultural 37, 129
comparability (see also comparable corpora) 38, 41, 43, 75, 112, 178
computer-assisted translation (CAT) tools 116
concordance(s)
　parallel 12, 179, 181, 183, 191, 193, 196
concordancing 4, 8, 10, 38
conversational routines 12, 68
corpora
　bilingual 114, 117, 153, 159
　comparable 9, 11, 38, 41, 112-14, 118, 120, 132, 178
　digital 10, 107, 115, 120
　electronic 110
　legal 11, 107-8, 110-17
　monolingual 7, 38, 153, 169, 183
　multilingual 8, 38, 112, 114, 116-17, 162
　parallel 8, 12-13, 38, 112-17, 120, 177-9, 181, 196, 203

　reference 6-7, 11, 48, 74, 100, 113, 178, 185
corpus linguistics
　corpus compilation 39, 41, 57, 183
　corpus design 4-5, 38, 43, 66, 111, 113, 179, 181
　corpus-assisted analysis 133
　corpus-based approach 4, 6, 28, 37-8, 70, 110, 169, 179, 193, 202
　corpus-driven approach 4, 6, 9, 12, 38, 65-9, 73-6, 110-11, 179
　corpus tools 37-8, 57, 181
crime drama series 202-3, 207, 208, 219
cross-cultural studies 9, 37-8, 41, 131
CSR reports 37-9
cultural context 37, 40, 44, 51, 58

digital humanities 1, 4, 8, 10, 19-22, 27, 30-2, 66, 107-9, 119-20, 129, 132, 143, 201
digital museums 127-9, 132-3, 143
digitalization 2, 12, 201, 203, 222
discourse
　academic 41, 65-6, 68, 71
　of good will 39
　legal 9, 11, 111, 113, 116, 215
　of promotion 39
　of self-justification 39
　specialized 6, 37, 66
distributional approach 10, 68-70
domain knowledge 155-8
dubbing 177, 184-5, 191-4, 196, 201, 204-5

e-health 10, 81, 83, 96
emotion 11, 128-31, 134, 138, 144-5
emotive language 11, 127-31, 139, 143-4
engagement 20-1, 40, 50, 54-7, 71, 130-1, 145, 164-5, 222
evaluation 38, 54, 72, 94-6, 131-2, 144, 160, 185, 189, 196
evaluative 39, 53, 187-8, 190

extended units of meaning 71, 85
extraction 10–12, 66, 70–1, 73, 117, 185, 196

fictive orality 12, 207, 221
film dialogues / speech 12, 177–8, 180, 196
formulaic expression(s) 66–8
formulaicity 67, 74
frequency data 47, 66

genre analysis 9, 37, 39, 41, 119
globalization 39–41, 145
glossary/glossaries 11–12, 45, 153–5, 160–6, 169
graduation 131

health communication 10, 81–3

idiomaticity 70, 212, 215, 219, 222
interpersonal meaning 46, 58, 131, 204, 206, 210–1, 221
interpreter training 11, 153–7

ketogenic diet 81–4, 88–91
keyness 38–9, 58, 86, 93–5, 187
keyword
    analysis 53
    negative 48, 51
    positive 49–51

learning analytics 11, 153, 158, 160, 164, 169
LearnWeb 153–4, 160–3, 168
lexical bundles 65–9, 75, 85, 96
lexico-grammar
    lexico-grammatical features 45, 47, 53, 57–8, 211
    lexico-semantic fields 49, 96
Linguee 117, 153, 162
local grammar 53–4, 203–4, 222
localization 12, 202, 205–7, 222
LSP 113

metadiscourse/metadiscursive 50, 53, 58
methodology 65, 70, 75, 129, 177, 185
migrants / migration 11, 117, 128–9, 130, 133, 138, 142, 210

mimetic isomorphism 40
move analysis 45

N-gram 73, 85, 88–9, 92
narratives 96, 127–30, 136, 138, 142–4
needs analysis 154
Nexis 117

operationalization 10, 73

pedagogy
    bottom-up approaches 73
    data tracking 12, 153, 163, 171
    learning dashboard 164
    pedagogical needs 157
    student dashboard 164–5
    teacher dashboard 165
    top-down approaches 9, 39, 44, 58, 69, 93
phrase frames 9, 65, 75
phraseological approach 10, 68–70
phraseology 38, 53, 66, 73, 76, 119, 156, 156, 162, 169
police procedurals 203, 207–8
popularization 10, 83
pragmatic functions 3–4, 53, 71, 76
prefabricated orality 207
professional
    needs and habits 154

quantification 1, 4, 10, 12, 58, 66

refugees 127–8, 139
register 5, 9, 65, 71, 112, 131, 156–7, 162, 212, 221
rhetorical structure 44

semantic
    preferences 6, 10, 38, 53, 55–6, 58, 85
    prosody 38, 85
sequence
    formulaic 67
    multiword 9, 65, 72–3, 75–6
    recurrent 69
    semantic 53, 69
SketchEngine 4, 10, 73, 81, 85, 88, 96 177, 181–3, 193
SLA 67, 73
social media 81–4, 96, 127

stakeholders 39–40, 46–50, 55–9
stance 72, 86, 119, 146

terminology 11, 116, 118–19, 153–5, 158, 163, 168, 171, 221
thematic categorization 50, 132
translation
    audiovisual 133, 178, 201, 205, 207
    corpus-assisted 112, 120
    legal 10, 107, 110–13, 119
    Memories (TMs) 116
    specialized 108–9

strategies 111, 179, 203, 211, 213, 215, 220
translation vs interpreting 12, 145, 153–7, 160–8
translator training 7, 118–19
Twitter 10, 81, 83–4, 96

variety/varieties 41–3, 178

Web 12, 81, 83, 153, 160, 163–4, 169
Westlaw 117
WMatrix 4, 10, 47, 81, 85–6, 93
Wordsmith (WM) 4, 73

www.ingramcontent.com/pod-product-compliance
Lightning Source LLC
Chambersburg PA
CBHW062214300426
44115CB00012BA/2056